093289

14.03

SW

D0536464

Powers of Persuasion

'Throughout the span of this book, Winston Fletcher has been both practitioner and respected commentator. No one could have been better qualified to write this valuable history–and as befits the subject, it's always readable and even at times engagingly racy.'
Sir Martin Sorrell, CEO WPP

'It's a ground-breaking book from a most authoritative pen which gives us the lowdown on British advertising, from the inside. Advertising is one of the most misunderstood forces in society–and *Powers of Persuasion* tells it like it is. It's frank, fast-moving and revealing. It contains that missing extra ingredient - real insight. Nine out of ten people should read it!'
Michael Grade, Executive Chairman, ITV

'Absolutely terrific. Fletcher is the consummate adman's adman, and he tells the tale with wonderful insight and vigour. I couldn't have enjoyed it more.'
Tim Waterstone, Founder of Waterstone's

'A great story, very well told. This readable account both has plenty for those who already know a lot about British advertising, and is also an excellent introduction for students and others new to the area.'
Patrick Barwise, Emeritus Professor of Management and Marketing, London Business School

Powers of Persuasion

The Inside Story of British Advertising: 1951–2000

Winston Fletcher

OXFORD
UNIVERSITY PRESS

OXFORD

UNIVERSITY PRESS

Great Clarendon Street, Oxford OX2 6DP

Oxford University Press is a department of the University of Oxford.
It furthers the University's objective of excellence in research, scholarship,
and education by publishing worldwide in

Oxford New York

Auckland Cape Town Dar es Salaam Hong Kong Karachi
Kuala Lumpur Madrid Melbourne Mexico City Nairobi
New Delhi Shanghai Taipei Toronto

With offices in

Argentina Austria Brazil Chile Czech Republic France Greece
Guatemala Hungary Italy Japan Poland Portugal Singapore
South Korea Switzerland Thailand Turkey Ukraine Vietnam

Oxford is a registered trade mark of Oxford University Press
in the UK and in certain other countries

Published in the United States
by Oxford University Press Inc., New York

© Oxford University Press 2008

The moral rights of the author have been asserted
Database right Oxford University Press (maker)

First published 2008

All rights reserved. No part of this publication may be reproduced,
stored in a retrieval system, or transmitted, in any form or by any means,
without the prior permission in writing of Oxford University Press,
or as expressly permitted by law, or under terms agreed with the appropriate
reprographics rights organization. Enquiries concerning reproduction
outside the scope of the above should be sent to the Rights Department,
Oxford University Press, at the address above

You must not circulate this book in any other binding or cover
and you must impose the same condition on any acquirer

British Library Cataloguing in Publication Data

Data available

Library of Congress Cataloging in Publication Data

Fletcher, Winston.
Powers of persuasion: the inside story of British advertising / Winston Fletcher.
p. cm.
Includes bibliographical references and index.
ISBN-13: 978-0-19-922801-0
1. Advertising–Great Britain–History–20th century. I. Title.
HF5813.G7F64 2008
659.10941–dc22 2008004129

Typeset by SPI Publisher Services, Pondicherry, India
Printed in Great Britain
on acid-free paper by
CPI Antony Rowe, Chippenham, Wiltshire

ISBN 978-0-19-922801-0

1 3 5 7 9 10 8 6 4 2

COLEG LLANDRILLO
LIBRARY RESOURCE CENTRE
CANOLFAN ADNODDAU LLYFRGELL

General   10\08

093289   659.1FLC

Contents

Plates

(Between pages 104 and 105, and 216 and 217)

Acknowledgements

Powers of Persuasion could not have been written without the information I gained from personal interviews and conversations with John Ayling, Alan Bishop, Martin Boase, Nigel Bogle, Tim Broadbent, Jeremy Bullmore, Barry Cox, Michael Garland, James Garrett, Andrew Green, Michael Hockney, Birger Jensen, Chris Jones, Ronnie Kirkwood, Simon Marquis, Chris Powell, Timothy Raison, Mark Ramage, Toby Reeks, John Ritchie, Jack Rubins, Ian Scott, Anthony Simonds-Gooding, Mike Waterson, and numerous others. Rufus Olins kindly helped me get started at the Campaign library. Philip Spink at the Advertising Association Library, the staff at St. Bride's Library, and everyone at the History of Advertising Trust gave me constant and unstinting help. Drafts of the text were read at various stages by Andrew Brown, Chris Cowpe, Jean Fletcher, Wally Olins, Andrew Robinson, and Jeremy Tunstall, all of whom suggested improvements, both minor and major. I am immensely grateful to them all but, as ever, any mistakes are entirely my own.

Winston Fletcher

The author and publisher are grateful to the History of Advertising Trust for their assistance in sourcing the advertisements illustrated in *Powers of Persuasion*. They would also like to acknowledge the following for their permission to use these photographs: Gallagher Limited and CDP Travis-Sully Limited for Benson & Hedges King Size; Premier Foods Limited for Cadbury's Smash; The Central Office of Information for the Clunk! Click! seatbelt and Pregnant Man campaigns; DSG International PLC for Dixons; The British Egg Marketing Research & Education Trust for Go To Work On An Egg; Cueta Healthcare Limited for Gibbs SR; Heineken (UK) Limited for Heineken; Yell Limited for Yellow Pages; The Conservative Party Archive for Labour Isn't Working; The Labour Party Head Office for Let's Go With Labour; The Dairy Council for Drinka Pinta Milka Day; The Ogilvy Group UK for Strand Cigarettes; M&C Saatchi (UK) Limited and Gallagher Limited for Benson & Hedges Silk Cut; Premier Grocery Products Limited for Oxo; Coca-Cola European Union Group for Coca-Cola; and the Brooke Bond PG Tips image is reproduced with kind permission of Unilever. Brooke Bond and PG Tips are registered trademarks.

There are instances where we have been unable to trace or contact the copyright holder. If notified the author and publisher will be pleased to rectify any errors or omissions at the earliest opportunity.

COLEG LLANDRILLO COLLEGE
LIBRARY RESOURCE CENTRE
CANOLFAN ADNODDAU LLYFRGELL

The Halcyon Years: Terms of Reference

Powers of Persuasion is a history of British advertising, not just of British advertisements. There is lots about advertisements—advertisements being advertising's *raison d'être*—but there is even more about Britain's advertising industry, and the ways in which it created advertisements during the second half of the twentieth century.[1]

During the second half of the twentieth century British advertising led the world, and *Powers of Persuasion* unashamedly bangs this British drum. As it happens Britain also led the world during the eighteenth and early nineteenth centuries, which is counter-intuitive because America is widely thought to be the heartland of advertising. Well, the United States is much the largest advertising market in the world, accounting for about 45 per cent of all global expenditure, and the level of advertising expenditure per capita there hovers around 60 per cent above the level in Britain. But from the late 1950s, and particularly from the early 1970s onwards, the British advertising industry not only produced innovative and brilliant advertisements, it also led the field in other important and influential ways—a surge which continued until the end of the century.

This was achieved despite the fact that during the second half of the twentieth century the British advertising industry was almost continuously under siege—certainly more so than the American advertising industry. Again, this started long before the twentieth century, and partly reflects the traditional British intellectual distaste for salesmanship. Advertising is not the only sector of commerce in Britain under siege, but

---

[1] Advertising in Britain is exceptionally London-centric. During the half-century there were brief flowerings of fine advertising in the Midlands and Scotland. But almost inevitably the best practitioners gravitate towards London, where the big business is.

because advertising is intrusive, and unavoidable, and an easy target—the most salient interface between commerce and society—during the latter part of the last century concerns about its powers grew, and there was almost constant pressure for those powers to be constrained. The pioneering originality of the British advertising industry has, in part, been a response to that pressure.

'The advertising industry' is a confusing phrase. There is no such entity as the advertising industry. What people call the advertising industry is an amorphous patchwork of different companies and specializations, broadly divisible into three sectors—usually called the advertising tripartite.

First, there are advertisers—manufacturers, retailers, the government, lonely lovers, and the rest—for whom advertising is a means to an end. They pay for all the advertising, but advertising is not their principal activity. Advertising is one of many things they do to achieve their aims. Though they are advertisers they do not think of themselves as being part of 'the advertising industry'.

Second, there are the media—television, press, posters, radio, the internet, and the rest—which carry the advertisements, in return for the advertisers' money. Television, radio, and posters carry, almost exclusively, 'display' advertising. Print media and the internet carry a mixture of display and classified advertising. This is an important distinction: there are advertisements which people look for (classified advertising), and advertisements which look for people (display advertising). Display advertising is necessarily intrusive, classified advertising is not.[2]

Most media would not exist if they did not receive hefty revenues from advertising, and they know it. But they do not think of themselves as being part of 'the advertising industry' either. They are purveyors of news, information, and entertainment to their many publics, and they are forced to carry advertisements to subsidize all this. In most media there is a rigorous separation between the advertising and the editorial operations, and that is the way the editorial people (and probably the public) prefer it. The advertisers and the media are by far the largest sectors of 'the advertising industry' even though, in both cases, advertising is not their industry.

The third leg of the advertising industry is the sector which produces the display advertising: the advertising agencies. Advertising agencies create

---

[2] As their name implies, 'semi-display classifieds', of the kind found in Yellow Pages for example, are perfect examples of advertisements on the borderline between the two types of advertising.

the advertisements, and buy from the media the space and time in which they appear. This is much the smallest sector of 'the advertising industry', but is the sector which wholly relies on advertising for its living. It is this sector most people think of, when they talk about people who 'work in advertising'. It receives the difference between what advertisers spend on advertising and what the media receive for space and time. Nowadays this difference amounts to about 10 per cent of the advertisers' total spend. It is the agencies upon which *Powers of Persuasion* will concentrate, as they are at the heart of the advertising process.

Advertising agencies measure their size in 'billings'. Until the 1980s their billings were the total value of the space and time they bought, in media, on behalf of their clients. This roughly equated to their turnover, or total sales. But during the 1980s media-buying began to split away from the creation of advertisements. Thereafter 'creative' agencies' billings became merely notional—the value of the space and time which carries advertise-ments they have created; they themselves do not buy the space and time. 'Media' agencies buy the space and time, and so their billings remained what they had always been—the total cost of the advertising they buy on behalf of their clients; but media agencies do not produce the advertise-ments. All agency billings figures, real and notional, are compiled by independent research companies. The research companies publish league tables which show what each agency's billings are—notional or not—and much attention is devoted to these tables (in the industry and in this book), because they show whether an agency is growing or shrinking, being commercially successful or not.

The agency sector directly employs about 18,000 people, but also em-ploys on a part-time or freelance basis a network of photographers, film directors and crews, illustrators, printers, and others—few of whom work solely on advertising, though some of them earn substantial sums from advertising. Additionally there is a bevy of specialists—market researchers, designers, marketing consultants, public relations experts, product devel-opment companies, and others—who may have an input into advertising campaigns, but who do not think of themselves as 'working in advertis-ing'. In the past, as we shall see, many of these specialists did work in agencies. Today they are either independent, or they may work for subsid-iaries of the large marketing communications holding companies—com-panies like WPP, Omnicom, and Interpublic. These holding companies are sometimes called 'super agencies', but this is a misnomer. They are invest-ment and management conglomerates, not agencies at all. Like most large companies they measure their size in revenue, or turnover, as much of their business is not media advertising, or billings, at all.

This agglomeration of businesses, specializations, and interests comprises the nebulous 'advertising industry', in this book and elsewhere.

And there is another complication to 'the advertising industry'. Historically advertising has been split into what was called 'above-the-line' advertising and 'below-the-line' advertising. Nobody knows where this mythical line originated, but it probably came from the way some large advertisers divided their budgets. 'Above-the-line' advertising comprised campaigns in press and magazines, television, posters, radio, and cinema. 'Below-the-line' advertising—which most of those working in above-the-line advertising have long regarded as below the salt—comprised sales promotion, in-store display, direct marketing, exhibitions, sponsorship, product placement: in fact any marketing communications which were not above-the-line. Today the above- and below-the-line nomenclature has generally been changed to 'prime media' and 'marketing services'. Research suggests the public sees little or no difference, and describes all of them as advertising. And increasingly the internet and other new media are blurring the division. But *Powers of Persuasion* will focus almost exclusively on prime media: above-the-line display advertising. This is not because I view either sector as more important or prestigious, but because it would have been impossible to encompass all these activities in one book of reasonable length.

Job titles within the advertising industry are often confusing too. Among advertisers, since the 1960s the most common titles for the people who control advertising are brand managers, product managers, marketing managers, and marketing directors. Within agencies, the executives who deal directly with clients are called account representatives, account managers, account executives, and account directors. In every case there are numerous refinements—but I shall try to stick to either brand managers or marketing directors (for advertisers) and account executives and account directors (for agencies).

I hope this has cut away some of the undergrowth that pervades and obfuscates the non-existent advertising industry.

* * *

A few words about times and timing. *Powers of Persuasion* begins in 1951, because that was the year when Winston Churchill's Tories ousted Clement Attlee's Labour administration, and came to power committed to competition and the economic forces which encourage advertising to thrive. However, it briefly looks back to earlier times, to embed recent history in its origins.

The main history then deals with the half-century after 1951, broken into decades. Any such divisions of time are arbitrary and deceptive. They imply the selected periods are watertight, which they are not. Decades, like all other eras, fade into each other. But for this particular sector of history, decades work as well as anything. To have used any other time periods would have imbued the bookend years with particular significance. In this story, there are no such years. Decades are rough and ready, but we are all used to dealing with them.

The history finishes around the end of the twentieth century. Any attempt to have brought it right up to date would have been journalism rather than history. However, it was written during 2006–7, and the occasional references to the way things are 'now' or 'today' should be taken to refer to the years 2006–7. There is also a fleeting glance into the future, as nobody writing about advertising can resist a little crystal ball gazing.

All important references will be found in the bibliography, listed alphabetically by author (or publication).

1951: Watershed Year

1951 was a watershed year for Britain, and for British advertising. It was the year which marked the beginning of the transition from the trough of the Second World War, and post-war restrictions and privations, to the sunny uplands of economic affluence.

Prime Minister Attlee's Labour government had always intended the year to be a watershed. On 3 May 1951, a century after the Victorians' Great Exhibition of 1851, large crowds congregated on the South Bank of the Thames to see the King and Queen open the Festival of Britain, which was designed to celebrate British post-war achievements—to advertise to the world that Britain had said goodbye to austerity and shabbiness, and was well on the way to recovery and prosperity. Deputy Prime Minister Herbert Morrison called the Festival 'the people giving themselves a pat on the back'.

The advertising industry took the opportunity to give itself a pat on the back too. In July 1951 it held what the trade magazine *World's Press News* dubbed 'The Greatest Ever Advertising Conference'—though whether this claim was strictly legal, decent, honest, and truthful is questionable. The great American advertising conference of 1924, also held in London, would—at the very least—have run it a close race. The 1924 American powwow billed itself as nothing less than 'The Greatest Event in Business History', and was opened by the Prince of Wales, but it was probably attended by fewer delegates than the 1951 event, so perhaps the *World's Press News* hyperbole was justifiable. Anyway, no British advertising conference of equivalent magnitude had been held before, or has been held since.[1]

---

[1] An international advertising conference held in London in 1965 was opened by Princess Margaret and attended by over 2,000 delegates, but turned out to be a damp squib.

The 1951 conference was organized by the UK industry's leading trade body, the Advertising Association, and it welcomed to Westminster's Central Hall 2,824 delegates from 38 countries, including such unlikely countries as Egypt, Japan, Kenya, Lebanon, and Uruguay. It was opened by the Duke of Gloucester, chaired by Lord Mackintosh of Halifax, and its declared theme was 'The Tasks of Advertising in a Free World'. The line-up of speakers, which included the Attorney General Sir Frank Soskice representing 'a government which at one time wanted to tax advertising', was illustrious, but none was more illustrious than Lord Beveridge. Beveridge had authored the great, eponymous 1942 report which laid down the foundations for Britain's Welfare State. With remarkable prescience, Beveridge ended his 1951 conference oration:

> In a free world the service of advertising to the community is to enable citizens to get the most and best out of . . . the consumer's freedom in spending his income. The condition on which alone this service can be rendered is that those who conduct advertising shall take service to the consumer as their over-riding purpose, and shall recognise responsibilities for what they say and how they say it.

What advertisements say, and how they say it, will—however obliquely—be twin themes of this history.

* * *

It was not only the Advertising Association's mammoth get-together and the Tory election victory which mark 1951 as a particularly significant year for advertising. In September the British market research industry, though still in its infancy, hosted the first ever joint international conference of ESOMAR (European Society for Market and Opinion Research) and WAPOR (World Association for Public Opinion Research). Though far smaller than the AA conference, this still attracted 120 delegates from 15 countries. They came to hear leading market researchers—including Dr George Gallup (who had worked with the Young & Rubicam agency in New York since 1932) and his protégé Dr Henry Durant—address the thorny issue: 'How can research help the creative side of advertising to produce advertisements that will have maximum effectiveness in creating sales'—another strand which will run through this book. Dr Durant warned that 'The limitations of copy testing[2] must be taken to heart to avoid disappointment', a warning as true today as it was then.

---

[2] 'Copy testing' is a general description of any market research in which members of the public are shown, and asked to respond to, an advertisement or advertisements. Copy testing can be used for advertisements in all media, and is usually carried out when the advertisements are still in a 'rough' stage, before they appear.

There was another way in which 1951 was a watershed year for both Britain and for advertising. Two years earlier the Labour government had appointed Lord Beveridge to chair an inquiry into the future of British broadcasting. Beveridge reported in 1951 and it is widely believed that, with one famous exception, the members of his committee were unanimously hostile to broadcasting being commercially financed. This is not true. The famous exception was Selwyn Lloyd, later Chancellor of the Exchequer and Foreign Secretary, who advocated the establishment of new radio and television services financed by sponsorship. But three other members of the committee, including Beveridge himself, said the total prohibition of advertising in broadcast media should be reconsidered. 'Is there any reason', they asked, 'why the most persuasive means of communication should not be used for this legitimate purpose?' The Labour government, knowing that many of its MPs and supporters were implacably hostile to the commercialization of broadcasting, shelved any decision about the Beveridge inquiry until 1952. But by then it was out of office, and an administration far more favourably inclined towards advertising was in power.

There was one important way in which 1951 was not a watershed year for advertising. To mark the great AA conference, the trade magazine *Advertisers' Weekly*—which competed with *World's Press News*, and claimed to be 'The Organ of British Advertising'—published a supplement it called a 'Portfolio of British Creative Advertising'. The introductory editorial was headlined 'British Creative Advertising Has Distinct Qualities', and went on 'The work of the best British agencies today can fearlessly challenge competition with that of any country in the world', a modestly phrased claim in the world of advertising—and rightly so. Few of the advertisements in the supplement display distinctive creative qualities. A handful from Crawfords, then one of the country's most creative shops—for Gillette, Martini, Daks, and KLM—were way ahead of the rest. But there was far better stuff before the war, and the halcyon decades of British advertising creativity were yet to come.

Antecedents: Look Back in Wonder

Advertising is popularly believed to be a modern—or at least a twentieth-century—phenomenon. Not so.

Shop signs existed in ancient Mesopotamia and Egypt, but the Athenians can probably lay claim to the invention of modern commercial advertising as we know it. In Athens there were town criers, chosen for their mellifluous voices and clear elocution, who interrupted their proclamations with paid-for advertisements (just as advertisements interrupt television newscasts today). Aesclyptoe, an early Athenian cosmetician, promoted his lotions and potions with consummate professionalism:

> For eyes that are shining, for cheeks like the dawn,
> For beauty that lasts after girlhood has gone,
> For prices in reason the women who know
> Now buy their cosmetics from Aesclyptoe.

This doggerel—which could have sprung yesterday from a highly paid copywriter's laptop—may well have been sung as a jingle, since the town criers were often accompanied by musicians. Following the Athenians, advertising burgeoned in Rome, Herculaneum, and Pompeii, where prostitutes' ads can be still seen carved into the stonework of the once-buried city. Thus was one of the world's oldest professions linked with another of the world's oldest professions, from the start.

This being a history of British advertising, I will skip from the ancient world to the earliest known advertisements in this country, again from town criers, who are first mentioned in 1299 but almost certainly plied their trade here much earlier. Printed advertising followed hard on Gutenberg's invention of the printing press in the middle of the fifteenth century. The first known printed advertisement in English, *The Pyes of Salisburi*—which was not, sadly, a puff for Salisbury pies but for a book of religious services—was printed in 1477 by William Caxton himself; he claimed 'The Pyes' was 'good chepe'. Thereafter royalty and other authorities, as well as the church, used advertisements in newssheets to impart information to the public—early public service advertising. The first magazine advertisements appeared early in the seventeenth century, and soon merchants were promoting patent medicines, property, and books (perfect targeting, as only those who could read bought magazines and newssheets). By then advertisements were so numerous that readers were already protesting there were too many of them.

Even then, as ever since, some questioned whether it was right to rely on advertising as the best way for sellers to communicate with buyers. The issue seems to have been first identified by the great French philosopher Montaigne, who raised it in his essay *Of a Defect in our Policies* (1595). How, he asked, can buyers and sellers successfully communicate with each other? The solution, he suggested, was for detailed lists of goods on sale to be published by objective third parties, without exaggeration or embellishment—a solution which would be endorsed by consumerists to this day.

Montaigne's idea for the publication of reliable lists was taken up in England in 1611, when Sir Arthur Gorges and Sir Walter Cope obtained Letters Patent for the launch of 'The Publicke Register for Generall Commerce'. The Letters Patent stated:

> A great defect is daily to be found in the Policie of our State for want of some good, trusty and ready measure of intelligence and intercourse between our said Subjects . . . By means whereof many men oftentimes sell landes, leases and other goods and chattels to great loss and disadvantage . . . to many that would (if they knew thereof) as willingly buy as the others would gladly sell.[1]

Interestingly, the buyer is here seen to lose out as much as the seller. However, the Publicke Register proved not to be one of history's great new product ideas. It flopped. Sir Arthur and Sir Walter relinquished their patent the following year. In the second half of the seventeenth century several other entrepreneurs tried to launch similar enterprises, equally unsuccessfully. For the great majority of goods and services such giant lists, packed though they may be with 'good, trusty and ready measures of intelligence' are plain boring, and few people can be bothered

---

[1] This is not a bad rendition of Lord Beveridge's peroration at the 1951 AA conference.

to pore over them. Instead, with the spread of literacy and the expansion of newspapers, commercial advertising increased. The difference between lists and advertising was defined with estimable accuracy by the essayist Richard Addison writing in *The Tatler* in 1710:

> The great Art in writing Advertisements is the finding out of a proper Method to catch the Reader's Eye, without which a good thing may be passed over, or be lost.

The underlying difference between classified advertising (lists) and display advertising ('catching the reader's eye') was thus unwittingly established. It will also be seen that Addison stresses the benefits which accrue to the buyer as well as the seller. It was not until the nineteenth century that it began to be felt that the benefits of advertising accrued almost entirely to the seller, usually to the detriment of the buyer. But already in 1759 there was a hint of another criticism to come, in the words of the great lexicographer Dr Samuel Johnson:

> Advertisements are now so numerous that they are very negligently perused, and it is therefore become necessary to gain attention by magnificence of promises, and by eloquence sometimes sublime and sometimes pathetic. Promise, large promise, is the soul of an Advertisement.

The 'now so numerous' advertisements were not only 'sometimes pathetic', they were not welcomed by the political establishment. This was not because of their content. It was because they subsidized the price of newspapers, and newspapers have never—then or now—been as subservient and sycophantic as politicians would like them to be. Nor have politicians' fears been groundless. Pamphleteers had played a major part in inciting public antagonism to Charles I: the beheaded king was described as having been defeated by 'paper bullets'. To control newspapers, in the seventeenth century editors were occasionally jailed. But taxes provided politicians with a subtler way to rein them in. In 1712 the government introduced a tax which levied a one-shilling duty—a sizeable sum—on every advertisement published. The duty was one of several taxes designed to retard the development of a free press in Britain, in this case by inhibiting advertising. Nonetheless, by the time of its repeal in 1853, just under 2 million advertisements were being taxed annually, a fourfold increase over the half-million at the start of that century, and a reflection of the resilience of advertising to restrictive pressures. Moreover, to get a complete picture of how advertising was thriving by the mid-nineteenth century, to those 2 million must be added advertisements in 'illegal' papers, which were not registered for the duty, plus posters, plus a panoply of other media which were then being discovered, or invented, by advertisers and their agents. Businessmen were quickly learning that advertising paid. By 1905 Clarence Moran was able to write in his book *The Business of Advertising*: 'There is, in fact, no class of consumers which cannot be affected through the medium of some section or other of the press.'

Magazines too were growing apace, likewise subsidized by advertising. Popular general periodicals like *Titbits* and *Answers* reached circulations of just under 1 million by the end of the nineteenth century.

Back at the beginning of the nineteenth century, the advertising industry had adopted the underlying tripartite structure that has survived to this day: the advertisers, the media, and the agencies. Almost certainly the first advertising agent in Britain (and therefore in the world) was William Taylor, who so described himself in an advertisement which appeared in 1786. Initially agents existed both to sell media space and to guide their clients towards the best media-buys. They were, effectively, media brokers. But by about 1800 agents were beginning to create advertisements, as well as place them. The essayist Charles Lamb raked in a little freelance cash by writing puffs for his friend the agent James White during the first decade of the nineteenth century.

Whether it was the government duty which drove advertisers to try media other than newspapers, or the energetic inventiveness of Victorian businessmen, the nineteenth century saw an explosion of new advertising media and methods on a scale certainly never seen before and arguably—with due respect to today's new media—never seen since. Many were admirably ingenious, many were wacky, many were effective and have survived the test of time, many were dodos and didn't.

Most of the basic techniques used by advertisers today were established in the nineteenth century. The Victorians were, for example, masterful at merchandising tie-ins with books and plays. Not only was there a striking 1871 poster campaign for Wilkie Collins's novel *Woman in White*—now often claimed to be the first modern poster design—but fans could also spray themselves with Woman in White perfume, dress themselves in Woman in White cloaks and bonnets, and dance to Woman in White waltzes and quadrilles. To promote his novel *Trilby*, author George du Maurier and his publishers offered Trilby sausages, Trilby ice-cream moulds, Trilby lapel pins, and Trilby hats, which have enjoyed impressive longevity. Eco-marketing arguably began on 2 July 1855 when Crosse and Blackwell announced, in an advertisement in the *Morning Chronicle*, that they were removing artificial colourings from their popular preserved foods. For Pears' soap Lillie Langtry, the most beautiful actress of the day, provided one of the first ever celebrity endorsements on a poster worded 'Since using PEARS' SOAP for the hands and complexion *I have discarded all others.*' The poster contained her picture and her signature.

In the middle of the nineteenth century Edward Lloyd, the owner of *Lloyd's Weekly Newspaper*, gave real meaning to the advertising jargon 'cost per thousand' when he stamped coins of the realm with the name of his weekly organ. The government took a dim view of Lloyd defacing British coinage, and made it illegal to do so thereafter. Consequently Thomas J. Barrett, appointed a director of the Pears' soap company in 1865, imported 250,000 French centimes and stamped 'Pears' on them. In those days French coins were legal tender here. The government retaliated by banning the centimes, and foreign national currency has never since been UK legal tender. Undaunted, Barrett badgered the government into letting him print Pears advertisements on the backs of postage stamps. He offered to sponsor and brand the 1891 census, but the government demurred. He was the first of the really big advertising spenders—petrifying Francis Pears, the chairman of the company, who felt it wise to resign from the family business in 1875 while (as it seemed to him) there was still a business to resign from. Barrett multiplied the brand's annual advertising budget from £80 when he joined to £126,000 in the 1890s. Despite Francis Pears' faint heart, Pears' soap cleaned up the market and Barrett built one of the world's first great brands. Yet he found himself constantly forced to defend his exorbitant advertising budgets, pointing out that the resulting economies of mass production made it possible to sell Pears' soap 30 per cent cheaper than it otherwise would have been. Barrett was dubbed 'the father of English advertising' by the first Lord Northcliffe, and 'the king of advertisers' by his contemporaries.

In addition to his more outlandish schemes Barrett firmly believed in using traditional advertising media. As well as using stage celebrities like Lillie Langtry, he employed leading artists to create his advertisements, and having bought Sir John Millais' painting '*Bubbles*' for £2,200 he used it on one of history's most famous posters. (Whether Millais was wholly delighted by this is disputed.)

'From an aesthetic point of view,' writes Professor Terry Nevett in his history, 'poster illustration in Britain reached a higher standard at the end of the 19th century than at any time before or since.' This is probably not a view with which the French would concur, since in Paris at the same time

Bonnard, Cheret, Manet, Mucha, and Toulouse-Lautrec were all designing magnificent posters.[2]

The long-standing overlap of advertising and art is spotlit in the 1896 Hamburg Poster Exhibition Catalogue:

> Art should be accessible to everyone... not only to those who can afford to buy works of art or have the time to seek them out in galleries... Art must go on the streets, where chance will bring it to the notice of many thousands on their way to work who have neither time nor money to spare. High ethical standards are fulfilled by posters created for everyday practical purposes—provided they are good posters.

But by no means all nineteenth-century advertising aspired to high ethical standards, as Leonard de Vries' *Victorian Advertisements* clearly reveals. To make the book fun, de Vries selects advertisements for the weirdest products he can find. But this can have presented him with few difficulties. From the eighteenth century onwards the media were replete with products promising incredible, not to say unattainable, benefits. Advertisers promised to cure every malady known to mankind and quite a few that are not—such as 'DEATH in the boot, the new affliction with which all who wear footwear are threatened' (safely cured, one is relieved to hear, by O'Brien's Patent Watertight Waist Foothold Golosh).

Apart from Barrett, probably the most inventive Victorian advertising man was the Glasgow grocer Thomas J. Lipton. He sent parades of skinny men through the streets carrying posters saying 'Going to Lipton's', followed by parades of fat men labelled 'Coming from Lipton's', and he drove home the message multi-media style by installing convex and concave mirrors in his stores, carefully placing them so customers saw themselves as skinny on the way in, and plump on the way out. He imported gigantic cheeses, each weighing 3,472 pounds, into which he stuffed coins which customers could win with their purchases. 'An illegal lottery!' cried the police, whereupon Lipton promptly ran advertisements asking the winners to bring their coins back. He publicly offered one of his cheeses to Queen Victoria to mark her Jubilee in 1885, but she was not amused. She could not, she sniffed, accept goods from people to whom she had not been introduced.

The theatrical impresario William Smith employed sandwich men for his shows, and touts to hurl flyers through the open windows of buses and

---

[2] Cheret is another contender for the title of 'father of modern poster design', partly because he developed high-speed colour lithography specifically for the poster medium, and partly because of his astonishing output. He designed more than 2,000 different posters, for a wide range of products, from cabarets to cough drops.

carriages, and had 10 million sticky labels stuck to 'omnibuses, cabs, vans, railway carriages, Windsor Castle, the Old Bailey, steamboats and glassware in public houses'. A tooth powder company devised a way to fire advertisements into people's gardens with a gun. An agent cut stencils into the soles of his boots, supplied them with ink via a tube running down the inside of his trouser leg and strolled around London stamping ads on the pavements. None of these was destined to become a major advertising medium.

Handbills, however, were a punchy medium from the start. In 1861 annual handbill distribution was estimated at 1.15 billion in London alone. William Smith, a novitiate market researcher as well as an impresario, established that during a walk through London the average pedestrian would have 250 handbills stuffed into his fist. A media guru of the time commented:

> Any man can stick up a bill upon a wall, but to insinuate one gracefully and irresistibly into the hands of a lady or a gentleman is only for one who, to natural genius, adds long experience.

Meanwhile direct marketing—usually thought to be a terribly modern medium—was booming. On 29 May 1864 leading Parliamentarians received hand-delivered telegraphs from 'Messrs Gabriel, dentists, Harley-street'. Messrs Gabriel were not, in fact, qualified dentists, but they were masterful marketing men, and their telegraphs were probably the first electrically-based marketing communications in history. From the 1870s postal advertising boomed. In 1907 the Reliable Addressing Service offered to advertisers a register of 30,000 car owners, and a list of 170,000 London suburbanites graded according to the value of their rent. Reliable Addressing could reliably address 250,000 catalogues a day, and despatched over 9 million mailings annually, even without the aid of a computer to botch things up.

This torrential flood of advertising was not universally welcome. There were business commentators who were concerned, even then, that the volume of advertising was impairing its own effectiveness. In *Hints on Advertising, Adapted to the Times* (1870) George Gentle wrote: 'There are some persons who entertain the idea that Advertising has seen its best days, that the public are tired of it and do not appreciate it.'

But more importantly, there were increasing numbers of influential people who felt the welter of advertising was despoiling Britain's towns and countryside, and the obscenity and mendacity of many advertisements had to be restrained. This view was underpinned by a widespread, intellectual and particularly British distaste for selling and salesmen. Macaulay wrote, for example, in the *Edinburgh Review* (April 1830):

> A butcher of the higher class disdains to ticket his meat...We expect some reserve, some decent pride in our hatter and bootmaker.

Thomas Carlyle was similarly sour about what he called the 'all deafening blast of puffery', and wrote in *Past and Present* (1843):

> There is not a man or hat-maker born into the world but feels, or has felt, that he is degrading himself if he speak of his excellences and prowesses, and supremacy in his craft...He feels that he is a braggart; fast hastening to be a falsity and speaker of the Untruth.

By the end of the century an influential pressure group called SCAPA (Society for Controlling the Abuses of Public Advertising) published a membership list which included such notable intellectuals as William Morris, Rudyard Kipling, Holman Hunt, Arthur Quiller-Couch, Robert Bridges, and Millais—perhaps still fuming about Bubbles—but also including Sydney Courtauld and members of the Fry (chocolate) family, showing that business people too were concerned about some of advertising's excesses. But the public was apathetic. There were 500 copies of a SCAPA pamphlet printed, of which only 30 were sold.

There is now a general belief that Victorian advertising was totally unfettered by controls of any kind. Not so. Exuberance and ingenuity in the service of Mammon have always needed to be restrained. There has been consumer protection legislation in Britain since Magna Carta. The mid-nineteenth century saw a succession of Acts which regulated sandwich men, billposters, noise, gambling, and indecent advertisements. To a lesser extent controls began to tackle advertiser dishonesty. Until nearly the end of the nineteenth century, however, the principle remedy for a customer was a Common Law action for breach of contract, requiring proof that the goods were either fundamentally different from what had been ordered, or that there had been a false inducement to buy them. Things changed in 1891 following a landmark case in which a Mrs Carlill bought a Carbolic Smoke Bomb advertised in the *Pall Mall Gazette*. The advertisement guaranteed her protection from influenza (among many other illnesses) or a £100 reward. The Smoke Bomb bombed. Mrs Carlill caught the flu, sued for her £100 and won—the court viewing the advertisement as a contract. Thereafter the Sale of Goods Act was passed in 1893 which greatly increased consumers' civil remedies over and above those provided by the Common Law. The twentieth century, and especially the second half of the twentieth century, saw a continuing escalation of the legal power of the consumer, against the advertiser.

All this took place against a background of rapidly escalating national wealth and—more importantly from the advertising perspective—a burgeoning of brands and branding. In the 1870s consumer choice began to increase for the working class, and advertisements started to appear for washing and cleaning products, as well as for sauces, relishes, and meat extracts to enhance what would usually have been very basic diets. Papers like the *Daily Telegraph* also carried advertisements for banking and insurance, auctions, charities, even horses-and-carriages.

Branding was developed during the nineteenth century, and with it brand advertising. Until then advertisers' names had appeared in their advertisements, but each advertisement was treated as an individual announcement. Each advertisement aimed to provide the public with new information, and each advertisement aimed to realize immediate sales. Brand advertising is not, essentially, immediate. It aims to build long-term reputation. And some of the very earliest brands—including Crosse and Blackwell, Lea & Perrins, Schweppes, and Wedgwood—built long-term reputations so successfully they are still with us two centuries or so later.

Branding guarantees to the public the consistent quality of the branded product. By advertising their brands direct to the public, manufacturers sought to force wholesalers and retailers to stock them. And while brands do not inherently need or depend upon advertising—today we recognize countless unadvertised brands of varying kinds—advertising is usually the most cost-efficient way for a brand owner to let consumers know about his brand. All this is easily understood today, but was utterly new two centuries ago. As Victorian businessmen grasped these commercial truths advertising truly began to boom—reflected in the fact that by the 1890s many major companies were using advertising agencies, including Players' Tobaccos, Colman's Mustards and Starch, Cadbury's, Fry's, Rowntree's, Suchard, Van Houten, Bovril, Liebig's (OXO), Pears, Wright's Coal Tar and Ivory Soaps— and a host of others, not all of which survived the twentieth century.

At the start of the twentieth century advertising in Britain took another leap forward, a creative leap, which was hardly noticed at the time but was to have long-term consequences. Until the late nineteenth century advertising was serious stuff. Much of it looks comic today, but it was not intended to be funny. It was intended to sell. Selling called for conviction and commitment. Humour was inappropriate. Until the end of the nineteenth century advertisements were often charming, and very occasionally light-hearted, but never deliberately amusing.

Around 1900, two fine British poster artists, Dudley Hardy and John Hassall, changed all that. Hassall's most compelling creation was the tubby, loveable fisherman 'Skeggy', whose uphill task it was to promote the northern seaside town of Skegness as a delectable holiday resort. Hardy's best known work was for theatrical comedies like *Cinderella*, *The Gaiety Girl*, and *Oh! What a Night!* in which he successfully developed a British comedic style in print. In introducing humour to commercial art, Hardy and Hassall established a strong tradition in British advertising which has, to a large extent, differentiated it from that of other countries. Most other countries now produce amusing advertisements occasionally. The British have been doing it longer, and still do it more often (Ch. 6, 'Laughing All the Way').

I have explored the late Victorian advertising scene at some length because so much of what was to happen in the second half of the twentieth century was unerringly foreshadowed during the second half of the nineteenth century. Already British advertising was exuberantly inventive, sometimes humorous, often outrageous. Already advertising was growing apace. Already it was being used by manufacturers to go over the heads of wholesalers and retailers, direct to the public. Already, along with its supporters, it had redoubtable antagonists. Already, senior businessmen were questioning its effectiveness. Already, for varying reasons, politicians and legislators felt the need to constrain its powers. All these phenomena seem to be intrinsic to advertising in Britain, part of its very DNA.

* * *

The first half of the twentieth century saw few equally radical innovations. Perhaps this is unsurprising in a period dominated by two world wars, and by the global recession of the 1930s which followed the 1929 international stock market crash. Though total advertising increased healthily during the 1920s, from £31 million in 1920 to £57 million by 1928, during the 1930s growth stagnated and by 1938 it had only reached £59 million. During both world wars advertising expenditure plummeted.

The most significant developments during the half-century included the creation of three new important advertising trade associations—what became the Institute of Practitioners in Advertising (IPA), the Incorporated Society of British Advertisers (ISBA), and the Advertising Association (AA). The AA coordinates the efforts of all the other trade associations (including the media trade associations) as and when they coincide. These advertising trade associations grew greatly in importance and influence

during the century, taking responsibility for much training and professional education, for lobbying, and for providing legal advice.

Other important developments during those years included the introduction of market research, the germination of commercial radio, the first
stabs at self-regulation, the use of advertising by governments during the
two world wars—and the consolidation of the agency commission system.

Commercial market research was born in the USA at the start of the twentieth century. It was brought to Britain by J Walter Thompson, whose London
office in 1923 introduced 'field research', which it had learned from its American parent. In Britain market research was initially greeted with scepticism
and derision, partly because this is the British way, but mostly because
research had been infiltrated by rogues and charlatans. Nonetheless, by 1935
Advertisers' Weekly wrote: 'It has survived the disparagement...its practitioners have vastly perfected their methods and have been gradually demonstrating the value of research in making methods more precise.'

Also during the 1930s commercial radio first began to reverberate a little,
accounting for around 2 per cent of total expenditure during the decade. UK-
based commercial radio was illegal. The BBC had a statutory monopoly.
However, in 1930 commercial broadcasters began beaming transmissions
into Britain from Normandy, Luxembourg, Paris, Madrid, and other spots
in Europe—and these transmissions quickly caught on. Two separate surveys
in 1935 showed about 60 per cent of households with radio sets listened to the
commercial channels. Such was their popularity that many believed commercial radio would be introduced in 1936, when the BBC's charter was to be
renewed. But the opposition to commercial radio was powerful—from the
BBC, but also from the NPA, whose members naturally had a vested interest
in blocking new competition. Legalized commercial radio did not come to
Britain until nearly 40 years later.

Cinema advertising, in contrast, had begun 40 years earlier, when a still
slide was shown at the Empire, Leicester Square in 1896. The first moving
cinema advertisement was for Dewar's Whisky in 1900, and sound came
along in 1927. But many cinema owners were leery of carrying advertising.
As late as December 1938 the large Associated British Picture Corporation
banned advertising in its 500 cinemas, its boss John Maxwell declaring, 'It
is unethical to take money from customers at the box office...then sell
them products from the screen. People come to be entertained, not to be
advertised at.' It is hardly surprising, then, that the cinema accounted for
only 1 per cent of total expenditure at that time.

Meanwhile the industry was starting to set its house in order. Ever
since the nineteenth century individual publishers had refused to carry

advertisements they disapproved of, for one reason or another, but in 1927 the Advertising Association set up the first self-regulatory National Vigilance Committee, which a year later was expanded into the Advertising Investigation Department. Though puny compared with today's Advertising Standards Authority, the AID helped drive shady operators out of the press, brought pressure to bear on agencies to stop them handling fraudulent advertisers' business, and dealt with 1,169 complaints from the public during 12 months in 1936–7.

The industry also set its house in order structurally. In 1930 the IPA proposed to the Newspaper Publishers' Association (NPA)[3] that the loose system of agency 'recognition' be formalized, and that newspapers should pay commissions only to agencies the NPA 'recognized'. Though newspapers had been paying agencies commission for bringing them business since the early nineteenth century, the practice had fallen into disuse (and misuse) between 1880 and 1920, when many agencies started to give the newspapers' commissions back to their clients. Indeed in 1909 the Thirty Club—advertising's leading dining club, then as now—held a debate entitled 'Should Agency Commission Be Abolished?' because some agencies were publicly offering to rebate commissions to advertisers and charge them instead a work-related fee (the common system today). Under the 1930 IPA proposal, agencies needed to provide details of their financial and professional competence to the NPA in order to be recognized. They would be legally liable for their clients' space bookings, and would not be permitted to rebate commissions to advertisers. In the event this recognition proposal was not enacted until 1941, but thereafter the system reigned supreme—policed rigorously by the media—and it moulded the shape and structure of British advertising agencies, and of the advertising industry, for almost 40 years.

While the two world wars resulted in a dearth of commercial advertising, they engendered a flowering of government advertising—perhaps more properly called propaganda—of unforgettable, and sometimes uncomfortable, impact. It was a corner of advertising in which Britain excelled. During the First World War, the War Cabinet set up a committee of advertising experts, and the military recruitment advertising they created has never been surpassed. Adolf Hitler himself paid tribute to Britain's propagandist skills, in *Mein Kampf*. Two campaigns were masterpieces of their kind. The first was 'Lord Kitchener wants YOU', which was written by Eric Field and designed by the artist Alfred Leete, though the idea came from Lord Kitchener himself. Following its publication 35,000 men were

[3] At that time called the Newspaper Proprietors' Association.

recruited in one month. The second campaign was Savile Lumley's notorious 'Daddy, what did *YOU* do in the Great War?' series, whose emotional blackmail provoked much public hostility. During the Second World War there was less emphasis on recruitment, as statutory conscription was enforced from the start. But the advertising was equally powerful. The government employed a team of 60 artists and designers within its newly formed Ministry of Information, and spent a massive £9.5 million on propaganda advertising, running some 80 campaigns designed to promote the conflict as 'a people's war'. Britain's leading designers, illustrators, and cartoonists provided a variety of exhortations from 'Dig For Victory' to 'Women Of Britain—Come Into The Factories', 'Look Out In The Blackout', and 'Careless Talk Costs Lives'.

During the following half-century, governments came to use advertising ever more extensively until, in many years, they were the biggest advertisers in Britain.

3

The Nineteen-Fifties: The Television Upheaval

'An Evil Machine'

Two years after 'The Greatest Ever Advertising Conference', in 1953 the Advertising Association held another grand jamboree. This was the era when large conferences, attended by 1,400 or more delegates, were an annual feature of the advertising calendar. Today such beanos are extinct. There has not been a national (let alone international) AA conference since 1989, and that one was an almost unmitigated flop, gathering a mere 400 or so delegates in Deauville. A successor, planned for 1992 in London, was cancelled for lack of support. But in leisurely times gone by, before 24/7 workaholism and financial accountability became the norms, advertising men—they were almost all men—liked nothing better than to whisk their compliant lady wives away each year for three or four days, to enjoy some tub-thumping, self-congratulatory oratory; a spot of golf; a white-tie ball with decorations and lots of convivial hobnobbing over a generous flow of cocktails and bubbly.[1]

Unfortunately the 1953 jolly was far from jolly. The organizers had invited firebrand Aneurin ('Nye') Bevan to be the lead speaker. Nye was a hard-line socialist. He personally launched the National Health Service, and famously resigned from the Attlee Labour government when it introduced prescription charges. Nonetheless, *Advertisers' Weekly* crowed enthusiastically when he accepted the AA's 1953 invitation: he was thought to be

---

[1] To some extent annual creative awards dinners in grand hotels, many attended by well over a thousand diners, have superseded conferences—reflecting the enhanced importance of creativity and creative people in today's advertising landscape.

a great catch. A stupendous orator, on 7 May the delegates in Eastbourne heard him thunder:

> I regard advertising as one of the most evil consequences of a society which is itself evil...you are harnessed to an evil machine which is doing great harm to society...the consumer is passive, besieged, assaulted, battered and robbed.

The reception to this onslaught was described by *Advertisers' Weekly* as 'cordial'. Possibly, but Nye's speech was publicized nationally, causing the delegates to round on the conference organizers. The organizing chairman, A. Everett Jones, responded by saying the advertising industry needed to know what socialists were thinking, in case they returned to power—a feeble defence, as the likelihood of this happening was nil.

People who work in advertising grow accustomed to being attacked, and hostility to advertising rears its head repeatedly throughout the second half of the twentieth century. As has already been seen, this is nothing new. Nor is advertising disparaged more than some other lines of business. But the great majority of people do not work in industries which are continuously disparaged. And working for an industry under attack has particular consequences. People develop a siege mentality, become unusually cliquey, inward-looking, defensive. Few if any other industries publish as many articles, pamphlets and books aiming to prove their work is truly worthwhile—honest, guv!

But between 1951 and 2000 there was a shift in the burden of the hostility. At the start, much of it, like Bevan's, was comprehensive and all-embracing: advertising was 'an evil machine', with no redeeming features. A round-up of opinion leaders in 1970 (Ch. 5, 'Let's Play Knock-the-Adman') elicited similar sweeping antipathies from most of them. Since then attitudes have changed, perhaps stoked by the modern fashionability of 'creative industries'. Today almost everyone accepts advertising provides economic and social benefits. Criticisms pertain to particular advertising sectors—alcohol, fattening foods, fast cars, ecologically damaging products, and so on; or to advertising's portrayal of particular social groups—the representation of women, or ethnic minorities, or the handicapped. Critics seldom now attack advertising as a phenomenon. But this does not make them less significant.

The New Bubonic Plague

When Winston Churchill swept back to power in October 1951—the first general election in which Margaret Thatcher stood—the Tory campaign promised to make Britain 'strong and free'. The Tories were determined to dismantle the plethora of economic controls the Labour administration had been forced to enact during the unremittingly tough post-war years. Despite the 1955–6 Suez debacle, the increasingly glacial cold war, the fear of H-bomb mushrooms blackening the skies, and the decline and fall of Britain's international power, under a series of Tory governments the 1950s was a decade of irrepressible optimism. Prime Minister Harold Macmillan exactly caught its zeitgeist when, in 1957, he proclaimed to the nation, 'You've never had it so good.' For the great majority of the population, this was the plain truth. After nearly thirty depressing years of recession, war, and the unexpected austerity of the war's aftermath, the feel-good factor ran amok.

Nye Bevan's AA conference tirade—in addition to being a venting of his natural spleen—was probably intended to abort the Television Bill, then in gestation. This Bill, when enacted, would bring commercial television to Britain. If this was indeed Nye's intention, he rather torpedoed his own case by admitting he owned no television set and had never watched a television programme in his life. Lord Reith's opposition to the Bill was more intimidating. Reith was the intense, puritan Scot who had been the driving force and guiding spirit behind the BBC from 1922 to 1938. In the House of Lords he compared the introduction of television advertising to the introduction into England of smallpox, the Black Death, and the bubonic plague. Other noble Lords felt similarly. Lord Hailsham likened ITV to 'a Caliban emerging from his slimy cavern'. Lord Esher forecast 'a planned and premeditated orgy of vulgarity'. Clement Attlee let it be known that if Labour won the forthcoming 1956 general election the proposed commercial television service would be dismantled.

Yet the commercial use of broadcast media had started long before. The first-ever entertainment broadcast in Britain was sponsored by the *Daily Mail*, on 15 June 1920. The British Broadcasting Company was the 1922 brainchild of a group of radio and electrical equipment manufacturers who wanted to promote their wares. It rapidly ran into financial difficulties, and in 1925 the government bought out the private shareholders. On 1 January 1927 it was transmuted into the state-owned British Broadcasting Corporation.

In November 1930 the hairdressers Eugene ('perfectors of the permanent wave') used a closed-circuit Baird system to transmit a demonstration at the Hairdressing Fair in London's Olympia. Eugene claimed they were the first 'to discover the real commercial use for Baird Television'. In the United States, television was commercial from its start, and from this side of the Atlantic it was thought ineffably vulgar. Horrific tales of crass programming, corruption, and interference by sponsors were legion.

Advertising on British television had been considered by the Selsdon Committee in 1934, but Lord Reith and the BBC had then kept the bubonic plague at bay. By the early 1950s the climate had changed, not least because there had been a good deal of quiet lobbying. James Garrett, whose company became one of the foremost makers of commercials, writes in Brian Henry's *British Television Advertising* (1986) that independent television was:

> carefully, skilfully, lobbied by a strange hotchpotch of people who knew that...there would be something in it for them. There was no real public clamour for an alternative to the BBC's service. The 'demand' was largely an invention of the self-interested.

Garrett was on the button. In the run up to the 1954 Television Bill which brought ITV into being, Labour MP Christopher Mayhew formed a National Television Council to block its launch. His Council included such distinguished figures as Bertrand Russell and E. M. Forster, and Mayhew published a polemical pamphlet called *Dear Viewer* which sold 60,000 copies. But the lobbyists on the other side had formed the Popular Television Association—astute naming—which was publicly launched in a letter to *The Times* on 19 July 1953. The PTA's 'strange hotchpotch' of supporters included Somerset Maugham, Rex Harrison and—astonishingly—both the idiosyncratic commentator Malcolm Muggeridge, and the celebrated Marxist historian A. J. P. Taylor (each of whom must have had his own personal reason for wanting to clobber the BBC). The PTA was backed by the advertising industry and by Conservative Central Office, and had raised a handsome £20,000 bankroll before its first meeting. Mayhew's NTC budget was a mere £840.

Opening the debate on the 1954 Television Bill, former Deputy Prime Minister Herbert Morrison opined that this was 'to be one of the—if not the—most important debates since the war. On it depends the future thinking of our people and our standards of culture.' Maybe this was a mite melodramatic, but certainly television in total has had an immeasurable impact on people's thinking and culture over the past 50 years, and commercial television has played a huge part in this. What is undeniable is that for 50 years commercial television has been one of the most powerful factors influencing the British economy, and the single most powerful factor influencing British advertising.

Commercial television was the high-octane fuel which powered the consumer society. Television is unquestionably the fastest-acting mass advertising medium, capable of building nigh on 100 per cent public awareness of a new product or campaign in a matter of days. In consequence it can generate mass sales far more rapidly than any other medium. This expedited the introduction of labour-saving appliances in the home, for example, which radically changed the role of women in the 1950s and 1960s. Television facilitated and expedited the growth of supermarkets and other mass national retailers—both by pulling manufacturers' brands off their shelves, and by helping them build their own brands and store traffic. It was the backbone of the massive privatizations which revolutionized the economic make-up of the country in the 1980s. It brought forward a generation of outstandingly talented British film directors, and energized Britain's creative reputation around the globe. Like an octopus with countless arms, it has reached out and entangled almost every aspect of our society.

Within the advertising industry, commercial television's intrusion into people's homes changed the relationship of advertisers with the public, and of the public with advertisers. Its use of sound and motion (and later colour) transformed the nature of advertising creativity and of agency creative departments. This fundamentally altered the power structure in advertising agencies. The complexity of buying television time, combined with the vast sums involved, transformed the nature of media-buying, and thereby the shape of the advertising industry. And the vast sums involved swiftly escalated the importance of market research in advertising.

All this muscle simultaneously endeared television advertising to businesses and made its antagonists fearful. Had commercial television not come to Britain, or had its launch been lengthily delayed—which would have been the outcome had Bevan, Mayhew, Reith, and their cohorts been victorious—the history of British society in the second half of the twentieth century would have been quite different, and the history of British advertising during those years would hardly have been worth writing.

The new Television Act received Royal Assent and became law on 30 July 1954, and it is now widely believed ITV was a storming success right from its start in September 1955. 'The advertising world was surprised by the speed with which the new medium established itself,' claims Terry Nevett, 'from the outset television advertising was remarkably successful.' And so it should have been. But it wasn't.

The auguries were excellent. Television set ownership was growing rapidly. The number of licences rose from 3 million in 1954 to almost 6 million by 1956. Advertising was booming. Between 1952 and 1955 advertising expenditure rose from £123 million to £176 million (up 43 per cent). From

1952 onwards the trade press was crammed with stories of big new campaigns. *Advertisers' Weekly* headlines like 'Hedley launch another new detergent—DAZ', and 'Branded Petrol Will See Biggest Advertising Battle For Years Joined' were par for the course. But national newspapers were still fettered by newsprint rationing, a hangover from the war, and so were unable to meet advertisers' swelling demands for space. For television, this left the door wide open.

In August 1955, the leading think tank Political and Economic Planning predicted ITV's advertising revenue would be £20 million in 1956, its first full year. In the event, in 1956 television raked in just £10.6 million, and the contractors lost £11 million in the first 18 months. 'The early backers of ITV had been hopelessly over-optimistic,' wrote Brian Henry. It was not until the end of 1957 that things perked up.

The reasons for ITV's slow take-off comprise an object lesson in advertisers' reactions to new media, and were broadly to be repeated when the internet arrived at the end of the century. Advertisers are, rightly, cautious about spending large sums of money on unproven media. Quite apart from the dottier media tried out in the nineteenth century, far better established media, which seemed likely to be perfect vehicles for advertising, have proved to be duds. Books, gramophone records, the telephone, recorded videotapes were all thought likely to be good carriers of advertising, but failed. (As late as 1960, 1,125,000 'advertising records' were distributed in Britain, carrying advertising spots for such major advertisers as Mobil, Pepsi, Nestlé, and McDougall's Flour among others. This was never repeated.)

True, commercial television had proved itself in America, but this was no guarantee it would work in Britain. Most people thought it would be a flash-in-the-pan: 'Just Radio Luxembourg with pictures', as one agency wag declared in 1955. A year after ITV's launch, in September 1956, the Incorporated Society of British Advertisers' conference was titled 'Does Television Sell Goods?' and the answer was a resounding 'Maybe'. The 600 delegates heard the highly respected S. H. Benson chairman Robert Bevan declare:

> We have proved television can sell some goods, but found it very difficult to prove it can sell others.

Nor, understandably, did the existing media make the importunate infant welcome. The embedded power of print media had been expressed at the great 1951 conference, when Lord Mackintosh declared: 'Advertising and the press are a partnership of enlightened self-interest.' ITV's first night,

22 September 1955, was damned by the press with faint praise. Of the opening night's commercials *The Times* sniffed: 'Offensive would be too strong a word by far for these comic little interruptions of the enter-tainment.' Some newspapers gave enthusiastic front-page prominence to sour comments made by the chairmen of Whitbread's and of Wadding-ton's, both of whom alleged their early television campaigns had been expensive and largely ineffective. And with nimble footwork Britain's leading advertising blockmaker C. & E. Layton, which naturally relied on print advertising, in 1955 launched the first properly organized annual British creative awards scheme—for print advertisements only. This was a wily pre-emptive appeal to agencies, and particularly to their creative staff: agency folk cannot resist gongs.

Neither the new television companies nor the agencies had prepared themselves properly for ITV's launch. There seemed to be a tacit assump-tion that everything would somehow happen of its own accord. It took some time for the TV companies to establish sales operations, to learn how to manage the complexities of spot scheduling, and to set up research systems for the measurement of audiences. Worse, *Advertisers' Weekly* did not report until 17 January 1955 that 'Agency Men Talk TV to their Cli-ents'—hardly long-term planning for a seriously important medium whose launch was nigh.

But things changed. On 20 March 1957, more than 18 months after ITV's start, *Advertisers' Weekly* reported, with breathless astonishment, 'TV Only For New Lever Product'. The largest ever launch of a new floor polish called DUAL was going to eschew print media altogether. This was unheard of. With its birth pangs over, in the late 1950s television's share of total adver-tising soared. By 1960 television had grabbed 22.3 per cent of total media revenue, equivalent to 29.4 per cent of all display advertising (excluding classifieds). Most of this revenue came from packaged goods (Table 1), which continued to be the dominant users of the medium until the late 1970s.

While television advertising was booming, the print media did not stand still. Though paper availability was restricted until 1956, in 1946 sales restrictions had been removed and circulations had rocketed to levels never reached before or since. In 1948 the *News of the World* reached a world record sale of 8 million copies weekly, the *London Evening News* became the world's biggest evening paper selling 1.5 million daily, and the *Daily Mirror* circulation topped 4 million. Aggregate national Sunday newspaper circulation figures totalled some 30 million, national dailies almost 17 million. As over 50 per cent of households took the *News of the World* and 25 per cent took the *Daily Mirror*, these were massively attractive

Table 1. Per cent of 1957 TV expenditure

Product category	%
Foods	22
Soaps and detergents	12
Confectionery	8
Non-alcoholic drinks	7
Medicines	7
Alcohols, cigarettes, and toiletries, each	5
All other product categories, less than	5

Note: It would have been good to be able to provide comparable figures for the entire half-century but this proved impossible, as category definitions changed repeatedly, and so did the companies providing the data.

Source: Brian Henry, *British Television Advertising*.

mass advertising media. And when all newsprint restrictions were finally removed in 1956, newspapers steadily increased their colour pages—a strong competitive advantage over monochrome television.

So television's impact on national newspapers' advertising revenue was far less than might have been expected. Display advertising in national and London evening papers increased healthily every single year from 1955 (£35 million) to 1960 (£62 million), an increase of 77 per cent. Each annual increase was greeted by the trade press—which may possibly have been a mite partisan—with headlines like 'Press Spending Hits New Peak' (*Advertisers' Weekly*, 7 September 1956, repeated word-for-word 7 March 1958).

Display advertising in provincial papers was also strong, growing by 23 per cent between 1955 and 1960. And the provincials were financially buoyed, as they have always been, by classified advertising. Approximately one-third of provincials' advertising revenue then came from classifieds, and classifieds were unaffected by the coming of television. (Today more than two-thirds of provincials' advertising revenue comes from classifieds, but this is falling sharply under pressure from the internet.)

Overall, magazines too survived the arrival of television, with display advertising revenue up 29 per cent between 1955 and 1960. But here the picture was patchy. In *The Business of Women's Magazines* (1979), authors Brian Braithwaite and Joan Barrell state: 'Women's magazines in the fifties were disappointingly lacking in innovation and adventure.'

Between 1955 and 1960 total circulations of weekly magazines fell by 8 per cent. For general magazines the position was still worse. These,

Table 2. Total advertising expenditure as % of GNP

	Expenditure (at current prices) £million	% GNP (at market prices)
1952	123	0.77
1954	157	0.87
1956	196	0.93
1958	249	1.08
1960	323	1.24

Source: Advertising Association.

predictably, were the real victims of television. All of Britain's leading general magazines—*Picture Post*, *Illustrated*, and *Everybody's*—were killed off between 1957 and 1959. However, the revenues of poster and cinema advertising held up, though television stunted their growth.

Throughout the 1950s advertising grew both in monetary terms and as a percentage of the Gross National Product (Table 2).

The 1.24 per cent of UK GNP reached in 1960 was the highest since the war, and probably the highest ever up to that time. (Early data, going back to 1907, suggests higher historical GNP percentages, but this data is neither directly comparable, nor wholly reliable.) With a strong growth trend, with more and more consumer goods flooding the market, with media now free of all wartime restrictions, and with increasing consumer affluence, in 1960 the future of advertising looked delightfully rosy. But for the next 15 years advertising's share of the GNP drifted downwards. It did not exceed the 1960 level of 1.24 per cent until 1984, almost a quarter of a century later.

'Loud Mouthed Salesmen'

In America, advertisers sponsored and produced the television programmes—Kraft Television Theatre, Goodyear TV Playhouse, Texaco Star Theatre, and the like. In the 1950s Coca-Cola alone sponsored over 30 of America's favourite shows. The programmes were frequently interrupted by so-called anchormen saying, 'And now for a word from our sponsor...'. Sometimes the 'word' would be a 60-second commercial, sometimes a sales pitch from the anchorman himself. When, in 1953, the NBC network tried to switch advertisers and agencies from sponsorship to spot advertising, they resisted. They liked the powers sponsorship gave them.[2]

In the UK, many in the advertising industry had expected, and hoped, British commercial television would be built around programme sponsorship too. A major company, Television Advertising Limited, was set up to produce sponsored programmes. But the industry did not get its way. Instead the 1954 Television Act enshrined precepts which reflected Britain's deeply held suspicions and fears of television advertising based on the American sponsorship model. The Act asserted that:

1. Funding should come from spot commercials, not from programme sponsorship, and programmes should be clearly separated from advertisements. Much emphasis was placed on this separation.
2. The channel should be run by an Independent Television Authority (ITA), and neither the ITA nor any programme contractor could act as an advertising agent.
3. The ITA would specify the total minutage of advertising to be allowed (initially 6 minutes per hour), be responsible for the approval of advertising rates, forbid political and religious advertising, and ensure the provision of facilities for local advertisers.
4. The ITA would appoint a statutory committee, the Advertising Advisory Committee, which would be concerned with standards of advertising, and would draw up a set of principles to be followed (this was published in June 1955).
5. Programme contractors would be legally responsible for the content of everything they transmitted, including the commercials. (This is very different from the situation in print media, where the advertiser rather than the publisher is legally responsible for the content of advertisements.)
6. Advertising would be restricted to breaks before and after programmes, and to 'natural breaks' within programmes.

All these rules were designed to protect British commercial television viewers from the excesses of over-commercialized American television—by forcing advertisements to comply with the ITA's Principles for Television Advertising; by insulating programmes from advertisements;[3] by

---

[2] It was not until 1958, three years after the launch of ITV, that the US broadcasting networks gained control of 75% of programming, and spot advertising became the norm.

[3] Until 1962 specific advertising 'programmes' were permitted, known as 'advertising magazines' (usually called 'admags'), in which actors promoted several different products in rather the same way as they do on shopping channels today. Admags, which were rather clumsy affairs, lasted 10 or 15 minutes and were designed to be suitable for advertisers with small

making the programme companies responsible for advertisement content; and by strict control of the quantity and timing of advertising.

The unpredicted outcome was the birth of the pre-recorded 30-second commercial. The Act's restriction of advertising time pressurized the broadcasting companies to limit the length of commercials. And until technology advanced, the only way the companies could meet their obligation to take responsibility for the content of advertisements was by getting scripts for commercials cleared in advance, and precisely executed on celluloid. To do this the companies set up a pre-vetting clearing house, now called the Broadcast Advertising Clearance Centre, which still does the job today. The BACC approves scripts, and then views the final commercial to ensure the approved script has been rendered faithfully. No commercial is ever transmitted which has not been passed by the BACC.

So it is hardly an exaggeration to say Britain invented the 30-second spot, in response to legal necessity. And before long the 30-second spot became the dominant advertising form internationally. Several academic studies, into the varying effectiveness of various lengths of spot, suggest shorter spots provide better value for money (see for example Burke and Stanton, *Journal of Advertising Research*, 1998). None of them has shaken advertisers' faith in the 30-second length. The 1954 Act gave the 30-second commercial to the world, and advertising industries throughout the world have willingly adopted it.

Why? First, whereas some countries did not initially restrict the volume of advertising on television (in 1974 a Venezuelan channel devoted 38.4 per cent of its transmission time to advertisements) total advertising time is now rationed almost everywhere, and this squeezes broadcasting companies to encourage short spots. But second, they would not have succeeded in doing so had not most advertisers discovered 30 seconds to be the optimal length for their needs. And third, this in turn would not have happened if viewers did not feel a 30-second sales pitch was sufficient to tell them all they need to know, in most cases, without boring them silly. In short, to coin a phrase, 30 seconds is both long enough and short enough. Consumers who wish to learn more about a product will use other means of finding out.

In 1980, to give advertisers and themselves more flexibility, the British programme companies introduced 20-second and 40-second time lengths— both derivatives of the 30-second spot. Today these three spot-lengths

budgets. They were discontinued because it was felt they too blurred the distinction between programmes and advertisements.

account for around three-quarters of all commercial airtime. Some £2,000 million is now spent annually in the UK on 30-second spots alone, far more than is spent on any other single mode of advertising. Over the years there have been some excellent longer commercials. But they were exceptions. For more than half a century, in Britain the 30-second commercial has been the foremost means of marketing communication. It must surely be the most potent mass-sales tool ever invented.

But the birth of the 30-second commercial was not easy. There were no real precedents. Small numbers of cinema commercials had been made over the years, but these had mostly been made by screen advertising sales companies like Pearl & Dean, rather than by advertising agencies. Now advertisers and agencies needed vast numbers of tiny filmlets for an infinitely more expensive and rapidly expanding medium going straight into people's homes, night after night. One major advertiser, Beecham, at first employed Pearl & Dean to write and produce all its television commercials, bypassing its agencies. Others looked to America, but what they found there was little help.

J. Walter Thompson's Jeremy Bullmore, later to be the agency's creative director and its chairman, recalls:

> At the start we imported quite a lot of US people to help us cope, but mostly what they knew was of no direct relevance at all.

Bullmore himself then visited America, but came away no better informed. There was nobody in the world with the know-how to produce 30-second advertising filmlets. In desperation British agencies hired a melange of photographers, BBC television directors, radio producers, film cameramen, theatrical set designers, anyone they could think of, and threw them in at the deep end. At the Robert Sharp agency, where I was a trainee, they even put me in charge. (My tenure in the job lasted less than four months.) Everyone involved in television commercial production at that time agrees it was a wonderful, exhilarating, frenetic, and terrifying experience. I'll say.

The early commercials, written by copywriters brought up on print advertising, were mostly wordy, earnest, and informative. Brian Palmer— later a founding partner of the Kingsley Manton & Palmer agency—wrote the first ever commercial to be transmitted in Britain, at 8.12 pm on 22 September 1955. It was for Gibbs SR toothpaste, and he admits it was hardly televisual at all. He later said: 'I look at it now as an illustrated lecture.'

Though a handful of the first commercials attempted to be light-hearted—usually using cartoons—most used presenters, talking to camera like anchormen. Everything was spelled out, with simple demonstrations, to ensure the audience understood. This condescension was misappropriated from America, where English was not the birth-language of much of the audience, and so simplicity of communication was essential. To increase memorability, some commercials appropriated crude American-style jingles. Ronnie Kirkwood, who was executive director in charge of television at the Colman Prentis & Varley agency, describes most early British commercials as intrusive and bad-mannered: 'loud mouthed salesmen who confused shouting with communicating, and bullying with persuading'.

Kirkwood was not the only leading figure then deprecating British commercials. Sir Kenneth Clark, who had been Chairman of the ITA since its launch, was the first of countless people over the subsequent half-century to declare television advertising was running out of steam. 'The novelty of TV advertisements is "wearing thin", and the appeal of the spot has begun to decline,' Clark opined in August 1957, adding 'the TV boom will not last.' Even the admen themselves began to worry about the deadening effects of too much television advertising. Mather & Crowther director A. Graeme Cranch made a major speech titled 'Will the public be immune to advertising in 5 years?'—blaming the cumulative, deadening impact of television commercials.

Nor was the rest of the world much impressed by British commercials. The Cannes Lions International Advertising Festival, as it is now called, had been set up in 1954 by Ernie Pearl of Pearl & Dean. Pearl pulled together an international consortium of cinema bigwigs to encourage movie advertising worldwide. Under threat of boycott by the production companies which produced commercials, the Cannes Festival had been forced—most unwillingly—to open its doors to television. In October 1957 the British sent more cinema and television entries to Cannes than any other country, 142 out of a total entry of 655. We failed to win a single award or diploma. Our ignominious tally was just two honourable mentions. 'British Ads Fail at Cannes' groaned *Advertisers' Weekly*, and the subsequent inquests generated much self-flagellating debate about whether British commercials were 'too hard sell'—too much like their American counterparts, in other words.

Ronnie Kirkwood and some of his creative colleagues in other agencies believed British commercials needed to be different, because British consumers were different, and the British cultural context was different. In America advertising had interrupted television programmes from the start. In Britain commercials were interrupting a medium in which there had previously been no advertising interruptions. So they needed to make themselves welcome—or at the very least, unobjectionable. And British consumers had long been used to a sprinkling of humour on their advertisements: hectoring salesmanship was not the custom.

British advertising took these issues on board. Soon British commercials would be winning far more than their fair share of international awards, and be admired for their creativity, craftsmanship, subtlety, and wit, throughout the world.

* * *

The impact of television on agencies went deeper than simply forcing them to discover how to make 30-second commercials. It shifted creative power from the copywriters to the art directors—or more accurately, to copywriter/art director duos. In the longer term it shifted power from the client service side of agencies to the creative side.

While the creation of posters had always been the preserve of artists and designers, the creation of advertisements for printed media—far and away the biggest advertising sector historically—was dominated by writers. At Mather & Crowther, where I worked for six weeks before moving to Robert Sharp, the copywriters and visualizers worked on different floors. (The term 'visualizer' is itself derogatory: it implies the person's role is to 'visualize' other people's ideas. And in those days, it was.)

When a new campaign was needed, the account executive would brief the relevant copywriter. When the copywriter had dreamed up an idea he would type out the copy and scribble at the top, 'Suggestion: show a pretty girl smiling', or—if he fancied himself as being visually creative—'Suggestion: show an elephant'. The copywriter might then stroll off to the visualizer for a chat about his idea, or he might give it to a messenger, who would deliver the scribbled idea for him. Uppity visualizers would sometimes ignore the copywriter's suggestions and proffer illustrations of their own—so there was always some needle between the two departments.

Large agencies employed about three times as many visualizers as copywriters, because once the copy was written and approved the writer's work was largely done, while the visualizer had to supervise and execute the advertisement's production right through to the printed page. This was how agencies had produced advertisements for over a century. It is all wittily depicted in *Murder Must Advertise* (1933) by Dorothy L. Sayers, who worked at S. H. Benson, and is credited with having created the

Guinness toucan. Sayers clearly looked back in umbrage on her time in advertising.[4]

Television upset the apple cart, though it took several years. Few copywriters knew how to write films. And if a script lacks visual oomph, it cannot be spiced up by sprinkling oomph on it like pepper. David Ogilvy, the brilliant Scot who launched Ogilvy Benson & Mather in New York in 1948 and was a consummate print copywriter, freely admits in his book *Confessions of an Advertising Man* (1963):

> In the early days of television I made the mistake of relying on words to do the selling...I now know that in television you must make your *pictures* tell the story; what you *show* is more important than what you say...Try running your commercial with the sound turned off; if it doesn't sell without sound it is useless.

The last sentence is a gross exaggeration—a characteristic Ogilvy provocative flourish—but his point is well made. As television grew in importance, the importance of the visualizers, now coming to be called 'art directors', grew too. Many art directors had an instinctive feeling for film. Agency managements stopped penning copywriters and visualizers on different floors. Instead writers and art directors began to work together. Soon it transpired that this was not only essential for television, it worked better for all media. Soon it no longer mattered whether the writer or the artist had the original idea. They developed ideas in tandem. Then the writer would write the precise words, and the art director would be responsible for its visual execution—though even those borderlines grew hazy.

The switch from copywriter/visualiser separation to integrated creative duos was imported into Britain by the Collett Dickenson Pearce agency in 1960, from Doyle Dane Bernbach in New York, with whom CDP had a trading relationship. At that time DDB was easily the most creative agency in the world, and its charismatic founder, Bill Bernbach, had introduced the 'duo' system into his agency in 1949. But I suspect the advent of commercial television, and the use of 30-second films, would inevitably have forced British agencies to adopt some such creative structure before too long. The old copy department/art department schism was out-of-time. It was broken and had to be fixed.

Within agencies, the knock-on effects of this structural change have been extensive. Increasing the power and authority of art directors altered

[4] Other notable ex-agency creative people include Len Deighton, Alec Guinness, Paul Jennings, Fay Maschler, Salman Rushdie, and Fay Weldon—whose attitudes to their advertising pasts are, well, varied.

the very tenor of agency life. During the second half of the twentieth century about half the outstanding agency creative chiefs started as writers, half as artists. John Hegarty, Colin Millward, and John Webster all went to art schools. David Abbott, Jeremy Bullmore, and Jeremy Sinclair all began as copywriters. (Charles Saatchi was a copywriter, but was never a creative director.) Most of the truly remarkable campaigns of the era were created either by or under the aegis of these six (or seven) individuals.

* * *

Commercials have always been made by small production companies which are independent of agencies. The production companies put together film crews, and provide the directors. The selection of the director is one of the key decisions the agency makes when producing a commercial.

And one of the inadvertent benefits Britain has derived from commercial television is the large number of highly talented feature film directors who have cut their teeth making commercials, and subsidized their careers with the cash they made from them. To name but a baker's dozen:

- Lindsay Anderson
- Stephen Frears
- Jonathan Glazer
- Hugh Hudson
- Richard Lester
- Richard Loncraine
- Adrian Lyne
- Alan Parker
- Karel Reisz
- Ken Russell
- John Schlesinger
- Ridley Scott
- Tony Scott

There were at least as many more again, slightly less well-known. Their cumulative contribution to Britain's international creative reputation—and to the British film industry's precarious coffers—has been colossal. Many began working in advertising because the British film industry was a strictly unionized 'closed shop', and it was all but impossible for a new feature film director to get into a union. Directing commercials provided a taut, highly disciplined training—and a speedy short cut to a union card.

'A Nondescript Term, Incapable of Definition'

In 1909, Samuel Herbert Benson, the ex-Bovril employee who in 1893 had founded the advertising agency which bore his name, wrote that 'advertising agent' was 'a nondescript term incapable of definition'—used as it then was by a motley assortment of traders including frame makers, newsvendors, railway companies, and refreshment contractors, as well as by space brokers who merely handled bookings, and those who in addition provided creative and other services. In the subsequent century the definition of an 'advertising agent' became a smidgeon more specific, but it has never been precise. Advertising agents were looked to for 'big ideas'—like those of Barrett, Lipton, and Benson himself. None of these was in modern terms a creative advertising man—but the creation of press advertisements was regarded as a fairly prosaic craft skill.

After the Newspaper Publishers Association embedded the agency recognition system in 1941, 'advertising agent' came to mean any company recognized by the media as a legitimate commission earner. In effect the media decided who was, and who was not, an advertising agent and only paid commission—commonly 15 per cent of the gross space rate—to agencies which they recognized.

This 'recognition' system was the framework on which advertising agencies were built for almost 40 years. But it brought complications. Forbidden to rebate commissions, agencies could not compete on price, and so competed by offering their clients a range of ancillary services (and generous entertainments). By the 1940s creative and media-buying services were universally accepted as core agency activities. But while agencies could claim to be more creative than each other, and/or better at media-buying, both of these were difficult to measure—in the case of creativity, impossible. The theatre of competition therefore became the ancillary services agencies offered. By the late 1950s advertising agencies were offering advertisers an abundance of services which were not intrinsically advertising at all. For example, in 1961 S. H. Benson bought three grocery shops to provide its clients with real-life, in-store, shopping research facilities.

Though it is unlikely any one agency would have provided all of them, the raft of services advertising agencies offered included:

- Direct marketing
- Door-to-door circular distribution
- In-store merchandising

- Kitchens run by home economists
- Market research
- New product development
- Package design
- Poster inspection
- Product sample distribution
- Public relations
- Sales conference organization
- Sales promotion
- Trade exhibition set-ups

Just about anything and everything, in fact, that would today be called marketing services, and would be handled by specialist companies. The advertising agencies provided these services for little or nothing. This was possible because the agencies were making fat profits, as their 15 per cent commissions more than covered the cost of creating and buying advertising campaigns. Even after offering their clients such ancillary services, in 1960 the average IPA agency made a lush 19.2 per cent profit on gross income, almost double the comparable percentage today. And if 19.2 per cent was the average, about 50 per cent of agencies must have been making still more.

As Jeremy Bullmore puts it:

> There was an obligation to over-service clients. You had to. Or at least you were wise to. At JWT we had two home economics units, an experimental film unit, a conference planning centre, a market research company. We ran the Cheese Bureau and the Butter Council from our own offices. They didn't exist separate from JWT. We were our own clients. There were 1200 people working for JWT in London then.[5]

Perhaps it is not surprising advertising agencies should have undertaken many of these services. They would indubitably have been viewed as 'advertising' in the nineteenth century. But because they were loss-leaders, giveaways, the agencies underfinanced them. Consequently the ancillary services provided by mid-twentieth century advertising agencies were not that great. But there were few specialist suppliers of marketing services available, so advertisers were more than happy to accept such services

---

[5] JWT was then Britain's second largest agency, as it is today. But today it employs just 280 people in London—a shrinkage of more than 75%, the significance of which will be explored below. Today Britain's largest agency, Abbott Mead Vickers BBDO, also employs fewer than 300 people.

from their agencies, on the cheap. It could not last. Long before the agency recognition system was finally dismantled in January 1979, specialist companies were emerging to handle public relations, new product development, market research, and the like. They were far more accomplished at their specialisms than the advertising agencies, mostly because it was the best specialists who quit the agencies to set up their own businesses.

As the non-advertising specialists drifted away, the agencies downsized and began to focus ever more narrowly on the creation of prime media advertisements, and on media planning and buying. Nonetheless, there are still advertisers who believe agencies should offer a multiplicity of marketing services, even though they do not employ the staff to do so. Counter-intuitively, small regional agencies, which work with small regional advertisers, still provide a multiplicity of services. Large national advertisers want, and can afford, the best specialists. Today these are not to be found in advertising agencies.

This being a history of advertising, not of marketing services, we can now say farewell to the specialists who themselves said farewell to the advertising agencies in the 1960s and 1970s, noting only that many of them have reappeared within holding companies like Omnicom, WPP, and Interpublic, an important point to which I will return.

Green Shoots of Creativity

The cat's-cradle of services agencies provided meant that until the mid-1960s most of the power in agencies was vested in account directors: the top client service executives. These were the men who nursed and massaged the agencies' clients, and provided for their every whim. If they were good at it, people would say they had their clients in their hip pockets. They managed and coordinated everything the agency did for the client, and ensured the client liked what he was getting. To do so they befriended their clients, ate, drank, and travelled with them, took them to Ascot, Henley, Twickenham, Wimbledon, Covent Garden, and Glyndebourne (if they were sufficiently big spenders), learned to understand their businesses and—in the era before management consultants—acted as their management consultants, or anyway as their management sounding-boards. Today, account directors tend to be advertising specialists; before the mid-1960s they were generalists, who gave clients advice on all aspects of their business.

Because creativity was not the be-all and end-all of agency performance, it is hard to say which were the leading creative agencies of the time—not that there would be universal agreement, even today. There never could be universal agreement on which agencies or advertisements are the best—the most creative, or the most effective—any more than there ever could be universal agreement on which architects and buildings, or film-makers and films, are 'best'. Today in advertising, as in other areas of commercial creativity, well-organized award schemes are the best measure of creativity, as they represent peer group judgement. And peer review is as reliable—and as unreliable—in advertising as in any other sphere. Today the trade magazines score agencies for their creativity, basing the scores on the awards each agency wins. This was unknown in the past.

Nonetheless, during the 1950s it was generally felt that two agencies led the field creatively: W. S. Crawford ('Crawfords'), and Mather & Crowther ('Mathers'). Crawfords was founded in 1914 by Sir William Crawford, who believed all copywriters should train themselves by reading the Bible. In the 1950s it was a medium-sized agency with several fashion accounts, on which it was relatively easy to shine creatively. Mathers, founded in 1850 by Edward Charles Mather when he was just 27, was then the fourth largest agency—though some way behind the big three: London Press Exchange, J. Walter Thompson, and S. H. Benson. Once the blockmakers C. & E. Layton launched their creative awards scheme in 1955, Crawfords and Mathers consistently came top of the class, bagging seven awards each in 1956, a particularly substantial achievement for the small Crawfords shop. Despite their creative reputations neither agency exists in its original form today. This should not be taken to confirm the commonly held view that advertising agencies come and go like sunshine and showers. Many agencies achieve enduring longevity. Founded in 1864, J. Walter Thompson is far older than the vast majority of its clients.

Both Crawfords' and Mathers' creative chiefs came from the art side: Ashley Havinden at the former, and Stanhope ('Shelly') Shelton at the latter. Maybe this proves other agencies would have been more creative had they ended the hegemony of copywriters earlier than they did. At the very least it shows outstanding 'visualizers' could, and occasionally did, break through their glass ceiling.

Havinden and Shelton epitomized two opposing approaches to creative leadership. Havinden was first and foremost a creator, Shelton a manager. Some creative directors lead by personal example, some by encouraging and motivating their staff. Some like presenting their own work at client meetings, some hate it.

Havinden was himself an innovative typeface designer, and two of his monotype faces—Ashley Crawford (1930) and Ashley Script (1955)—are still in use. The publication *Art & Industry* (January 1957) claimed he had done 'more than any other artist to bring new visual conceptions to the layout of press advertisements', and he was then the most famous advertising creative man in Britain: in modern terms a celebrity adman. He became a toff, buying a farm in Hertfordshire, where *Country Life* pictured him late in his career, spruced up in a three-piece suit with a handkerchief in his top pocket and an immaculately groomed moustache, looking quite like the Major in *Fawlty Towers*—difficult to reconcile with today's image of the creative director in expensive sloppy gear. Shades of Charles Saatchi, Havinden was a notable art collector, and held exhibitions of works by his friends Barbara Hepworth, Ben Nicholson, Henry Moore, and others. His most famous 1950s campaigns, most of which won him Layton Awards, were for Pretty Polly, Wolsey, Daks, KLM, and Chrysler Cars. All were strong graphically but weak on sales propositions (at least in modern terms).

Compared with Havinden, Shelton was relatively unknown outside advertising. He was Mathers' creative chief for 21 years, from 1948 to 1969. He built a huge creative department, eventually of over 200 people, and his success rested on his brilliant management rather than his personal creative output. As Stanley Piggott writes in his book *OBM—125 Years* (1975):

> He coaxed, wooed, goaded and encouraged his artists and writers and typo-graphers to produce work of a standard Mathers had never known before. And he defended them like a terrier. . . [He had] the gifts of an impresario, a Diaghilev, able to attract disparate talents and excite them to work together.

During my six-week stint at Mathers as a trainee copywriter I only once glimpsed Shelly's Diaghilevian management style. We had both arrived back from rather bibulous lunches—customary then, rare today—and he rejected a commercial the agency had made for a margarine brand called 'Magic', in which a well-margarined bun floated magically through the air. The commercial was ham-fisted, he declared, it must not be shown to the client. Those who had made the offending little movie sat gloomily silent, so I patiently explained to him that it was rather better than he thought.

'Have you read my book?' he asked affably.

I hadn't.

'Read it tonight and report to my office at 8 o'clock tomorrow morning,' he beamed.

The 'book' was a photocopied collection of his *pensées* about advertising. In my wisdom, they seemed sensible enough, and I duly reported to his office to tell him so. He was far too busy to see me. He remained far too busy for a fortnight, at which point I quit Mathers to join Robert Sharp and Partners—but not because of Shelly, whose response to my bumptiousness had been charming, even if not quite Diaghilevian.

Neither Havinden nor Shelly welcomed the coming of television advertising. Havinden refused to have any truck with it at all, forcing Crawfords to set up a separate and almost independent television division, an agency within the agency. Shelly held out against it for several months,[6] then caved in, and by the late 1950s Mathers had become the foremost creative agency in London in television, as well as in other media. Many Mathers campaigns from those years are still popularly remembered, however vaguely. In *The Advertising Man* (1964) Jeremy Tunstall writes: 'Mather and Crowther has a reputation as the leading creative agency, and creative people in other agencies think very highly of their advertisements.'

Mathers' reputation was largely built on generic (non-branded) campaigns. It had pioneered generic advertising in the 1920s with 'Eat More Fruit', claimed to be the first ever cooperative campaign. ('An apple a day keeps the doctor away' was a Mathers slogan.) In the 1950s the agency handled a rich smorgasbord of generic accounts including Bananas, Eggs, Fish, Fruit, and Milk, as well as Coal, Electricity, and Gas. Their slogans for the Milk Publicity Council ('Drinka Pinta Milka Day') and for the Egg Marketing Board ('Go To Work on an Egg') quickly became popular catchphrases.

The Egg campaign, created by Fay Weldon and Mary Gowing, with commercials starring Tony Hancock, was a forlorn attempt lasting 14 years and costing £12 million, to reinstate cooked breakfasts into lifestyles which already lacked either the time or the inclination to indulge in them. And whether the 'Drinka Pinta Milka Day' campaign was either as original or as successful as was claimed is debatable. The slogan came from the client, Bertrand Whitehead, who said it was a 'bathtub inspiration'. The line was initially resisted by the Mathers creative department—as clients' creative ideas almost always are—but they were overruled from afar by David Ogilvy. David was the brother of Francis Ogilvy, Mathers' chairman. Back in his bathtub, Whitehead may have been mulling over a United Fruit Company campaign of three years earlier—'Havabanana', 'Drinkabanana', and 'Mashabanana'. In any event, both 'Go To Work' and 'Drinka

---

[6] Havinden and Shelton were by no means the only top creative men to rebel against the coming of commercial television. Similar revolts occurred in many London agencies. Even the mighty S. H. Benson was at first forced to set up a separate television unit.

Pinta' achieved high levels of public awareness and won countless creative awards. But this had nothing to do with sales results. As the Layton Awards rules made abundantly clear:

> In judging advertisements the attention of the panel is confined by the Rules to aesthetic considerations only...Copy and campaign considerations are not taken into account.

(How 'copy' can be excluded from 'aesthetic considerations' is less abundantly clear.)

In *Advertising in a Free Society* (1959), authors Harris and Seldon—despite haughty reservations about 'the use of pidgin English'—make a valiant attempt to prove the Drinka Pinta campaign 'helped keep up the consumption of milk', which would otherwise have fallen. Their case is far from convincing. It can be difficult to measure any correlation between advertising and sales, but it is especially difficult for generic campaigns. Early in the second half of the twentieth century there were many such campaigns—for wool, men's hats, bread-baking, cream, beer, leather, bacon, and fresh meats as well as those mentioned above. Almost all of them were intended to arrest long-term sales declines: declines unite competitors who in happier times would not dream of cooperating. Today such generic campaigns are unfashionable, and are likely to remain so until, and if, researchers can prove they achieve anything. However, as always with high-profile award-winning campaigns, whatever their effect on sales, their effect on the agency which creates them is likely to be beneficial—as it was for Mathers, which enjoyed considerable success in the early 1960s.

While the campaigns for Milk and Eggs probably attained greater popularity than any other advertising of the period, it would be remiss to leave the 1950s without mentioning three other seminal campaigns which influenced British advertising in subsequent decades.

OXO had always believed in advertising. It was one of the 23 advertisers on ITV's opening night in September 1955. But its advertising had been serious, not to say austere, and by spring 1958 sales were starting to slide. The brand needed beefing up. To do the job OXO appointed J. Walter Thompson.

If Crawfords and Mathers were quintessentially British agencies, JWT was quintessential Anglo-American. It would be unfair to say Crawfords and Mathers disregarded market research, but they were agencies driven by creative flair. At JWT market research was a key element in its operations. JWT had brought market research to British advertising in 1923, and its subsidiary the British Market Research Bureau (BMRB), founded in 1933, had grown into one of the strongest research companies in the country. JWT worked to disciplined systems, which relied upon research data, in a systematic American way. None of this should be taken to detract from JWT's creativity. While JWT has never been the most creative shop in town, at no time has it produced less than top-notch work, quietly pocketing as many creative awards as many of its more famously creative competitors.

One of the fundamental changes in advertising practice during the second half of the twentieth century was an emphasis on the strategic 'brief'. The brief spells out the objectives of each campaign: exactly what the advertising is intended to achieve, what the advertisements are intended to communicate, and to which target market they are addressed. Campaigns had always had objectives, of course, but in earlier times these had been loosely defined, often in conversations between advertisers, account executives, and copywriters. With the growth of market research, it became standard practice to spell out the objectives more precisely, on paper, and often quantitatively. This paperwork makes people think hard about the objectives of the campaign before there is any creative input, which minimizes any waste of the creative people's time—an expensive resource to waste. Today all agencies, and many advertisers, have their own approach to the campaign briefing process—indeed most agencies believe their own briefing process to be superior to all others. Be that as it may, in few if any agencies will new creative work now be undertaken until a written brief has been produced, and signed off by all concerned. JWT was one of the first agencies to adopt this discipline.

JWT's researches showed OXO's image to be blurred—some people drank OXO in hot water, others used it as a stock—but either way OXO was seen as synthetic, not real beef (which it was), cheap, and used by the old and the poor. If OXO were to be revitalized, these prejudices would need to be dispelled, its image as a stock clarified, and the brand's image modernized. This was the gist of the brief.

JWT's solution was to create a mini-soap opera series, depicting the mealtime dramas and traumas of a young, middle-class couple. The husband would manifestly think his wife both enticingly sexy and a great cook—qualities then perceived to be oxymoronic. The pithy plot of each commercial would require the trusty little meat cube to act as a *deus ex machina*, and the sexist slogan 'OXO gives a meal man appeal' rounded off each story. Thus were Katie & Philip, the OXO couple, born. Though not stunningly creative, the idea was strong, relevant, intriguing—and it fashioned a new genre. It blazed the trail for many subsequent advertising 'soaps'. But few of those that followed were a patch on Katie & Philip.

For the OXO commercials to succeed, the production values would be all-important. JWT's production values are generally spot on. Katie & Philip were meticulously delineated and ideally cast, the sets were flawless, the camera work flowed smoothly, the scripts were chatty but crisp. As was appropriate in the late 1950s, Katie was subservient to her man in a caring, tolerant, gently derisive way. Katie & Philip were the first characters in commercials with credible lives of their own. Viewers wrote to Katie as though she were an agony aunt, telling her about their problems and asking for advice. When, in one commercial, Philip scolded his wife, the female staff at an electronics factory came out on strike. When Philip greedily mopped up his OXO gravy with a hunk of bread, thousands wrote in complaining about his bad manners. When Katie started cooking as soon as she entered the kitchen, viewers tut-tutted because she hadn't washed her hands.

Nonetheless the campaign took a while to bite. When it hit the nation's screens in October 1958 the OXO sales graph hardly flickered. JWT's research expertise now came into its own. Consumer research early in 1959 showed public attitudes to OXO were indeed changing, in the desired ways. But changes in purchasing behaviour frequently lag behind changes in attitude. Client and agency stuck to their guns. By the end of 1959 OXO sales started to reflect the public's changed attitudes. During subsequent years Katie & Philip grew older, bred a son David—who materialized without his mum ever having been pregnant—and their relationship blossomed. True to their values, JWT steadily researched and monitored the campaign, honing and adjusting it as time passed. At first Katie & Philip were studiously middle-class, but in the early 1960s they became upwardly mobile, with Katie serving wine, putting candles on the dinner table, and going to the ballet. When this alienated many OXO users, Katie's salt-of-the-earth dad was hurriedly unearthed. To keep the campaign fresh, in the autumn of 1967 the couple moved to the country, this being the thing to do, then moved to America, and then came back again.

Meanwhile Katie, ably supported by the OXO marketing chaps, was running a one-woman, interactive, multi-media campaign. She opened new stores, published cookery books and articles, wrote to butchers, made special offers to OXO customers, and kept up a voluminous correspondence with her countless fans.

Katie & Philip were symbols of their era. By the early 1970s, when family meals were no longer social norms, their selling-by date had passed. Still,

Katie & Philip had sold OXO for 18 years, demonstrating how successful an unadventurous campaign can be. The Katie & Philip campaign never won a creative award, certainly not one of any significance. But it proved that well-crafted, rather mundane advertising can be remarkably effective and memorable.

Katie & Philip also demonstrated the astonishing durability of strong campaign ideas. After they passed away, there was a gap of a decade— which came to be known at JWT as 'the wilderness years'—when OXO was family-less, orphaned. But Katie & Philip were deeply embedded in viewers' affections. So in 1983 OXO acquired a new, up-to-the-minute family, with Linda Bellingham in the Katie role. This family survived a further 16 years, until it too was polished off, in 1999. Even then the OXO family refused to lie down and die. Three years later in 2002, after the account had moved from JWT to its new agency Abbott Mead Vickers BBDO, a third generation OXO family, with scripts written by Richard Curtis, hit the air, picking up the baton Katie & Philip had long since dropped. It is a remarkable tale of campaign longevity.

The Strand cigarette launch campaign was in every sense a darker story. It was created in 1959 at S. H. Benson, which had been one of the most creative British agencies—maybe the most creative agency—in the 1930s, when Dorothy L. Sayers worked there. By the 1950s its glory days had passed. Like Mathers, with which it later merged, it was a very British agency, but more genteel and traditional—that is, old-fashioned.

The Strand cigarette campaign was the brainchild of John May, then Benson's copy chief and one of the agency's most notable talents. May's most successful creation was 'Mrs 1970'. Mrs 1970 promoted Shell-Mex & BP central heating as the avant-garde form of home heating in the 1960s. But May's most famous creation was the Strand man. The Strand man was a Frank Sinatra lookalike, modelled on Sinatra in *Pal Joey*—who wandered lonely as a smoker, at night, through certain half-lit desolate streets, in a trilby and a white overcoat bought from Cecil Gee, accompanied only by his comforting gasper. But his comforting gasper was all he needed. 'You're never alone with a Strand,' intoned the voice-over huskily, the only words spoken in the commercial.

The launch was a multi-media blitzkrieg, using television, print, posters, and point-of-sale. The Wills company, Strand's makers, were so confident of success that the first commercial was publicly previewed in a London dance hall, to generate instant publicity. Public awareness of the brand, and of its advertising, rocketed to over 90 per cent within weeks. This was unprecedented, and has rarely if ever been surpassed. Like Katie & Philip, the anonymous Strand man, played by jobbing actor Terence Brook, acquired a life and a fan club of his own. The black-and-white cinematography was stark and compelling. The *Lonely Man* soundtrack hit the pop charts—the tradition of commercials using and promoting pop songs goes back a long way—and it might have reached the very top of the pops had the BBC not banned the disc when it belatedly realized it was promoting a cigarette brand. Suddenly everyone was talking about the Strand man. The word-of-mouth publicity—what today would be called viral marketing—was noisome. Like Sinatra himself, the confident, casual Strand man oozed sex appeal. Terence Brook received letters offering marriage 'and several less respectable forms of enjoyment'. Brook was headed for stardom. The Strand brand was headed for stardom. Neither made it.

As John May said later:

> It sank without trace. The most memorable campaign since the war and it failed in only one thing. It just didn't sell the product. Otherwise it was perfect.

With everything going so well, what went wrong? For one thing the product may not have been up to much. Advertising storytellers often underestimate the crucial importance of product quality. The reality is that potent advertising merely expedites the demise of a poor product, by persuading people to try it and discover its shortcomings. Certainly some people said Strand was a lousy smoke—but as most of those people were not the target market for a small, cheap smoke their views may be irrelevant. Anyway the putative quality of the cigarette was not the whole story. The Strand advertising failed to persuade many smokers even to try it. At its peak Strand was bought by 0.3 per cent of men and 0.7 per cent of women.

Advertising mythology has it that the lonely man had been lurking in the recesses of May's mind for ages, but he thought he would never find an advertiser brave enough—or reckless enough—to use it. This may have been true. May whisked up the campaign in 24 hours, after Wills had rejected all S. H. Benson's earlier efforts as too pedestrian. Wills demanded something outrageous and audacious. The speed with which May responded to this challenge suggests the idea had long been simmering. Nothing unusual there. Most professional writers and composers carry ideas in their notebooks and in their heads until they find a home for them, and many advertising creative people do the same.

May admitted the campaign was based on pure hunch. It was not researched before Strand's launch, and if a post-launch inquest survey was carried out it has never been published. Consequently all kinds of urban myth have emerged to explain the campaign's dismal failure, from the social ('who wants to identify with a man who has no friends?'), to the psychological ('he may enjoy being a loner, but I don't'), to the addictive ('solitary smoking is like solitary drinking, it tells everyone you're hooked'), to the depressing ('it was more likely to make you phone the Samaritans than to buy the brand'), to the sexual ('solitary smoking is like masturbation—maybe you do it, but you don't want people to know'). Doubtless all played their part.

In my view—though opinions differ—the Strand flop left British advertising two major legacies. First, it spotlit the difference between creativity and effectiveness. The Layton Awards had it right. It is entirely possible to assess an advertisement's creativity without reference to its effectiveness. If, that is, you accept the common usages of the word creative: original, innovative, imaginative, intriguing, perhaps stylish and unusual. The Strand campaign was all those things, but was ineffective. The difficulties arise because advertising practitioners imbue the word 'creativity' with far more weight than it will bear. Because advertising creativity is the means to an end, not an end in itself, practitioners try to equate creativity with sales effectiveness, with functionality. Probably the extreme example of this was the slogan of the American international agency which claimed: 'It's not creative if it doesn't sell.' Codswallop.

In no sphere of creative endeavour is creativity synonymous with functionality. In 'pure' creativity—painting, music, literature for example—functionality has no role: the artefacts are their own justification. In 'applied' (or commercial) creativity—architecture, fashion, advertising for example—the artefacts can be functional without being creative, or creative without being functional. No proficient chair designer would deliberately produce a beautiful but uncomfortable chair, and no proficient advertising practitioner would deliberately produce a creative but ineffective advertisement. But both might bend the rules a tad, to produce work which was just a little less comfortable—or effective—than it might be, in order to be just a little more aesthetically pleasing. This is the way designers and creative people are—and should be.

Strand's second, also arguable, legacy was that in the wake of Vance Packard's *The Hidden Persuaders* (1957), many people, both inside and outside the industry, were starting to believe that if enough money were spent the power of advertising was irresistible. Strand very publicly proved this to be tosh. As John May had admitted, the most memorable campaign since the war—was a dud. For me, this was one of the most important lessons of the era.

COLEG LLANDRILLO COLLEGE
LIBRARY RESOURCE CENTRE
CANOLFAN ADNODDAU LLYFRGELL

093289

Today everyone in advertising accepts that new campaigns and new products have a high failure rate. The sophisticated market research and pre-testing techniques now routinely employed can reduce the likelihood of catastrophe. But the 1951 words of Dr Henry Durant still hold true: 'The limitations of copy testing must be taken to heart to avoid disappointment.'

The third seminal 1950s campaign was the Tory party's victorious 1959 general election campaign. Conventional wisdom now has it that Saatchi & Saatchi's 1979 advertising for Margaret Thatcher was the first significant political campaign in Britain. Far from it.

Political advertising dates back at least to Roman times. But when democracy disappeared from Europe, the need for political advertising went with it. In Britain the Reform Act of 1832, and its extension of the franchise to less wealthy sectors of the (male) population, spurred a resurgence. In that year Sir Edward Knatchbull and Sir William Geary each spent more than £100 on election advertising in newspapers. Such lavish expenditure raised questions in Parliament. Nonetheless politicians continued to advertise heavily in the press, as well as on posters and handbills, throughout the nineteenth and twentieth centuries. For the 1929 general election the Tories appointed S. H. Benson to design and run a massive poster campaign, and Benson continued to handle the Tories' advertising during the 1931 and 1935 elections, using the press, posters, and—most innovatively—cinema advertising. Far from politicians emulating baked beans and detergents, as the cliché has it, baked beans and detergents have long emulated politicians. This should not be surprising. Persuasive communication is the essence of politics, and always has been.

In 1959, the genesis of the Tory campaign was the party's slump in popularity following the disastrous Suez invasion of October 1956, and the subsequent economic recession. In September 1957 opinion polls showed Labour 13 per cent ahead. To recover from their unpopularity the Tories built up a publicity war chest, which financed a pre-election campaign costing £468,000, an unprecedented sum in UK politics. The advertising began in June 1957, and the Tories had recovered their lead in the polls by May 1958—but this may have had nothing to do with the advertising, as by then the UK economy had anyway recovered. Thereafter the Tory's advertising continued intermittently until the announcement of the general election. In July 1959 the Tory party was the largest press advertiser in Britain.

With the UK economy now flourishing, the Tories ran with the slogan 'Life's Better With The Conservatives. Don't Let Labour Ruin It.' This encapsulates a positive–negative message used repeatedly ever since by British parties seeking re-election: a boast followed by an overt or covert threat. In 1979 the Labour government proclaimed, 'Keep Britain Labour And It Will Keep Getting Better.' In 1983 the Tories said, 'Britain's On The Right Track—Don't Turn Back,' and in 1987 Margaret Thatcher went back to basics with 'Britain Is Great Again. Don't Let Labour Wreck It.'

The value of the Tories' 1959 campaign was much enhanced when Labour attacked it. Many Labour politicians, like Nye Bevan, viscerally disliked advertising and fervently believed it had no place in politics. This was exacerbated by Labour's envy of the Tories' bankroll. In 1959, goaded beyond endurance by the Tories' heavy expenditure, Labour unwisely laid into the campaign itself. This was counterproductive. As David Windlesham wrote in his book *Communication and Political Power* (1966):

> The angry reactions provoked in the Labour party (by the Tory advertisements) may have encouraged more people to look at them.

This is a truth politicians have yet to grasp.

In 1959 the Tory agency was Colman Prentis & Varley. CPV was one of the five largest agencies in Britain, and it had a strong creative reputation, rather like Crawfords, mostly built upon its work for fashion advertisers—though, unlike Crawfords, CPV also handled such major advertisers as Unilever, Shell, Austin cars, and British European Airways, as well as the Tory party. While Crawfords' reputation was closely linked to Ashley Havinden, CPV's reputation was closely linked to its celebrated founder, Colonel Arthur Varley. Varley, a Wykehamist, was a major figure in post-war British advertising, and was variously described by his staff as 'so jolly clever he gets bored if things start running smoothly . . . that's when the trouble starts', 'the sharpest mind in London', and 'a megalomaniac'. CPV was a breakaway from Crawfords, and was founded in 1934 by Varley, R. H. Colman, and Terence Prentis. At that time Varley was 31, and the oldest man in the agency.[7]

By the late 1950s Varley, a formidable trencherman, was a portly fellow with a pipe, a tweed suit, and a pince-nez, and was said to prefer talking about his garden to talking about business. If this portrays him as an old buffer that may have been his intention, as he was uncommonly sharp, irascible, and manipulative. To have built one of the top five agencies from a standing start, particularly during those war-fractured years, was a substantial feat.

---

[7] When he quit advertising to enter politics, the late Senator William Benton, joint founder of the Benton & Bowles agency, said: 'I sold my interest in Benton & Bowles when I was 35, and I'd been taking three or four hundred thousand dollars a year out of it. Any business where a kid can make that kind of money is no business for old men.'

At the same time he put together a robust international operation, well ahead of any other British agency; and in 1957 he established an American link via a share exchange with the large New York agency Kenyon & Eckhart. Varley's great strength was his ability to spot and recruit talented people—both creative and managerial. His great weakness was his inability to hold onto them. He said of himself that he 'picked the liveliest minds he could find and taxed them to the utmost'. Maybe he taxed them too hard, or too ungenerously, as most left his agency—several to build triumphant shops of their own. The CPV offspring included John Hobson & Partners and Collett Dickinson Pearce, two of Britain's most successful twentieth-century agencies; plus Robert Sharps and others which shone more briefly.

As we shall see later, the evidence suggests the power of political advertising is marginal, at most. However, having been deep in the mire two years earlier, the Tories swept back into government in 1959 with a substantially increased number of votes. Much of this success was attributed—by friends and foes alike—to the CPV advertising. And as with another election campaign agency two decades later, Colman Prentis & Varley became the most famous, and most talked about, agency in the country.

* * *

The Eggs, Milk, OXO, Strand, and Tory party campaigns together throw light on the vexed question of whether advertisements lead, reflect, or follow social changes. The simple answer is that there are too many advertisements, and they are too heterogeneous, for there to be a simple answer. Some advertisements (perhaps like John May's Mrs 1970, and certainly like many fashion advertisements in glossy magazines) lead change. Many advertisements—like Eggs, OXO, and the Tory campaign—reflect social changes, in OXO's case tracking them constantly, in the Eggs case aiming to reverse social change. But for the great majority of advertisements social change is irrelevant. Inevitably the ways performers and models (if any) dress and speak, the nature of the sets and props used, all reflect particular social milieus: it could not be otherwise. The products advertised similarly reflect the then current usage of that kind of product: it could not be otherwise. But with a little amendment all five campaigns could have appeared at almost any time throughout the entire half-century. The OXO campaign very nearly ran throughout the entire half-century.

With the exception of certain government campaigns, advertisements exist to sell goods and services, not to effect social engineering.

Uncreative Advertising

In *On Creativity: Interviews Exploring the Process* (2003), John Tusa writes:

> 'Creative', 'creation', 'creativity' are some of the most overused and ultimately debased words in the language. Stripped of any significance by a generation of bureaucrats, civil servants, managers and politicians, lazily used as margarine to spread approvingly over any activity with a non-material element to it, the word 'creative' has become almost unusable.

Tusa is palpably right. And as the twentieth century progressed, advertising did more than its fair share to contribute to the words' debasement. Nonetheless, 'creative' and 'creativity' continue to be used, incessantly, because there are no satisfactory substitutes.

In the Covent Garden pubs and chichi Soho clubs advertising people chit-chat endlessly about highly creative campaigns, and why they are so often highly effective. They almost never talk about uncreative campaigns, and why they too are so often highly effective. Writing about advertising of the past—or advertising of the present for that matter—it is easy to forget that high-profile, popular, award-winning, highly creative campaigns comprise but an infinitesimal fraction of the total. It would be futile to hazard a guess as to what this percentage is, as it would depend on the definitions of high-profile and award-winning: there are countless tiny advertising award schemes run by different media, and different sectors of the industry, often in different localities.[8] But however you define high-profile and award-winning, if the percentage is more than 0.01 per cent of the total, I'll hunt out a mouldy pack of Strand and chew the tobacco.

Nobody knows how many new advertisements are produced each year. The Broadcast Advertising Clearance Centre vets approximately 50,000 new television commercials, a figure which has risen steadily over the years. The figure is approximate because many 'new' commercials are merely minor amendments of old ones. Still, it means about 900 new commercials appear each week. Nobody has any idea at all how many new posters and print advertisements appear each year. A figure of 25 million used to be quoted, but this was the merest guess. As around 2 million press advertisements were being taxed in 1853, 25 million must be

---

[8] While advertising may have more than its fair share of awards, there can hardly be an industry in Britain that does not now have its own awards scheme(s), as nightly awards dinners up and down Park Lane and awards events in every county town attest. And all of them are built upon the same underlying thesis: 'While we do our jobs for money, it is the quality of our work which, deep down, really matters to us.'

a gross underestimate. As with television, what is 'new' raises definitional problems—even more acute in print than on television, as tiny changes are more commonplace. To all those must be added new radio, cinema, and now internet advertisements. It is the sheer quantity of new advertisements produced in Britain which ensures that far fewer than 0.01 per cent ever win awards (of even the most trivial kind) or achieve much profile.

This does not mean the remaining 99.99 per cent or so are ineffective—as Katie & Philip proved. Take detergents. The 1950s and 1960s, as *Advertisers' Weekly* had heralded, were the heyday of detergent commercials, reflecting both rapid technological improvements in the products, and a rapid growth of washing machine ownership. In 1957 soap powders and detergents accounted for 12 per cent of all television advertising. Until the 1970s, three or four of the top half-dozen television spenders every year were washing powders. With the arguable exception of Persil, which was an old-fashioned soap powder, the great majority of the commercials were archetypes of distasteful advertising: brazen, patronizing, charmless, employing seemingly specious science, often comparing their brands with an apparently bogus 'Brand X', always derided, always good for a comic joke. And while some of the campaigns were undeniably memorable while they were on air, most were swiftly forgotten soon after. With so many shortcomings, did they work?

Between 1950 and 1961 total sales of branded detergents in Britain increased by over 50 per cent. In 1950 there were several hundred brands on the market. By 1961 the market was dominated by four heavily advertised detergents from just two manufacturers: Daz and Tide (Hedley/Procter & Gamble), Omo and Surf (Levers/Unilever). It should be noted that old-fashioned Persil was still overall brand leader in the washing powder sector—supported by J Walter Thompson's emotive 'washes whiter' campaign.

The detergent manufacturers, and the ITA, were neither unaware of, nor blasé about, the public's antipathy to the commercials. But all attempts to advertise detergents more subtly proved ineffective. This may in part have been due to the somewhat mechanical means P&G and Unilever employed to research the effectiveness of their commercials. But the research was substantiated by the sales results. So the abrasive commercials continued and the viewers' complaints did likewise. In response, in 1960 the ITA introduced controls regulating the number of washing powder commercials which could be broadcast hourly, and banned side-by-side whiteness comparisons. This neither mitigated the number of complaints nor hampered the two manufacturers' growth. Their market dominance was so strong that in 1967 the Monopolies Commission investigated whether their heavy television advertising had prevented competitors entering the detergent market, or had increased prices to consumers. Following its investigation the Commission recommended that selling costs, including advertising, should be slashed by 40 per cent and consumer prices cut by 20 per cent. The government agreed. The two manufacturers did not. After some negotiation the manufacturers brought out low-price, minimally advertised brands, which failed.

During the 1970s washing powder commercials ceased to dominate commercial breaks. In 1980 not one was to be found among television's top twenty spenders. However, they represented, and for many continue to represent, the antithesis to the subtle, witty, beautifully produced commercials for which Britain became famous.

Detergents are far from the only field where prosaic, uncreative advertisements prove highly effective. As Giep Franzen shows in his magisterial work *Advertising Effectiveness* (1994),[9] a raft of studies have established that what consumers want from advertisements differs markedly from product to product. For some products information is all important, for others originality and imagination are what matter. Franzen writes:

> Viewer appreciation of the advertising itself can be an important factor for advertising effectiveness, [but not if] subordinated to forced originality.

Retailers' line-and-price press advertisements—like those used for decades by Dixons, MFI, and other electrical goods and furniture stores—are jammed full of information consumers want when they are considering a purchase. Agency creative people view them as deeply dreary, but this misconstrues their nature. They are quasi classified advertisements, like Montaigne's lists. In effect, the retailer buys a large space and crowds it with his own tiny classifieds: this works because intending purchasers are willing to pore over the advertisements searching for the best prices. The advertisements do not have to seek out customers; customers seek out the advertisements. (This 'search' aspect of retail line-and-price advertising explains why so much of it is migrating to the internet.)

Similarly, direct response press advertisements, which sell goods off-the-page—for certain financial products, book clubs, replicas, holidays—are

---

[9] Giep Franzen's *Advertising Effectiveness: Findings from Empirical Research*, summarizes and references some 400 studies into detailed aspects of advertising effectiveness, and is much the most authoritative single book on the subject.

notoriously lacklustre. New brooms starting out in direct response marketing regularly try to sweep away existing shibboleths, and make direct
response advertisements more 'creative'. Why should direct response
advertising, they ask, be unlike other advertising? Surely greater creativity
will bring greater sales? Time and again uninformed advertisers, or downright ignorant agency creative departments, try to break the mundane
mould of direct response advertising and run radically new approaches.
Instead of breaking the mould, they usually break the bank.

Direct response advertisements are—to return to Giep Franzen—instances of consumers wanting information rather than originality. Seeking
to generate immediate, off-the-page sales they do not need to be memorable. They do their job there and then, or not at all. So the advertisements
must provide all the information needed for an immediate purchase. This
normally necessitates detailed copy. The same does not apply to inexpensive branded consumer goods. Their advertisements rely wholly on memory, which is why they can be (indeed must be) less detailed, more imagist,
more distinctive—more memorable.

The vast majority of advertisements always have been and always will be
run-of-the-mill. Most are creative in their own little ways, but neither
advertising professionals nor the public think them original or imaginative. Like the clothes most of us wear, and the houses most of us live in, they
are not terrifically creative or exciting. But they do their job perfectly well.

Where Have all the Blockbusters Gone?

Nobody writes blockbusters about advertising any more. That is not to say
authors don't try. They just don't succeed. During the half-century only
four really huge sellers were published, all of them between 1957 and 1963.
These were the years when advertising began to boom again after the
Second World War, when television advertising took root, when advertising became increasingly involved in politics, when market research
emerged as a powerful tool for honing and sharpening advertising techniques, when detergent and similar commercials appeared to be able to
pummel people into acquiescently buying their brands, despite being
disliked and even despised. As a consequence of this confluence of historical factors, these were the years when the public, politicians, some academics, and many social commentators grew increasingly concerned
about advertising's power to manipulate people like puppets. This percep-
tion was fuelled by many leading advertising men keen both to convince

their clients they should be advertising more heavily, and to massage their own macho egos.

The four blockbusters were:

- Vance Packard: *The Hidden Persuaders* (1957)
- Martin Mayer: *Madison Avenue USA* (1958)
- Rosser Reeves: *Reality in Advertising* (1961)
- David Ogilvy: *Confessions of an Advertising Man* (1963)

All were global bestsellers, three of them running into numerous editions and many languages. All were written and published in New York, but were hugely influential in Britain, and the first and last of them remain influential to this day. Though Naomi Klein's *No Logo* (2000) has its devotees, no recent book about advertising has remotely approached the big four's impact and success.

Even now, if you ask most people outside advertising if they have ever read a book about advertising, there is a fair chance they will name *The Hidden Persuaders*. Its title has entered the vernacular, and the concept the title expresses still dominates the thinking of most of those hostile to advertising. Whether or not they use Packard's exact words, advertising's antagonists continue to believe advertising is a means of 'hidden persuasion'—a paradoxical notion, since display advertisements go out of their way not to be hidden, but to be publicly seen and remembered.

The paradox is resolved as soon as you open the book. For although everyone thinks *The Hidden Persuaders* is about advertising, it is not really about advertising at all. *The Hidden Persuaders* is about market research. More particularly it is about motivational research—the branch of market research which seeks to uncover people's 'deepest' motives for acting in the ways they do, by penetrating their rationalizations with pop-psychology. As one of its exponents put it: 'We undress people in terms of their rationalisations.' Its principal practitioner in those years, and the principal bad hat in *The Hidden Persuaders*, was the Vienna-born Dr Ernest Dichter, a jaunty American who opened a modestly successful London branch in 1959.

Motivational research is, indeed, relatively hidden. It is carried out privately, and its commercial findings are usually confidential. Moreover, it claims to reveal people's 'hidden' motives, by delving deep into the subconscious. Its practitioners have undoubtedly provided advertisers with original, often radical, insights—though these insights more frequently concern products than advertisements.[10] The early motivation

---

[10] Dichter's most celebrated dictum compared a sports car to a mistress. Whether or not this is true, it has little or nothing to do with advertising—nor did much of his other work.

researchers liked to imply their findings could provide advertisers with mesmeric powers to make customers do whatever they want them to. This is twaddle. But Packard's views were symptomatic of a strand that runs through the four books, and helps explain their massive popularity.

Each of the four authors believed, as did almost everyone at that time, that there was some kind of 'Golden Key' to effective advertising, and if you discovered it you could unlock the secrets of sales success. Most outsiders still believe there is a single Golden Key to successful advertising. Anyone who works in advertising will have been asked countless times, 'What makes a successful advert, then?'—usually by questioners eager to advance their own pet answer.

The questioners look disbelieving when they are told there is no single, straightforward answer.

For Vance Packard the Golden Key was motivational research. For Martin Mayer, who was much more subtle—Packard was only interested in writing a provocative potboiler (and he hit the jackpot)—the Golden Key was 'added value'. Mayer saw, correctly, that advertising can, and does, add value to brands. This was not an entirely new thought. In 1909 Unilever's founder William Lever said, 'The whole object of advertising is to build a halo round the article.' The halo is the miasma of thoughts, beliefs, and feelings 'the article' (in modern terms 'the brand') conjures up in consumers' minds. But building a halo is not precisely the same as adding value. Adding value involves building a particular kind of halo. Adding value, when it succeeds, ensures consumers feel that the brand is worth its price. The value added can be measured by testing consumers' reactions to the exact same product formulation when it is (a) anonymous, and (b) in its brand pack. The increased percentage who prefer the branded formulation over the anonymous formulation—if this percentage does indeed increase, as it usually does—quantifies how much value has been 'added' to the brand. The process can be further refined by asking consumers to price the anonymous and branded products. The maestro of the subject was the late Stephen King of JWT.

In his search for the Golden Key, Mayer had arrived at the right answer for much, but not all, advertising. And being a journalist rather than an advertising man, he did not quite understand the process by which value is added. Adding value is indeed a Golden Key, but it constantly needs to be recut: every brand is different, and the ways in which value is added to brands differ. There is no universal formula: adding value is itself a creative process.

For Rosser Reeves, boss at Ted Bates, then a tremendously successful global agency, the Golden Key was the Unique Selling Proposition—another great phrase still widely used (and frequently misused). Reeves had been closely involved in Eisenhower's 1952 presidential campaign, and laid personal claim to its success. ('If only Dewey had known these things he too would have been president,' Reeves boasted, inaccurately, referring to Thomas Dewey's failed shot at the presidency in 1948.) *Reality in Advertising* was an unabashed puff for Ted Bates and its USP philosophy (the USP being itself a USP for the agency). The USP discipline insists all advertising should search for, and single-mindedly hammer home, the unique fact about a brand which differentiates it from its competitors and will make consumers buy. Though it often leads to the kind of piledriver advertising exemplified by the worst detergent commercials, it can be potent for packaged consumer goods, and held sway over the development of many campaigns in Britain until the late 1970s. By then marketers were beginning to focus on brand images (and added value) instead of concentrating exclusively on product specifications. But USP analyses still remain an integral part of most campaign briefs. The approach does not, however, work for anything and everything, as Reeves postulated.

Just as Martin Mayer was far more subtle than Packard, David Ogilvy was far more subtle than Reeves. During his lifetime David Ogilvy became the most celebrated advertising man in the world. Much of his fame emanated from the success of *Confessions of an Advertising Man*, which he freely admitted was, like *Reality in Advertising*, a puff for his agency Ogilvy Benson & Mather. David—charming, talented, egocentric, and autocratic—was the younger brother of Francis Ogilvy, who had become head of Mather & Crowther in London in 1937. Together with S. H. Benson, Mather & Crowther backed David's New York agency from its start in 1948. In 1964—eight months after Francis Ogilvy died—Mather & Crowther merged with Ogilvy Benson & Mather to form Ogilvy & Mather International,[11] which David Ogilvy then built into the sixth largest agency in the world. As a book, *Confessions* massively outsold *Reality*. But as an agency Ted Bates outperformed O&M, eventually becoming the second largest in the world—though this was after Rosser Reeves had retired.

In his book, Ogilvy confesses there is no single Golden Key which will unlock all of advertising's secrets. Instead there are, as it were, a host of small Golden Keys, each of which provides different solutions to different advertising problems. Understanding the heterogeneous nature of advertising far better than Reeves, Ogilvy provides a bouquet of rules and

---

[11] Now renamed Ogilvy & Mather Worldwide.

guidelines for effective advertising, many of which flower to this day.[12] As we saw earlier, Ogilvy understood print advertising far better than television, and he hated posters as he felt they defiled the landscape. Nonetheless, and despite its shortcomings, *Confessions* remains the best popular book ever published about the ways in which advertising works.

Why, in the forty or so years since, has none of the plethora of books about advertising become a comparable blockbuster? Partly because, between them, Packard, Mayer, Reeves, and Ogilvy answered many of the fundamental questions about advertising, and since then people have merely refined their answers, tinkering at the edges. Partly, no doubt, because nobody since has written a sufficiently good book. But mostly because advertising has become so normal a part of everyday life that few people outside the business believe it to be worth reading books about. They may get hot under the collar about particular campaigns, like Benetton, or particular market sectors, like alcohol, but few get impassioned about advertising as a whole. They'll read trendy features, watch television programmes about funny commercials, chat about advertising—briefly— to their friends. But take the time and trouble to read a book? It seems not.

Meanwhile the four great blockbusters remain well worth reading, with several pinches of salt.

---

[12] This is, it must be said, a fairly traditional approach in books about advertising, many of which proffer 'XXX Ways To Create Great Advertisements'. But Ogilvy's subject matter and his insights are far wider-ranging and more perceptive than any others.

4

The Nineteen-Sixties: 'You've Never Had it So Good'

Swinging Britain

In April 1966 *Time Magazine*'s cover story was 'Swinging London', and it editorialized: 'Every decade has its city, and for the Sixties that city is London.' But it wasn't only London that was swinging. For the first time in Britain's history there was widespread private affluence (combined admittedly with public squalor, in J. K. Galbraith's plangent phrase).

In the 1960s Britain witnessed an unparalleled explosion of innovation in almost every sphere of culture. This was the natural reaction to thirty years of depression and gloom. It was the decade when the contraceptive pill transformed women's lives—with incidental and immeasurable long-term consequences for advertising—and also transformed both sexes' attitudes to . . . sex. It was also, perhaps partly as a result, the decade when young creativity supplanted the old, and disrespect for the past supplanted respect. From the Beatles and the Stones to Britten, Tippett, and Maxwell Davies; from Pinter and Joe Orton to Lionel Bart and Joan Littlewood; from Quant and Hulanicki to Conran and David Bailey; from Francis Bacon to 'Young Contemporaries' Hockney, Blake, and Caulfield; from the *Beyond The Fringe* quartet—Alan Bennett, Peter Cook, Jonathan Miller, and Dudley Moore ('they don't know the meaning of good taste,' quoth a critic)—to Glenda Jackson and Judi Dench; from *Private Eye* to the new *Sunday Times* Colour Magazine; from *Till Death Do Us Part* to *That Was The Week That Was* . . . wherever you looked young creativity burgeoned. And so it did in advertising.

On 21 June 1961 *Advertisers' Weekly* was able for the first time to proclaim joyfully, 'Sweeping Successes for UK at Cannes.' A Schweppes commercial had won the Grand Prix de la Television, and Britain raked in twenty-four other awards and diplomas. From then on the international gongs and garlands kept coming.

The precisely distilled advertising of the Ashley Havinden era—based on cubism, futurism, and Bauhaus typography—suddenly looked dated. In less than two years it breathed its last. In 1960 and 1961 Crawfords was still scooping up Layton Awards, with stylish advertisements for Shell and Associated-Rediffusion.[1] By 1962 Crawfords had disappeared from the Layton Awards listings, and a bright new agency called Collett Dickenson Pearce entered the ranks with a trio of awards for Whitbread, Charles of the Ritz cosmetics, and Rayne shoes.

However, the Layton Awards were themselves about to breathe their last. In 1962 Britain's leading young designers and art directors got together and formed the Designers and Art Directors Association, to celebrate and encourage excellence in creative communication by awarding their own garlands. They were enraged that the Layton Awards were, from their point of view, just a blockmaker's sales promotion, and still more enraged that they were excluded from the judging panels. In November 1963, after ten bumpy years, the Layton Awards passed away. C. & E. Layton said they were no longer willing to foot the entire cost of their award scheme— though this seems odd, as the awards had in some years made a profit, which the blockmakers had generously donated to the National Advertising Benevolent Society. Whatever Layton's reason for pulling the plug, the D&AD awards took over without missing a beat. D&AD hit the ground running, attracting 25,000 visitors to its very first show.

More than four decades later D&AD is still fulfilling its original role, but has expanded its activities and gained an enviable reputation that extends far beyond its original Soho backstreets. From its beginning D&AD insisted creative work should be peer-judged, and the peers who judged should be leaders in their field. Today more than 300 D&AD jurors fly into London annually, from all over the world.

Despite the apparent specificity of its name, from the start D&AD harmoniously invited into full membership—in addition to designers and art

---

[1] In 1960 Prince Philip handed out the Layton Awards, and with characteristic tact plunged into the creativity versus sales effectiveness debate by announcing at the ceremony that 'Commerce, not art, is the test of an advertisement'—exactly the opposite of what the Layton Awards were about.

directors—all those involved in the visual aspects of commercial communications: especially photographers and television producers, directors
and cameramen. Though copywriters and copywriting were also involved
from the start, copywriters were not invited into full membership until
October 1968, and only then after 'rowdy meetings'. However, D&AD's
broad inclusiveness helped make it one of the world's two leading advertising awards ventures—the other being the Cannes Lions International
Advertising Festival launched by Pearl & Dean in Monte Carlo in 1954.
Both have been major British contributions to global advertising creativity.

The Cannes Festival is more highly regarded by international marketing
and media people—17,000 of whom now use the Riviera venue for networking and glitzy entertaining each year. D&AD is more highly regarded
by creative practitioners. Cannes used to focus on television and film, but
now covers all advertising media, as D&AD did from its start. Each year
there are now over 23,000 entries for D&AD awards, approximately 6,000
from Britain, over 4,000 from the USA, with the rest coming from 60 or so
other countries. The Cannes Festival similarly receives about 25,000
entries, from 80 countries. In London D&AD employs more than 50 full-
time staff, and is an educational charitable trust, financing 18 educational
courses to the tune of £2.5 million a year. Being a not-for-profit educational charity, D&AD is a rare bird among awards schemes: most are run
for commercial gain. To fulfil its educational commitments, D&AD runs
exhibitions, lectures, and courses throughout the world. Its awards—
called Yellow Pencils—are immensely coveted, and look much the same
today as when designer Lou Klein designed them in 1966. Each year since
its inception D&AD has published a lavish album reproducing every piece
of work its juries have cited. This album—known to cognoscenti simply as
The Book—is the world's most influential annual record of topflight advertising and design.

The Two Johnnies

The 1960s' two most influential and successful new British agencies were
both founded by men who had worked for Arthur Varley, a remarkable
tribute to his strengths—and weaknesses. In 1955 John Hobson left CPV
to launch John Hobson & Partners, in 1960 John Pearce left CPV to
launch Collett Dickenson Pearce. What is still more remarkable is that
they and their agencies embodied divergent and conflicting extremes in
advertising beliefs and principles. They represented the two inimical ends

of a spectrum of approaches to advertising whose protagonists on either side were in constant dispute throughout the half-century. It is often dubbed the conflict between effectiveness and creativity—but that is far too simple a description of the battleground.

John Hobson's agency deprecated creative awards, cared little or nothing about whether its advertisements were liked by the public, and made no bones about being first, last and only, committed to sales results. The agency quickly built a reputation for producing hard-hitting, hard-selling campaigns which really did the business. John Pearce's shop believed advertisements were ambassadors for their brands, and that like ambassadors they should be friendly, courteous, and well-mannered. The agency produced award-winning campaigns by the bucketful, and for three decades was a byword for British creativity throughout the world. The Hobson agency believed uncompromisingly that advertisements should be based on professional market research and testing. The Pearce agency believed uncompromisingly that advertisements should be based on professional instinct and gut-feelings.[2] John Pearce wanted to enhance the status of advertising by producing advertisements the public liked, enjoyed, and admired. John Hobson wanted to enhance the status of advertising by getting the public to appreciate the essential contribution advertising makes to commercial success and economic growth.

By 1970 Hobson's agency was the 5th largest in Britain, Pearce's agency 11th largest. For the next twenty years the two agencies played leapfrog. By 1980 CDP had ousted Hobson's agency from 5th position, and Hobson's shop had fallen back to 8th. By 1990, following a succession of mergers and acquisitions, Hobson's agency (now called Ted Bates, Hobson having retired a decade earlier) had climbed to 3rd position, while CDP had dropped back to 11th, following a breakaway which ripped out a hunk of its business. Both then fizzled out, and today only their rumps remain.

John Hobson's agency opened on 30 September 1955, with Hobson's definition of the agency's philosophy:

> Advertising is as much a part of the formula of a product as the texture of a food, or the scent of a soap, or the line of a car... this is a fresh approach to the purpose of advertising.

Remembering William Lever's definition of advertising as 'building a halo round the article', this was not as fresh an approach as all that. But in

---

[2] This dichotomy is not unique to advertising. It now bedevils all the creative industries, not to mention many aspects of manufacturing—and politics.

launching his agency a week after the start of ITV, Hobson's timing was immaculate.

The agency was driven by Hobson—who owned a dominating 44 per cent—and his creative partner, a third but less significant John, John Metcalf. Metcalf was the second largest shareholder in Hobson's agency, but owned just 10 per cent. So there was no doubt who was boss. Theirs was a marriage of opposites. Hobson, tall and gaunt, seemed to me, on the few occasions I met him, improbably to combine languor and stress. A reticent intellectual from an academic background, he gained a first in Classics at Cambridge. Metcalf, short and tubby, was also at Cambridge, where he read English under F. R. Leavis. Unlike Hobson he was a gregarious extrovert, a roue, a literary critic and broadcaster. Hobson was patrician; Metcalf was witty and waspish. Hobson was abstemious; Metcalf was a gourmet and toper, which later did his career no good. When they started the agency Hobson was already 46, had published a leading textbook, *The Selection of Advertising Media* (1955), and was one of advertising's most highly respected and awesome practitioners: a prototypical business consultant rather than a words-and-pictures adman. Metcalf, still 32, was in public relations, an intellectual gadfly with countless contacts, working for CPV's PR subsidiary, Voice and Vision. Both had been goaded beyond endurance by Colonel Varley's dictatorial management, but they were not close friends. Metcalf later described their relationship as that of 'great opponents within the company'.

It is typical of Hobson's attitude to advertisement creativity that he should have appointed a public relations man—who had never created an advertisement in his life—to run the agency's creative department. Neither of them was much enthralled with advertisements per se. One suspects that, for different reasons, they both felt advertisements to be beneath them. Like a margarine manufacturer who is brilliant at making the stuff but wouldn't dream of eating it himself, Hobson was profoundly intrigued by the advertising process but not by advertisements—a common phenomenon among top advertising men of that era, but unknown today. Metcalf, a denizen of London's artistic and cultural world, probably found his involvement with advertisements a trifle embarrassing. Both cared a lot about what advertisements said, but far less about how they said it—unless this interfered with their clarity.

In time-honoured fashion Hobson launched the agency by hip-pocketing two major CPV accounts with which he had worked closely: Cadbury's drinking chocolate (which the agency still held when I became its boss some 30 years later), and Lyons' Sunfresh squashes (which it had long since lost). After a brief period of consolidation, the new agency swiftly began to win clients. Early on it beat its alma mater CPV to the Gold Cup Margarine account, and not long afterwards pulled in Antussin cough treatment, Captain Morgan Rum, and the launch of a cigarette called Bristol which, unlike Strand, was a fair success.

Hobson's donnish image provided the agency, not unfairly, with a reputation for rigorous and reliable analytical thinking. He said:

> Our aim has always been to minimise the area of uncertainty in advertising . . . In advertising there are always dozens of ways of doing any job. We consider them all and then test and test and test until we get the right one.

These sentiments were music to the ears of many advertisers. But they would not have endeared him to a headstrong and impassioned creative director. Happily, Metcalfe was not a headstrong and impassioned creative director. Here is Metcalf's view of creative awards: 'I think awards take us away from what our job is. They take us away from the judgement of effectiveness.'

Quite suddenly, following a car crash in which Hobson nearly died, in 1959 Hobson and Metcalf sold their shop to Rosser Reeves and the Ted Bates agency, and changed its name to Hobson, Bates and Partners. The Americanization of British advertising was then a tender topic, and their sell-out was viewed by some as treachery. Shortly afterwards *Advertisers' Weekly* led its front page with 'Slashing Attack on American Influence on Advertising in Britain'—by London agency chief Carl Brunning.

'To stop the American influx' as he put it, Brunning soon broke totally new ground. In June 1961 he floated his agency group on the London stock market. The Brunning Group owned seven companies in different marketing sectors—including a door-to-door distribution company, a research company, and a commando sales force company—and the share offer was oversubscribed $31\frac{1}{2}$ times. Regarding the public flotation Brunning said: 'This was a step that had to happen . . . I happen to be the first.' (Before going public Brunning was forced to obtain permission from the NPA, a mark of the power of the agency recognition system at that time.) Brunning's flotation was swiftly followed in December 1961 by the flotation of the C. J. Lytle agency, which was similarly oversubscribed, the share offer opening and closing within 60 seconds. Charles Lytle, too, claimed he had gone public in order 'to remain British', a cheeky claim in his case as he was himself American. Anyway this was all spin. Though the Brunning and Lytle agencies were well-run businesses, they were far from being high-flying agencies of the kind American agencies would be willing to pay a healthy premium for—as John Hobson & Partners was.

Hobson and Metcalf could not have cared less about remaining British. Many of the largest advertisers in Britain were already American, and to them it looked as though US-led globalization was on the near horizon. 'We knew the big clients of the future would want an international agency,' said Metcalf, 'and joining the Bates Group was the fastest way of becoming one.'

The globalization of advertising has been much more tardy in coming than Hobson and Metcalf—and many others since—predicted. Still, for them the move to American ownership paid off handsomely. Almost immediately they acquired billings worth £1 million from Ted Bates's US clients, among them the Mars Corporation, which was to be the global agency's largest client for the next 30 years or so. Mars was followed by another major Ted Bates client, Colgate, which appointed Hobson Bates to handle its male toiletries in Britain. But even more important than clients, Hobson Bates acquired the Ted Bates USP philosophy.

Most advertising agencies feel an irrepressible yearning to have their own philosophy. Their philosophies are intended to differentiate them from other agencies. But as the late Charles Channon showed, in his 1981 paper 'Agency Thinking and Agencies as Brands', while different agencies approach the creation of campaigns in different ways, these differences are usually instinctive, and merely reflect the personalities of the top management. They are not based on philosophies. Most agency philosophies amount to no more than highfalutin platitudes, proclaiming the agency's extraordinarily passionate commitment to extraordinarily creative and extraordinarily effective advertising.

The USP philosophy—though hardly what philosophers would call a philosophy—is undeniably meatier. It differentiated Ted Bates from other agencies in a way that was real and was, as mentioned, highly attractive to many advertisers. It involves studying every detail of a product—this is often called 'interrogating the product'—to discover any attributes which can be claimed to be unique. These attributes may be genuinely unique, or may be attributes the product shares with its competitors, but have never been promoted. When the attributes have been identified, one (and only one) will be selected for its sales power—called 'pulling power' in Bates argot—and turned into a memorable slogan. This will be the Unique Sales Proposition. Classic Bates USPs include 'Cleans Your Breath While It Cleans Your Teeth' (Colgate), 'Melt In The Mouth, Not In The Hand' (M&Ms), and 'Top Breeders Recommend Chum'. A winning USP, Bates claimed, should be used forever and a day—repetition, repetition, repetition. Consequently many of Bates's USPs achieved astonishing longevity. Cynics, however, whispered ungenerously that the principal winner from such repetitiousness was the agency, which had no need to create a new campaign as long as the old one could be kept alive.

The USP philosophy has notable weaknesses. It is built around the concept of a verbal proposition, and much successful advertising—fashion advertising, for example—may have no verbal proposition. It is circular, being based on the identification of a 'selling' proposition, and it is impossible to say whether or not a proposition is a 'selling' proposition until it has proved to be a seller. It works well for consumer brands which change little over time, but not nearly so well for, say, electrical or electronic goods, or even cars, whose specifications constantly change, and it is the changes which need to be advertised. But none of this detracts from its effective use for many brands, in many situations.

Ted Bates's USP discipline gelled perfectly with the Hobson agency's own hard-nosed creative style. It was applied successfully to several of their British clients, including Cadbury's Bournvita, Tuf boots and shoes, and Double Diamond beer. Occasionally it needed to be bent a trifle. The agency's long-running campaign for Manikin small cigars, which showed sultry semi-naked females rolling cigars on their upper thighs in glamorous locations, was a fantasy campaign, with no hint of a USP. The Manikin slogan was 'Sheer Enjoyment'—which the agency post-rationalized as 'a pre-emptive USP for the entire product category'. Hobson and his team were astute enough, and Jesuitical enough, to prove all their campaigns were USP campaigns, even those which were patently not USP campaigns. Consequently, by the mid-1960s Hobson Bates was known to be an agency which had a USP of its own, a USP which achieved great sales results.

Superficially, John Pearce and John Hobson would have been thought quite similar. Neither, as it happens, reflected Swinging London—but then there are exceptions to every *Time* generalization. Both were distinguished, gentlemanly middle-aged British chaps. Both were exceptionally intelligent workaholics, though in later years Pearce's post-lunch work rate decelerated, more than somewhat. Both believed totally and passionately in the power of advertising to build great brands. Both inspired great loyalty from clients and staff—and both came from CPV.

There the similarities end. Hobson was stiff and correct, unlikely to roll up his sleeves and do dogsbody jobs. Pearce would potter around his agency in his socks, shirt sleeves, and red braces, helping with paste-ups and having a drink or several with the staff at almost any time of day.

Hobson believed in well-organized meetings and the orderly conduct of business; Pearce hated meetings and held them in corridors. In 1965 Hobson became President of the IPA, a role Pearce would not have touched with a well-crafted barge-pole. Pearce was invited to be a member of the very first D&AD Awards jury, an invitation which would never have been extended to Hobson no matter how many brands he built. Pearce turned down clients if he felt their brands were beyond salvaging, or anyway beyond CDP's desire to salvage them. Hobson would have viewed this as unprofessional—not simply because he was greedy for business, but because he would have thought it defeatist: a competent agency should be able to undertake any advertising challenge and make a fist of it. Hobson was formal; Pearce maverick. One evening Pearce invited two senior Harvey's executives to dinner. Harvey's was a major CDP client. The three met up at Pearce's West End flat. Having downed a few drinks Pearce went to his bedroom, undressed, and went to sleep. In the sitting room the Harvey's men sat forlornly, getting hungry. Hobson would have viewed this as unprofessional, too. But the story comes from Harvey's, and is told with amused affection.

To obtain media recognition John Hobson launched his shop with outside capital, which he had difficulty raising. John Pearce and Ronnie Dickenson bought into Pictorial Publicity, a small agency which already held media recognition. This was a common practice at the time. Pictorial Publicity, owned by John Collett, had a few clients but was going through a rough patch. Messrs Collett Dickenson and Pearce opened their agency on 1 April 1960.

Pearce and Dickenson had worked together at Hulton's Press, and were boozing as well as business partners. John Pearce's widow says launching CDP was Dickenson's idea, but Pearce was its indisputable leader. The vision he brought to British agencies was an uncompromising focus on advertising, at a time when other agencies were still mucking around with a miscellany of marketing services. An internal CDP memorandum dated August 1961, presumably drafted by Pearce, states:

> Our business is advertising. We stick to it. After all, a client knows his business better than we do. What we can do better than the client is:
> (a) Provide outstanding advertisements;
> (b) Offer shrewd media buying;
> (c) Service the account.
> If these things are done properly, the agency will earn its 15% commission.

No mention, note, of any activities other than the creation of advertisements and the buying of media. The allusion to clients knowing their 'business better than we do' is an indirect—maybe not so indirect—dig at the increasing propensity of agencies to get involved in marketing and market research. The final line is a dig at clients who wanted additional 'free' or cheap services for their money. The agency invested its time, and when necessary its own money, perfecting every single advertisement it produced. All had to be unremittingly superb.

So the most important decision Pearce made at the start—perhaps ever—was to haul from CPV the art director Colin Millward 'to look after the ads'. Millward, a curmudgeonly, nail-biting, cruel-to-be-kind Yorkshireman, had excelled at Leeds College of Art and had wanted to be a painter. He spent some years in a Paris garret before renouncing the Bohemian life and switching to advertising. Starting at C. J. Lytle, he moved first to Mather & Crowther and then to CPV, where he met John Pearce. Though hardly known outside the advertising industry, within it he is recognized as one of the handful of people who immeasurably influenced British advertising creativity during the twentieth century. In its 1993 Silver Jubilee list of the 50 most important people in British advertising, *Campaign* magazine placed Millward first—ahead of Charles Saatchi (second), or anyone else: a somewhat idiosyncratic anointment which nonetheless reflected Millward's contribution to British creativity. Under Millward CDP recruited most of the most talented creative advertising people of the era, and gave them the freedom to maximize their talents, simultaneously bullying them and protecting them, like a disciplinarian parent. No other British agency—probably no other agency in the world—has ever employed anything like so glittering, and so costly, a galaxy of creative people.[3]

Just about every one of them admits that when CDP offered them a job they could not believe their luck. David Puttnam says:

I was 21 when I saw my first CDP ad ... I didn't know it was a CDP ad but I found out who had done it ... I wrote three letters before I got an interview.

---

[3] The creative people Millward brought to CDP, and directly or indirectly trained, include Tony Brignull, Rooney Carruthers, Ron Collins, Rita Dempsey, Graham Fink, Max Forsythe, Richard Foster, Malcolm Gluck, Neil Godfrey, Derrick Hass, Dave Horry, John Horton, Gray Joliffe, Tony Kaye, Terry Lovelock, Alfredo Marcantonio, Barbara Nokes, John O'Donnell, John O'Driscoll, Alan Parker, David Puttnam, David Reynolds, Nigel Rose, Charles Saatchi, John Salmon, Geoff Seymour, Alan Waldie, Tim Warriner, Paul Weiland, and Robin Wight.

Millward was a laconic, brutally exacting taskmaster—an intimidating perfectionist with perfect visual pitch. He inspired terror in young account executives, who were far more frightened of him than of their clients. It was their job to sell to the clients the work Millward and his team created: to fail was unacceptable. Puttnam, with manifest fondness, dubs him a tyrant and a bastard who 'taught me more than anyone I ever met'. Frank Lowe, Robin Wight, and other leading advertising men of the era have said much the same. And while the creative department at Hobson Bates would be preparing, in Hobson's words, dozens of ways to do any job, in order to 'test and test and test', CDP clients were only ever presented with one creative idea, the idea Millward and the agency believed to be the right idea. Peter Wilson, then Cigarette Marketing Manager of Gallaher and later Chairman of the Gallaher Group, for many years CDP's largest client, says they were

> a highly autocratic agency... They had their own very clear rules about what was right for the brand and nothing would sway them from their opinion.

Nor would they be rushed. The creative department was massively indulged. Their clients knew, as Wilson also said, 'they like to take their time.' This was only partly due to their eternal quest for perfection. CDP was shambolic. Rudeness and lateness were routine, lingering lunch hours were chronic, decadence all but encouraged. 'The amount of drinking that went on was astonishing... with Pearce and Dickenson leading by example,' says John Salmon, later CDP's creative director and chairman, in Sam Delaney's book *Get Smashed* (2007). 'John Pearce was knocking back a bottle of whisky a day,' confirms Alan Parker, the CDP copywriter who became a film director.

In this milieu the role of market research in campaign development was nugatory. John Salmon and John Ritchie write in their panegyric *Inside Collett Dickenson Pearce* (2000):

> If we agreed on anything it was that formulas and rules don't lead to great advertising. We were sure we could tell a good ad from a bad one and fortunately, most of the time, we were right.

CDP's first research director was John Wood. When Wood joined, Colin Millward told him the appointment had been made 'over my dead body'. Millward's disdain for research and researchers was legendary. Millward believed—everyone at CDP believed—that the merit of their work was (and should be) self-evident. Wood was only appointed, reluctantly, when the agency was forced by certain of its clients to use market research—and even then the research was used as a prop for their creativity, rather than a provider of new insights.

CDP's creative work sparkled from the start. Pearce liked to claim his agency specialized in 'booze, fags, and fashion', and in the first few years its innovative campaigns for Whitbread beers, Harvey's sherries, Gallaher's Benson & Hedges and Hamlet, Acrilan synthetics, and Dunn & Company clothes became instantly famous. But CDP was soon doing much more than booze, fags, and fashion, working with Aer Lingus, Ford, Selfridges, Vogue, Unilever's Birds Eye and Van den Berghs. A blue-chip client list, built in no time.

* * *

Which of the two Johnnies was right? If only advertising were that simple. The relationship between creativity and effectiveness preoccupied British advertising during the latter part of the last century. Over recent years more than forty academic papers[4] have been published on the subject, particularly by Alex Biel, Erik Du Plessis, and D. A. Aaker. Most focus on the relationship between likeability and effectiveness, using likeability as a surrogate for creativity. The great majority of these papers have shown consumers recognize, and do not like, advertisements that are dull, forgettable, or phoney. They like advertisements they find meaningful, believable, and convincing. They also like advertisements which are imaginative, clever, original, and amusing, but they insist that these attractive qualities should not obscure the product message.

At the same time a slew of attempts have been made by non-academic advertising practitioners to prove award-winning advertisements are more sales-effective than others. Some of these attempts were circular, and focused on campaigns which were known to have both won awards and built sales; some got bogged down in semantics. (Academics fall foul of this too—see for example 'Creativity Vs. Effectiveness' by Kover, Goldberg, and James, 1995.) Most were heavily biased towards proving the case they wanted to prove. In 1995 Donald Gunn,[5] the worldwide director of creative resources at global agency Leo Burnett, compiled a list of the 200 most creative international campaigns during 1992 and 1993 (as anointed at

---

[4] This academic work has been summarized in the *Journal of Advertising Research* (2006) by Erica Smit, Lex Van Meurs, and Peter Neijens, in 'Effects of Advertising Likeability: A 10 Year Perspective'.

[5] Gunn is now President of the Cannes Festival (page 253).

creative awards festivals throughout the world) and sought to check their sales effectiveness. He telephoned the 103 agencies and advertisers responsible for the 200 gong-laden campaigns, and asked if they had met their sales objectives. Gunn himself admitted, 'This isn't 100% scientific.' (Who'd have guessed?) Nonetheless, he went on to claim his survey proved an award-winning advertisement is two-and-a-half times more likely to be sales-effective than one that has won no awards. What hogwash. Nobody doubts many highly creative campaigns make cash registers ring, but that does not prove a correlation, let alone a causal relationship.

From a historical perspective I believe it to be justifiable to concentrate—but not exclusively—on the minute number of award-winning, high-profile campaigns. It is justifiable because they occupy a greater share of public interest than their commercial importance dictates, because they influence future creative trends, and because they are more stimulating, more engaging, and more fascinating than the prosaic stuff. But prosaic should never be mistaken for trivial.

Advertising's *raison d'être* is to sell things. That is not debatable. But advertisements which sell things charmingly and attractively are more likeable, more welcome, more socially desirable than those which do not. To bastardize John Keats, an advertisement of beauty is a joy for quite a while.

Creativity Germinates

From the moment the D&AD awards got going in 1963, the advertising sector was dominated by CDP. By the end of the decade CDP had bagged a mind-boggling bouquet of awards and citations for their work for:

- Aer Lingus
- Chemstrand/Acrilan
- Dunn & Company
- Ford cars
- Gallaher—Benson & Hedges/Hamlet cigars
- GEC
- Harvey's sherries
- Lewis's stores
- Lovable bras
- Martell
- Selfridges

- Vogue
- Whitbread
- Van den Bergh

But CDP had no monopoly. Creativity in London advertising, as in other cultural spheres, was blooming. Three established American agencies—Benton & Bowles, McCann–Erickson, and Young & Rubicam—all hauled in awards. At Mathers, Shelton was still delivering the goods. In addition to its Milk and Eggs work, in 1960 Mathers crafted the romantic People Love Players campaign to revitalize the ailing Player's Navy Cut cigarette brand (it failed), and three years later Mathers launched the 'Schhh . . . you-know-who' campaign to revitalize the ailing Schweppes mixer brand (it succeeded, and ran for nearly a decade).

Almost simultaneously four new agencies leapt impressively from their starting blocks—though none of them as impressively as CDP. Three were British: Davidson Pearce Berry & Tuck, Kingsley Manton & Palmer, and Geers Gross (though Geers and Gross were Americans). All forged celebrated creative campaigns. The fourth start-up agency was the offspring of New York's Doyle Dane Bernbach, then still the most creative agency in the world—and from day one, DDB's London office was a fine chip off the old block.[6]

The influence of DDB on British creativity at this time, both from New York and via their London agency, cannot be overestimated. From New York, reproductions of DDB's 1950s and 1960s advertisements for Avis, El Al, Levy's bread, Uttica Club beer, and above all Volkswagen sped round the globe, inspiring veneration and envy in every advertising creative guy who saw them. They still do. All were beautifully designed, by some of the world's finest art directors and typographers, marvellously photographed, by some of the world's finest photographers, and wittily written by some of the world's finest copywriters. But their particular appeal was that they didn't shout, brag, and ram home their sales pitches like 'loud mouthed salesmen', as other American advertisements did. Almost to a fault they were cool and honest about their products' faults—or anyway about some of them.

Self-denigration, of even the mildest kind, was then almost unknown in advertising—it isn't exactly commonplace today. But DDB's VW

---

[6] DDB's London agency immediately launched a flurry of stunning campaigns for Avis UK, the ASTMA, British Gypsum, Chivas Regal, Christian Aid, Gillette, Jamaica Tourism, London Weekend Television, Lufthansa, Polaroid, Remington Shavers, Tern shirts, and Uniroyal.

advertisements ingenuously mocked the funny little car. One was head-lined 'Lemon' and admitted the VW production line was not always faultless; another headlined 'Think Small' admitted VWs were tiny com-pared with the gross American leviathans of the time. Such admissions would traditionally have been sacrilege in American automobile adver-tising. For Uttica Club, DDB wrote 'Our Beer Is 50 Years Behind the Times', a perilously un-American admission. Naturally these advertise-ments turned their negatives into positives, and the candid honest-to-badness approach made them all the more believable—at least that was the stratagem. 'The public are hungry for the truth,' declared Bill Bernbach, and when they are given it 'the public say to themselves, "there's an honest advertiser"'. In DDB's celebrated Avis campaign, based on the strapline 'We Try Harder. We're Only Number Two', not only did Avis admit Hertz was larger (and therefore more popular), but admitted Avis occasionally over-booked, and even sometimes hired out poorly serviced cars with dirty ashtrays. Unsurprisingly DDB had a par-ticularly tough time selling this advertising to Avis. And while VW sales in America grew strongly during the 1960s, the Avis campaign was dis-continued quite quickly and—for whatever reason—DDB was fired by Avis soon afterwards.

The vogue for honest-to-badness advertising crossed the Atlantic. In the late 1960s several British advertisers and agencies bought into it with gusto. Its nadir was the Austin Maxi car launch, which was headlined 'What's New About the Austin Maxi?' before answering, all too honestly: not a lot. It ended, 'Will you like the Maxi? We don't have a clue.' Well you can't say less than that.

A modicum of self-denigration in advertising, as in life, is charming and attractive. It works best when the humility is expressed wittily—at which DDB New York were masters. But it is a dangerous stratagem. The public knows what advertisements are for. Advertisements are there to sell things. Honest-to-badness advertising makes people suspicious: advertisements do not do self-denigration. Moreover, advertisements are seen by the brand's existing customers—existing customers are often the prime target audience for a campaign—and it is doubly risky to draw your product's weaknesses to the attention of your customers. People like to be reassured they are making the right buying decisions—and advertising plays a key role in providing such reassurance. Honest-to-badness advertising as-sumes consumers always take thoughtful analysis and rational judgement with them when they go out shopping. They don't.

But consumerism makes similar assumptions.

The Day the Pigs Refused to be Driven to Market

The 1960s were the heyday of consumerism—consumers acting in pressure groups to influence the products and services they buy. The movement started in America in 1927, when Stuart Chase teamed up with F. J. Schlink and published *Your Money's Worth*, which reported the results of tests carried out by the US National Bureau of Standards and became a mammoth bestseller. In 1969, 89 per cent of readers of the *Chicago Daily News* voted for Ralph Nader—the consumerist scourge of General Motors—to be the next Democratic Presidential candidate. (He wasn't.)

Consumerism in Britain never soared to the giddy heights it reached in the USA. It took thirty years for the idea even to get here. In 1957 Michael Young, the sociologist who later fathered the Open University and the Open College of the Arts, founded the Consumers' Association and produced the first copy of the consumerist monthly *Which?* in a garage in Bethnal Green. Its first print run was 10,000, which quickly sold out. By the late 1960s the circulation of *Which?* was around 600,000, and as many of its reports were publicized by the news media its influence extended far more widely.

In 1959 the government set up a committee under Mr Justice Moloney QC, to consider 'the protection of the consuming public'. In 1962 the Moloney Committee published its 242 conclusions and recommendations. Its main proposal was for a Consumer Council to be created to coordinate all consumer protection activities, supported by public funds. This was enacted by the Tory government in 1963, but was given a miserly annual budget of only £210,000 and abolished by a subsequent Tory government not long afterwards, to save money!

The Moloney Committee rejected any overall statutory regulation of advertising, arguing that self-regulation should be given 'a fair trial'. The advertising industry responded by setting up an Advertising Standards Authority. This new ASA would enforce in non-broadcast advertising a Code of Advertising Practice to which Moloney had given the nod. (Under the 1954 Act the control of broadcast advertising already came within the remit of the Independent Television Authority, and that continued.) The ASA would investigate consumers' complaints about advertisements, allowing advertisers to defend themselves before deciding whether or not any advertisement should be banned.

The first ASA was chaired by the distinguished economist Professor Sir Arnold Plant, of the London School of Economics. Its Council included Vic Feather, the General Secretary of the Trades Union Congress, and four other independent members, but these were balanced by five members from advertising and associated businesses—with the independent chairman having a casting vote. Its powers were far from awesome. The best *Advertisers' Weekly* could claim in July 1962 was that: 'Constituent members of the Advertising Association are virtually pledged to abide by decisions of the Authority.' As neither all advertisers nor all media were members of the Advertising Association, and as even members only 'virtually' pledged themselves to abide by the Authority's authority, the ASA could hardly throw its weight about. It was a step in the right direction—but inevitably it soon ran into controversy and criticism, both within the advertising industry and without. Within three months, in October 1962, *Advertisers' Weekly* grumbled that the performance of the infant ASA was 'not over-encouraging'. The next year Plant was forced to defend the ASA against accusations of 'dragging its feet'. The ASA had drawn the teeth of advertising's consumerist antagonists, but only for a while. In November 1973 the main session at the IPA's National Conference was 'Consumerism—A Threat or a Challenge?' In 1974 the ASA had to be fundamentally refinanced and restructured.

Advertising and consumerism are endemically inimical. Many in advertising, and a few consumerists, deny this on the grounds that advertising and consumerism fulfil complementary roles. They certainly fulfil different roles, but the roles are rarely complementary—more rarely still complimentary. Consumerists believe advertisers will always be as deceitful and unscrupulous as they can get away with being; advertisers believe, as industrialist Sir Miles Thomas claimed in a tirade against *Which?* in 1964, that consumerists deliberately undermine people's faith and confidence in the products they buy, and so retard economic growth.

Advertising aims to make goods and services attractive and appealing, while consumerism aims to tell the whole truth, warts and all. Indeed consumerists like to concentrate on the warts, because they believe it is the warts consumers most need to know about, and won't learn about from any other source. From the consumerist perspective, advertising misleads by committing sins of omission; from the advertising perspective, consumerism misleads by suggesting people buy things only for rational, measurable, reasons, whereas the truth is that people buy things—have always bought things—for an abundance of reasons, rational and emotional, quantifiable and unquantifiable. This is why, *pace* Ted Bates's USP philosophy, many advertisements contain no facts whatsoever—something which is intrinsically wrong, not to say iniquitous, from the consumerist perspective (see also Ch. 6, 'An Insane Irrelevance?').

But during the late 1960s one of British advertising's most talented and flamboyant youngsters—a dandy whose suits and bow ties have always been best viewed through dark glasses—was single-handedly plotting to persuade his industry that the consumerists were basically right, and that the advertising industry had better come to terms with them. Robin Wight, an amiably eccentric Cambridge agriculture graduate and award-winning copywriter, who had set up his first agency while he was still an undergraduate, was drafting a pro-consumerist book: *The Day the Pigs Refused to be Driven to Market: Advertising and the Consumer Revolution* (1972).

Wight argued—and few today would disagree—that companies which deal helpfully with aggressive and militant consumers are more successful, and more profitable, than companies which do not. Wight wrote to a score of British companies asking them to justify their advertising slogans—including 'The Best Sherry in the World' (Harvey's), 'The Most Welcoming Pub in the World' (Bass Charrington), and 'The Happiest Sounds Come From Babies Fed With Heinz'. Their offhand, tardy, and sometimes contemptuous replies revealed all too plainly the attitude of many manufacturers to irritating customers. Few advertisers would respond so disdainfully today.

Unsurprisingly—though he himself seemed surprised—Wight's book was not greeted with universal acclaim by the advertising industry. It was a backwards step in his long career, which has had as many ups and downs as a giveaway yo-yo. Wight had gone native: he had drunk too deeply from the consumerist well. Responding to consumerism, John Hobson had written in November 1956: 'Consumers are seeking experiences, not things . . . advertising adds subjective qualities to a product, for example in giving a feeling of smartness, cheerfulness, rightness, well-being etc . . . and thus increasing its ability to satisfy a yet more ramified, but just as real, complex of wants.'

From their very earliest existence, human beings have always added 'subjective qualities to a product'. Primitive man enhanced and adorned his flints and bone tools. Advertisements similarly enhance and adorn material objects, polishing Lever's halo. Wight had briefly forgotten it. But he remembered soon enough, and his career began one of its long upward trajectories. His agency Wight Collins Rutherford Scott, launched in 1979, became one of the shooting stars of the 1980s.

Brands and Bad Habits

Consumerists were not alone in their hostility to advertising. In November 1955 future Labour Prime Minister Harold Wilson described advertising, in the House of Commons, as 'a wasteful use of national economic resources'. In 1959 a public meeting called by Labour MP Francis Noel-Baker set up the Advertising Inquiry Committee, an independent body designed to keep under surveillance 'all kinds of socially harmful advertisements'. The Labour Party Political Broadcast in May 1961—itself a form of advertising, of course—was entirely devoted to an attack on advertising, led again by Harold Wilson. In April 1962, Labour Party leader Hugh Gaitskell set up an Advertising Commission under Lord Reith—who had previously compared television advertising to the Black Death and bubonic plague, so his objectivity may not have been wholly objective. In 1966 Reith's Commission recommended there should be a statutory code of advertising practice supervised by a body, appointed by the government, with legal power to enforce it—a proposal the Moloney Committee had rejected. The Reith Commission also recommended there should be a tax on advertising, to finance both the control of advertising and the setting-up of a National Consumer Board. Harold Wilson, who had become Labour Party leader when Hugh Gaitskell died suddenly in 1963, remained convinced advertising was a waste of economic resources, and while in opposition strongly backed the taxation of advertising—though he did nothing about it when he came to power.

The desire to control advertising was not restricted to Labour politicians. During this period an abundance of statutes were enacted by governments of both hues, to enhance consumer protection and restrict different aspects of advertising.[7]

But increasingly the cause célèbre, on which public attention focused, was cigarette advertising. Advertising and smoking first became a major issue in March 1962, when the Royal College of Physicians published 'Smoking and Health'. This established a statistical correlation between

---

[7] These included the Food and Drugs Act, 1955; the Prevention of Fraud (Investments) Act, 1958; the Consumer Protection Act, 1961; the Building Societies Act, 1962; the Protection of Depositors Act, 1963; the Weights and Measures Act, 1963; the Trading Stamps Act, 1964; the Advertisements Hire Purchase Act, 1967; the Marine Broadcasting Offences Act, 1967; the Misrepresentation Act, 1967; the Gaming Act, 1968; and particularly the Trades Descriptions Act, 1968, under which a false or misleading trade description in an advertisement would be subject to criminal penalties. These joined over forty statutes previously enacted, to form a sprawling, and often confusing, corpus of restrictive legislation.

cigarette smoking and carcinoma of the lungs, emphysema, and bronchitis. The tobacco manufacturers swiftly responded that no causal link had been established, but there was an outcry in Parliament. Parliament pressed for cigarette advertising to be restricted, particularly advertising aimed at children. The ITA ruled that tobacco advertisements should be banned from children's programmes. The tobacco companies went further and voluntarily ceased to advertise before the 9.00 pm 'watershed'. The ITA also ruled that all performers in cigarette commercials should clearly be aged 21 or older, that commercials must no longer connect smoking with social success, nor with manliness, nor romance, nor employ 'heroes of the young'.

Two years later, in January 1964, the US Surgeon General published his report on the connections between smoking and health. In Britain the pressure for a total ban on television advertising now intensified. The broadcasting companies resisted, arguing that people saw cigarette advertisements in many other media, and so a television ban alone would be ineffectual. Nonetheless the pressure escalated, and in March 1965 the Labour government announced that all television advertising of cigarettes and hand-rolling tobaccos would cease on 1 August that year. Advertising for cigars and pipe tobaccos, which had been pretty well exonerated in the health reports, could continue. It was relatively easy to ban cigarettes on television, as television was under statutory control. A ban in any other medium would require new legislation, and the government knew the print media would fight tooth and nail to protect their revenues.

The banned cigarette and tobacco categories accounted for 7 per cent of all television advertising revenue, £5,250,000, and represented the third largest advertising sector, behind washing products and confectionery. However, the Minister of Health opined in Parliament: 'I rather doubt whether this intensification of the campaign [against smoking] will result in any sudden or dramatic drop in cigarette consumption.' He was right. Cigarette smoking in Britain continued to rise until the mid-1970s.

Cigarettes were not the only goods, or services, banned from advertising on television. Nor were they even, as cigarette advertising protagonists often claimed, the only goods banned from television which could be legally bought and sold. Breath-testing devices, matrimonial agencies, fortune tellers, undertakers, and even (at that time) charities, as well as politics and religion—all of which could be legally advertised in other media—had been banned from television from the start. But it was not unreasonable to view cigarettes as a special case. Nothing similar had ever occurred before. Cigarettes were a highly popular, mass consumer product used by the majority of the population, heavily taxed and therefore providing the state with considerable cash, providing income and employment to hundreds of thousands of people—perhaps millions, indirectly. There was no evidence a television advertising ban would have any effect on consumption. In imposing the ban the government was feigning social responsibility, while in reality engaging in cosmetic gesture politics: appeasing vociferous pressure groups whether or not their arguments had substance.

Banning cigarette advertising appears to have had no effect in any country where it has been tried. In Italy cigarette advertising was totally banned in 1962, and consumption increased almost every year for the next two decades. Cigarette advertising in Poland was banned in 1972, and by 1980 cigarette sales had increased by 30 per cent. In most other communist bloc countries cigarette advertising had been banned for even longer, but smoking increased unabated. In Norway cigarette advertising was totally banned in 1975, yet manufactured cigarette sales grew 27 per cent by 1980, while hand-rolling tobaccos declined by just 3 per cent. In the USA the ban on television advertising in 1965 had no perceivable effect at all.

Inevitably the effects, if any, of an advertising ban cannot be disentangled from the host of other anti-smoking factors almost always introduced at the same time. In Britain, since the 1960s there have been fierce taxation/price hikes; health warnings on packs and in all advertisements, while they were still permitted; continuous advertising of smoking's health risks; a constant stream of medical reports publicizing the dangers; a steady reduction in public places where smoking is permissible; the developments of new and better addiction treatments; and a mounting hostility by individuals to anyone smoking near to them. Despite all these pressures, some forty years after the television ban about 10 million people—25 per cent of the adult population—still smoke, and this figure has been fairly static for more than a decade. Among 16–24 year olds over 30 per cent smoke—the largest fall in smoking has been among the elderly.

Underlying the debates about the influence of advertising on smoking are fundamental questions regarding the influence of commercial advertising on social behaviour. Increasingly, people have come to believe that while the generality of advertising is fine and dandy, particular advertising sectors—like cigarettes—should be constrained or completely banned. In the same way that many believe cigarette advertising must surely make people smoke, many believe alcohol advertising makes people drink, car advertising makes drivers speed, toy and confectionary advertising makes kids pester, fast food and carbonated drink advertising make people obese, slimming product advertising makes people anorexic, and medicine advertising makes people hypochondriac. It seems perverse—not to say self-serving—for the advertising industry to deny all this. If advertising does not build these markets, and these habits, why do advertisers advertise?

This history is not the place to rehearse the pros and cons of each case: protagonists on both sides have been batting the arguments back and forth for ages, and a surfeit of books, theses, and articles have been published by both sides. However, the issue has impinged substantially on British advertising over recent decades, so it can hardly be ignored.

In 1997, as these sectoral attacks were growing in number and frequency, the AA Economics Committee researched and published a report called *Does Advertising Affect Market Size?* The objective was to determine whether, for example, advertising for alcohol brands makes people drink more, toy advertising makes parents buy more—or toilet soap advertising makes people wash more. As with most advertising studies there was no simple, definitive answer. To quote the report:

> There is always a possibility that advertising affects the size of a particular market, but its scale and significance are highly variable.

Brand advertising, the research showed, is unlikely to increase the size of the market (or product category) if the market is large, well-established, and already satisfies a basic and satiated need. In these circumstances advertising's effects on the size of the market will be minimal, if they occur at all. On the other hand, markets (or product categories) are more likely to respond positively to brand advertising if they are small, or new, or are dominated by a single brand, or if the market is already growing for other reasons.

New electrical and electronic goods, new snack and hobby products belong in the 'more likely' category. Cigarettes, alcohol, confectionery, toys, slimming products, and most foods (not to mention toilet soap) belong in the 'unlikely' category. This is not as strange as it may appear. Large, long-established markets will contain a multiplicity of brands, whose advertising will be specifically designed to achieve brand share increases. Market movements are generally minimal, and slow, and are therefore unimportant to the brand advertiser. This does not apply in small and new markets, where market expansion may be crucial to a brand's success.

Most studies which seek to correlate brand advertising with a product category's sales investigate only one product category at a time—as though there were not a welter of advertising for brands in other product categories running simultaneously, competing for every penny in the consumer's purse. If huge campaigns which specifically aim to increase consumption in large, long-established markets fail to do so—think 'Drinka Pinta' or 'Go To Work on an Egg'—it should not be surprising that brand campaigns which have no such intention have no such effects.

Nonetheless, pressure groups constantly call for the advertising of product categories of which they disapprove to be restricted. Such restrictions cease to be evidence-based. They become political. At a private AA dinner at the end of the last century, when the question of totally banning all cigarette advertising was discussed, government minister Margaret Beckett made clear the argument was over. Whether brand advertising did, or did not, encourage smoking could not be conclusively proved either way, she said. But the government—and most of the population, she believed—felt cigarette advertisements to be obscene, a public affront: that was why they had to be stopped. It was a political decision.

On a different occasion David Abbott, the gifted writer who co-founded Abbott Mead Vickers, argued that until it could be shown that cigarette advertising had never persuaded a single child to start smoking, it was indefensible. Abbott's father, a smoker, had died of cancer. His agency refused ever to handle a tobacco account, and instead created powerful anti-smoking campaigns for the Health Education Council.

I do not accept either Margaret Beckett's or David Abbott's arguments. But smoking is lethal, and everything that can be done to discourage it should be done. If banning cigarette advertising deterred people from smoking I would endorse it unreservedly. But there is no evidence the ban has made a jot of difference.

Somewhat at Sea

During the 1960s total advertising expenditure grew (at current prices), but this represented a decline in advertising's percentage of the Gross National Product (Table 3).

While total advertising's share of the GNP fell by 14 per cent, display advertising fell still faster, by 21 per cent. The difference was accounted for by classified advertising, which did tolerably well. As advertising agencies mostly handle display advertising, the decline in that sector hit them hard. The number of people employed in agencies dropped sharply. But despite these staff reductions, agency profits as a percentage of turnover more than halved, falling from 19.2 per cent in 1960 to just 9.3 per cent in 1970.

Table 3. Total advertising expenditure as % of GNP

	Expenditure (at current prices) £million	% GNP (at market prices)
1960	323	1.24
1962	348	1.19
1964	416	1.23
1966	447	1.15
1968	503	1.14
1970	554	1.06

Source: Advertising Association.

These depressed advertising figures were largely caused by a slowdown in the growth of the UK economy, particularly when compared with the rapid expansion of the 1950s. Slow growth, however, is not the same as recession, and throughout the decade wages and consumer expenditure in Britain grew, so the public's economic optimism remained steadfast, and upbeat: these were, after all, the Swinging Sixties.

Within the overall figures, television's growth continued until its share levelled off at around 37 per cent of display advertising (around 25 per cent of total advertising). Print media lost some display advertising to television but, as in the 1950s, they lost less than many had predicted. And they were buoyed up by the classifieds' strong showing. Consequently print media's share of advertising remained steady.

But the resilience of print's revenue masked a period of turmoil. The early 1960s saw the closure of four national newspapers: the *Sunday Graphic*, *Sunday Dispatch*, *Empire News*, and *News Chronicle*—plus *The Star* (then London's third evening paper), as well as other locals and provincials. A newspaper called the *New Daily* was born but quickly died. In 1962 *Reynolds News* was relaunched as the *Sunday Citizen*, but it, too, quickly died. In 1964 the moribund *Daily Herald* was relaunched as *The Sun*, and lost £12.7 million in the following six years. The escalating cost of newsprint, falling circulations, and the uneconomic production costs engendered by the printing unions' restrictive working practices all conspired against the publishers.

Fortunately not all the newspapers' news was gloomy. Colour advertising was growing steadily. In 1959 the *Manchester Guardian* was successfully relaunched in London as *The Guardian*, which boosted its circulation and advertising revenue. In 1961 the *Daily Telegraph* successfully launched the *Sunday Telegraph*. And on 4 February 1962 the Canadian media entrepreneur Roy Thomson launched the *Sunday Times* Magazine, to widespread scepticism from both the public and the advertising pundits.

Roy Thomson was one of several commonwealth men who brought fresh ideas and fresh impetus to British media—his fellow Canadian Lord Beaverbrook preceded him, the Australian Rupert Murdoch followed him. Thomson was a modest man, with little interest in the trappings of wealth, who often journeyed to and from work on the London underground. His only apparent interest was reading balance sheets, which he read like novels, his eyes twinkling through his pebble-glass spectacles whenever he spotted the promise of a profit.

Nostalgia for his origins brought Thomson back from Canada to Scotland, and in 1952 he bought *The Scotsman*. Thereafter his rise in British media was swift. In 1957 he successfully bid for the Scottish Television contract, later quipping that owning a British television franchise was like having a licence to print your own money—a quip he must often have regretted. In 1959 he bought Kemsley Newspapers, the largest newspaper group in the UK, for £5 million, and changed the name to Thomson Newspapers. The *Sunday Times*, a Kemsley title, came with the deal. In 1966 he bought *The Times* from the Astor family. During the 1960s, while many provincial papers were closing down, Thomson opened new ones. He had an instinctive sense of the advertising revenue media can generate— among his many other ventures he launched Yellow Pages in the UK. His interest in editorial content was minimal. He referred to editorial as 'the news hole', a phrase his journalists found less than inspirational.

The *Sunday Times* Magazine was Britain's first free colour supplement, supported entirely by advertising, and Jeremiahs predicted it would bomb, bringing the *Sunday Times* crashing down with it. British readers, the prophets prophesied, were unwilling to spend their Sundays drowning in so much newsprint. On the single occasion I met him I asked Thomson if he felt there was any validity in this argument—which seems puerile now (and was puerile then, come to that). Rubbish, he growled, buyers need not read the Magazine if they don't want to; he had never heard of anyone getting upset because they were given something for nothing, even if they didn't want the something they were given.

But Thomson did not take the Magazine's success for granted. He knew that, like all new media, it had initially to overcome the inertia of the advertising agencies. He invited the boards of London's leading agencies, one-by-one, to private lunches in his boardroom; he threw lavish champagne parties at the grandest West End hotels, exclusively for agency creative people, knowing creative people influence media selection more than is commonly supposed; in February 1963 he flew top advertisers and agency bosses to icy Moscow—an innovative and much-publicized freebie. He backed up these trade promotions with striking advertising aimed squarely at his Sunday competitors. 'The Sunday Times—The Only One With Colour,' proclaimed his posters, which were created in-house at the *Sunday Times* by art director John Donegan. Though it did not emanate from Ted Bates, 'The Only One With Colour' is a fine USP.

It did not take long for the *Sunday Times* Magazine to become a success. Tagging along behind, the *Observer* Magazine was launched in November 1964, and the *Daily Telegraph* added a magazine in 1966, which was transferred to its Sunday sibling ten years later. Today the weighty plethora of giveaway supplements and colour magazines published by the national and provincial papers is taken for granted—and all of them are paid for by advertising.

At the end of the 1960s colour was also the big story on television. November 15, 1969 saw ITV's first colour broadcasts. After considerable debate, the television contractors decided against seeking a premium for colour advertising—although colour has always commanded a premium in the press (where it costs more to print). The contractors' decision rapidly proved wise, as ITV's advertising revenue started to fall, for the first time since its launch. In 1969 television advertising revenue fell by 1.2 per cent, and in 1970 by a further 2.9 per cent. Any attempt to charge higher rates for colour at that time would have been strongly resisted by advertisers, and would almost certainly have worsened the falls, as smaller advertisers would have migrated to the press. In 1971 television advertising revenue recovered, with a healthy increase of 14.7 per cent. This pushed television expenditure through the £100 million barrier, and that year ITV pocketed a record £108,633,692. More than three-quarters of this came from the half-dozen product sectors which dominated television advertising (Table 4).

Meanwhile television audience research was growing increasingly sophisticated. Audiences were being measured on a national basis by meters plugged into sets in a representative sample of UK homes. This research was carried out by Television Audience Measurement Limited (TAM)—whose first contract with independent television had been signed, as a temporary expedient, in January 1956. 'Tam Ratings' became the standard unit of audience measurement.

Table 4. Per cent of television advertising by product sector

Product sector	% of total
Food	38.5
Household products	14.7
Drink	9.1
Toiletries and cosmetics	7.4
Household appliances	3.4
Publishing	3.3
TOTAL	76.4

Source: Advertising Association.

A decade later, in January 1965, after a trial run in the Midlands, the Television Consumer Audit (TCA) was extended to all major areas during 1966 and 1967, costing the contractors more than £200,000 a year. TCA was the first research methodology which attempted, however imperfectly, to correlate spot transmissions with consumer sales, and it became a powerful weapon in the ITV sales armoury.

One other advertising medium made waves in the 1960s: commercial radio.

Having stopped during the War, Radio Luxembourg restarted transmissions in 1946, and while post-war newsprint was in short supply it flourished. But after 1955 commercial television stole its audience. Deftly, the station changed tack. Redefining its target market, Luxembourg aimed solely at teenagers, broadcasting late at night when television had shut down. The teenagers listened in their bedrooms, on their new transistor radios. Transmitting only pop music, which the BBC disdained, Luxembourg rapidly built up a sizeable young audience of substantial interest to advertisers.

Luxembourg's ploy was soon spotted by others. In 1964 a young Irishman named Ronan O'Rahilly launched Radio Caroline. Caroline was targeted at the selfsame teenage market, transmitting its programmes from a 'pirate' ship anchored three miles off the Essex coast, just outside British jurisdiction. Other offshore pop music stations now dropped anchor, thick and fast. Within two years Radio Caroline (now with two ships) was joined by American backed Radio London; Radio 390; Radio City; Radio Scotland; Radio 270; Radio Essex; and Radio England/Britain Radio. A survey carried out by National Opinion Polls in May 1965 showed that Caroline and

London reached 13.1 million listeners between them. The pirate ships were registered in Panama, flew the Panamanian flag, and paid the record companies no royalties. This was unacceptable. Something, the UK government felt, must be done. In 1967 the Marine Broadcasting Offences Act made it unlawful either to buy or to supply pirate advertising from the British mainland. Thus were the pirates put to the sword.

Though they were a fleeting phenomenon, the pirates had revealed a latent demand for popular music which the BBC was failing to meet. They had also shown there was plenty of advertising available. Eventually the government got switched on, and in 1972 it passed the Sound Broadcasting Act. This allowed for 60 local commercial radio stations to be launched, and the Independent Television Authority (ITA) became the Independent Broadcasting Authority (IBA), to regulate both commercial sectors.

Now all Britain's major media sectors could carry advertising.[8]

The Groves of Academe

In November 1963 leading businessman and industrialist Donald Stokes won the first ever National Marketing Award, conferred by the Institute of Marketing and Sales Management. In his acceptance speech Stokes bewailed the low status of selling and salesmanship in Britain, and urged universities to offer degrees in marketing—which he felt would increase selling's prestige. Within four months, in February 1964, Advertising Association President Lord Robens announced that the AA would finance a chair of marketing at London University. The AA would provide £100,000 in ten annual instalments of £10,000 to fund a professorship at the London School of Economics.

Enthusiasm for the idea spread. In July 1964 the lead headline in *Advertisers' Weekly* was 'Advertising Education To Get A Big Boost.' The story continued: 'Degrees in advertising and marketing . . . expected in the near future.' The University of Lancaster, it transpired, was to be the second British university to establish a chair in marketing. The Institute of Marketing was furnishing Lancaster with an annual endowment of £10,000 for seven years to establish a Department of Marketing Studies. But despite the confident words, funds for the project came in at little more than a snail's pace. By September 1964, £25,000 had been raised, and the university did not give its formal go-ahead until October that year, by which time the

---

[8] But not of course the BBC.

fund had climbed to £33,000. Meanwhile, over at Manchester, Viyella's mercurial boss Joe Hyman modestly announced he would sponsor the Joe Hyman chair of marketing, to the tune of £5,000 annually for the next seven years. Back in Lancaster, like a church steeple collection, the fund had climbed to £67,000—including less than magnanimous gifts of £1,000 from Ford and IBM.

In October 1964 Britain's first ever European Marketing Course was announced. It would be based on a similar module at Harvard, and be run annually. There would be four weeks' coursework at Oxford University, and a three-week 'coalface' tour of Western Europe. The Steering Committee would comprise only people living in Britain who had been on the Harvard course, and to clinch Harvard's commitment the director-in-charge would be Professor Edward C. Bursk, editor and publishing director of *Harvard Business Review*.

Things were accelerating. In July 1965 *Advertisers' Weekly* announced Lancaster had pipped the London School of Economics, and won the blue riband for appointing Britain's first professor of marketing. He was Raymond John Lawrence, an Englishman aged 40. He had taken a first in classics at Cambridge, then worked with Unilever for twelve years, before spending three years at the University of California. Not unreasonably, Lancaster professed itself well pleased with its new professor: to have found a British national with Lawrence's blend of academic and business experience, gained in both Britain and the USA, was a coup.

At the end of October 1965 Lancaster's Vice Chancellor Charles F. Carter proudly announced his university would be offering MA degrees in marketing, and that Lancaster was to become 'a central point in marketing and research'. In just two years, advertising and marketing had trampled into the serene groves of academe. Today there are more than two dozen professors of advertising and/or marketing at British universities. Three of them, Professor Patrick Barwise (London Business School), the late Professor Peter Doyle (Warwick), and Professor Andrew Ehrenberg (London Business School and South Bank) have directly influenced advertising practitioners' thinking and practice though, sadly, they are the exceptions. The gap between academic studies of advertising and practitioners' day-to-day activities seems well nigh unbridgeable.[9] A 2007 paper by Sheila Keegan in the *International Journal of Market Research* shows, perhaps more surprisingly, that much the same pertains in market research.

[9] There is a fine analysis of the reasons for this by Nyilasy and Reid in the *International Journal of Advertising*, 2007.

The *International Journal of Advertising*, launched here in 1983, is now one of the world's top three academic journals in the field. And at the end of the last century the World Advertising Research Center (WARC)—a wholly British venture, despite the Americanized spelling of 'center'—opened for business. WARC began building its databank in 1997, and was launched in 1999. Today WARC is used by academics and businesses in 192 countries. It contains papers and articles by 16,000 authors, is consulted in over 10,000 on-line sessions each day, and despatches 125,000 requested news reports each week. It is now the world's prime source of advertising and marketing research information, and the world's largest on-line advertising research databank. Another British advertising success story.[10]

To Market, To Market

In 1966 David Ogilvy took Ogilvy & Mather International public in London and on Wall Street simultaneously. It was the first agency to be quoted on both markets. Then, in Britain, during the last few months of 1969, a surge of UK agencies went public. KMPH (previously Kingsley Manton & Palmer), S. H. Benson, Geers Gross, and Collett Dickenson Pearce came helter-skelter to the stock market. As we have seen, they were not the first British agencies to go public. The Brunning Group had been the pacesetter in 1961, closely chased by C. J. Lytle, both of them claiming—disingenuously—they were floating to avoid being bought by Americans. Over the next few years Brunning and Lytle were followed by Dorland,[11] Pembertons, and Stowe & Bowden.

The first slew of agencies to go public were solid, stolid, dependable businesses which had built their assets and proved their ability to trade over the long haul: the kind of businesses the stock market traditionally liked. Brunning, Lytle, Dorland, Pembertons, and Stowe & Bowden had grown, and were expected to grow, steadily but unspectacularly. Among these agencies only Brunning had seen that internal, organic growth would not be sufficient to satisfy the stock market's hunger for soaring profits. Immediately after flotation Brunning went on a shopping spree, buying five agencies in 1962—a precursor of public agencies to come. The

---

[10] I should perhaps declare an interest here, as I was WARC's founder chairman—but Mike Waterson was its progenitor, and remains its guiding spirit.

[11] Lacking Charles Lytle's cheek, Dorland never claimed to be escaping Americans, as it had been founded by an American named John Dorland in Atlanta City in 1886—though the London agency had bought out its parent in 1917, and then closed down the US offices.

other early floaters made few acquisitions, and their growth rates were far from dazzling.

With the exception of S. H. Benson, the class of 1969 were birds of a very different feather. S. H. Benson resembled the early floaters, though it was older, grander, and had a more formidable reputation. But by 1969 it had become a stuffy if reliable old shop. In contrast, CDP, KMPH, and Geers Gross were thrusting creative newcomers, winning awards and setting the pace. They were fashionable, savvy, and skilled at self-publicity. (KMP's take-off in 1964 was a masterclass in the orchestration of publicity, as they dribbled out gobbets of news week-after-week during their deliberately attenuated launch.) All three agencies had started in the 1960s, so had short trading records and minimal assets. But this meant they were still small enough to be able to grow by leaps and bounds. The stock market did not, however, buy blindly into all their puffery.

KMPH (David Kingsley, Michael Manton, Brian Palmer, Len Heath) was the most businesslike of the floaters, and its shares were eight times oversubscribed. Collett Dickenson Pearce was the most established of the three, but Collett, Dickenson, and Pearce were no longer in the first flush of youth, and the agency's financial record was distinctly patchy: the offer was about 100 per cent oversubscribed. Geers Gross was the riskiest of the three, being the smallest and heavily dependant on its two American partners, Bob Geers and Bob Gross, with little management underpinning (though Tim Bell—later to become Margaret Thatcher's favourite adman— was their media-buyer). Worse, the Geers Gross business was dominated by just two large clients. Consequently, to quote *Campaign* magazine, its stock market debut was 'sadly depressed'. The stock market's caution was vindicated when Geers and Gross more or less split up in April 1974 (though they tried hard to obfuscate the break).

The stock market's overall judgement of the three newcomers was sound. As an investment, KMPH was the best bet—at least initially. The agency was producing high-profile creative work. All four partners were young and energetic but already experienced businessmen, who had forged successful separate careers before they teamed up. After floatation the company changed its name to Kimpher, to accommodate a fifth partner, George Riches, who was only with them briefly. Like Brunnings before it, Kimpher went on an acquisition spree, and within four years owned eight advertising agencies, including five in London, two in Manchester, and one in Australia. They had minority interests in agencies in Sweden and Ireland. They owned companies in market research, sales promotion, design, and recruitment advertising, plus a successful media-buying specialist, The

Media Department. By 1974 Kimpher was the fifth largest agency group in Britain, with billings of £23 million. This was its zenith. Though its billings were growing its profits were crumbling. In 1975/6 Kimpher lost £372,000, of which £210,000 was accounted for by a bankrupt client, whose media bookings they had been forced to pay for, plus £72,000 for termination payments to two of the key partners, Brian Palmer and Len Heath, who left for pastures new. A succession of unsuccessful financial rescue deals followed, and in 1983 the group found itself owned, indirectly, by Saatchi & Saatchi, which had itself followed the Kimpher path, with considerably more success.

Apart from putatively helping them to duck being bought by Americans, the agencies which floated claimed they did so for three reasons. First, public companies find it easier to raise capital for acquisitions. Second, public companies have more businesslike reputations. Third, public ownership puts a realistic value on their shares, so they can be traded at a fair price. But the realities were that with the exception of Brunning and KMP—and for them only briefly—these agencies made few acquisitions; if their reputations improved (which is questionable) it did not help any of them win business; and there are cons as well as pros to having your shares valued fairly—it may leave you prey to takeovers, as several of them painfully discovered. In 1971 Dorland was snapped up by financier John Bentley so he could strip out its valuable property assets. Bentley then stated openly and insultingly, 'The [Dorland] top management cannot run this group as a business,' and having extracted the properties, he flogged the rest of the company within six months at the best price he could get.

At the end of 1969 there were nine publicly quoted British agencies in London. The IPA house magazine, in chorus with many others, predicted a torrent of agencies would soon flood the stock market. This did not happen, though in 1972—in a move that was to have long-term repercussions—the London offshoot of a large American group, Compton UK Partners, backed into the London stock market via the reverse takeover of a publicly quoted shell company called Birmingham Crematorium (whose only remaining, and possibly symbolic, asset was a grisly bone-crushing machine). Instead of the predicted torrent, Dorland and Stowe & Bowden both soon returned to private ownership, while S. H. Benson was hoovered up by Ogilvy & Mather International. None of the British agencies which floated during the 1960s still exists in its own right.

Not all talented advertising men, however, were thinking of going public in 1969. One who was uncompromisingly uninterested was a youngster then working in a creative consultancy which had broken away from

CDP. The talented youngster was a copywriter named Charles Saatchi, aged 26. He and his partner, art director Ross Cramer (31), were already running one of the most successful advertising creative consultancies of all time. Their consultancy, Cramer Saatchi, employed such creative men as John Hegarty, Alan Parker, David Puttnam, and Jeremy Sinclair. Occasionally they worked directly for advertisers, and their powerful advertisements for the Health Education Council (the Pregnant Man among many others) were already winning them shedloads of kudos and publicity. More often, and more covertly, they created campaigns for agencies. The agencies paid them generous fees, both to produce great campaigns and to keep their mouths shut. This is what advertising creative consultancies do, and Charles Saatchi was happy doing it. 'We don't want to get bigger', he insisted in a *Campaign* article on 22 November 1969, 'because as soon as we became an agency we'd get bogged down with a load of useless paraphernalia . . . caught up in the administration bog.'

On 14 September 1970, Charles and his brother Maurice launched Saatchi & Saatchi Limited.

Publish and Be Read

At the end of the 1960s British advertising underwent another tectonic change. On 6 September 1968 the moribund trade magazine *World's Press News & Advertising Review* was transmuted by its owners Haymarket Publishing into *Campaign*. *World's Press News*, together with its rival *Advertisers' Weekly*, had sleepily documented the ups and downs of British advertising since early in the century. Their content could be better described as anti-journalism than as journalism. They were devoid of investigative reporting, nearly always kowtowed to the industry's leaders, printed PR handouts almost unchanged, and rarely unearthed scoops or published news which agencies did not want published.

Campaign came in like a depth charge, exploding without warning from beneath the trade press Plimsoll line. Its groundbreaking design by Swiss typographer Roland Schenk, and its punchy, aggressive reporting sent shock waves through the industry. Its first editorial promised it would be 'undeterred by bluster, unseduced by handouts', and it was true to its word. Early on its journalists were rather too prone to bite the hands that fed them—many in advertising felt they were innately hostile to the business they were being paid to write about. But they got the griff, and they published it. *Campaign* was an overnight financial success, and was soon making profits of more than of £1 million a year. As if hit by a fusillade of torpedoes, *Advertisers' Weekly* first changed itself to *AdWeek*, then tried to respond by publishing more statistics and hard business data, then gave up the ghost. Competition, red in tooth and claw, had quickly killed off a publication that had, all too cosily, served its market since 1913.

The industry had been accustomed to a servile trade press for nearly threescore years and ten, so *Campaign's* publish-and-be-damned aggression provoked a love–hate relationship which still simmers. Like politicians—like everyone—advertising people prefer media to flatter them. They like good news about themselves ('ABC wins huge account') and hate bad news ('ABC loses huge account it won last week'). *Campaign's* guts and assertiveness have made it extraordinarily influential. It influences agencies' reputations, individuals' careers, advertisers' hirings and firings, and investors' views of the business. Many advertising and marketing people believe *Campaign* breaks embargoes, publishes unsubstantiated rumours, and is utterly untrustworthy. For many years the routine advertising conference joke ran: 'We should stop knocking *Campaign*. Two facts on the front page are always absolutely accurate. The date and the price.' None of that has been my experience. But *Campaign* has its favourites, and for others it has little time: perhaps this is unavoidable.

Campaign's effect on British advertising has not been entirely beneficial. It has helped make it more introverted and self-important. It has fostered trendy agencies and trendy creative work, to the detriment of sound, hardworking agencies and campaigns. It has exacerbated advertising's predisposition to be a celebrity culture, and promoted colourful personalities at the expense of humdrum businessmen: for years it excoriated Martin Sorrell. And though its reporting is generally good, its judgements, as we shall see, are frequently wonky.

But for advertising people, it's a great read.

5

The Nineteen-Seventies: Britain Takes the Lead

Climbing the Peaks

For British advertising, the 1970s—and a few years either side—were golden years, when we forged ahead of the world. The other decades were not barren. But more creativity, more innovations, and more attainments were crowded into and around those ten or so years than any others—partly in response to economic, political, and commercial pressures; partly because the structure of agencies changed; and partly fortuitously, in that there happened to be a bunch of extraordinarily bright, talented, and ambitious people working in the industry at that time.

British creative work was the best in the world, and it was then that our international creative reputation reached its peak. In *Campaign*'s selection of 'The 100 Best British Ads of the 20th Century', published in December 1999, more than 20 per cent came from the 1970s. But this creativity was enhanced and underpinned by a host of structural developments which contributed to its strength, and to the strength of the business. At Boase Massimi Pollitt and J. Walter Thompson, more or less simultaneously, a new system of campaign development—misleadingly called 'account planning'—was invented and came to fruition. This system integrated market research into the creative process in a fertile way, and is now used by leading agencies throughout the globe. From the first months of 1970 media-buying specialists became increasingly powerful, and captured an increasing share of the media-buying market. Specialist media-buyers were not new—they had existed in both Britain and the USA a century earlier—but in London they soon became more adept and more sophisticated than ever before. During 1974–5 Britain developed the best form of advertising self-regulation yet seen, which remains basically unchanged more than thirty years later, and is widely admired abroad. In 1975 an optimistic group of advertising folk founded the History of Advertising Trust (HAT), to preserve Britain's advertising heritage for study and reference. HAT is now the largest advertising archive in the world. At the end of the decade, the IPA launched the first authoritative Advertising Effectiveness Awards— for campaigns that could establish their sales achievements, beyond the shadow of a doubt. These too have been emulated in other countries, and by other industries. And commercially towering over all this, Saatchi & Saatchi came from nowhere in 1970 to become the biggest agency in Britain within ten years and, without stumbling, two years later acquired control of one of the largest international American agencies—a previously unimaginable feat for a British shop—to emerge as one of the world's dominant advertising powers.

For British advertising agencies it was a heady, thrusting decade— though not an especially profitable one, because for British society, British politics, and the British economy, things went from bad to worse. In April 1970 The Beatles' acrimonious break-up semaphored both the end of the swinging sixties and the start of a fractious and fissiparous ten years— dubbed somewhat melodramatically by American commentator Joseph Alsop as 'The very worst decade since the history of life began on earth'. The intensifying Vietnam war provoked public protests in Britain and around the world, until the Americans accepted a face-saving peace treaty in 1973; the same year, after the Egyptians attempted a lightning strike on Israel, the Israelis won the Yom Kippur war, and Arab oil-producers retaliated by cutting oil production and hiking the oil price by 70 per cent. The resulting runaway inflation led to bitter strife between trades unions and Ted Heath's Tory government, which in turn led the country into darkened 3-day working weeks in the winter of 1973, followed by two successive General Elections in 1974—the first won by nobody, the second providing Labour with a hardly workable, wafer-thin majority. In 1974 the Retail Price Index leapt by 16.9 per cent, and in 1975 by a scary 23.7 per cent, the highest rate of inflation in Britain since the Napoleonic wars sent prices rocketing by 36 per cent in 1800. Britain's economy sank deeper into debt. Local councils failed to pay employees and streets were defiled with rubbish.

It wasn't all gloom and despondency. In 1972 Tory leader Ted Heath finally led Britain into the EEC, our entry ratified by an overwhelming

67 per cent to 33 per cent majority in a 1975 referendum held by the Labour government; North Sea oil began to flow; the first ever test-tube baby was born in Manchester; and our prestigious white elephant Concorde started transatlantic flights. In 1976 Britain's first and only Minister for Drought was appointed and delivered unto us rainstorms in no time. The next year we celebrated the Queen's Jubilee with a week of festivities.

Against this mostly catastrophic background, advertising initially held up surprisingly well, largely because business optimism was buoyed by our Common Market entry and by North Sea oil, while raging inflation kept consumer expenditure increasing and profits rocketing, at least in monetary terms. Consumer expenditure and company profits are the key determinants of advertising buoyancy.

But by 1975 the economic havoc brought advertising expenditure as a proportion of GDP down to its lowest ebb for thirty years. That year advertising accounted for just 0.91 per cent of the GNP—a level not plumbed since 1955, before commercial television. The recovery began in 1976 (Table 5) and continued gingerly, year by year without a break, until the 1989–91 recession.

The long upward trend from 1976 was bolstered by the landslide victory of Margaret Thatcher on 3 May 1979, when—looking back on the 'winter of discontent' just passed—she proclaimed from the steps of 10 Downing Street, 'Where there is discord may we bring harmony... where there is despair may we bring hope.'

She did not add, 'and where there is a Tory victory, may we give thanks to the advertising folk who got us elected'—but perhaps that was because they didn't.

Table 5. Total advertising expenditure as % of GNP

	Expenditure (at current prices) £million	% GNP (at market prices)
1970	554	1.06
1972	714	1.09
1974	907	1.06
1976	1,205	0.95
1978	1,869	1.10
1980	2,604	1.12

Source: Advertising Association.

Let's Play Knock-the-Adman

In 1970 the hard-hitting new trade magazine invited twenty-one influential opinion leaders to publish essays titled 'What I Think About Advertising'. The list included Labour politician Christopher Mayhew, economists Sir Roy Harrod and Joan Robinson, moral crusader Mary Whitehouse, television dramatist Ted Willis, academics John Cohen and Raymond Williams, the Bishop of Peterborough, and a newsroom full of top journalists including Richard Clements, Richard Ingrams, Brian Inglis, Peter Jenkins, Jill Tweedie, and Peregrine Worsthorne. Several were well-known enemies of advertising—particularly Mayhew, Clements, and Williams. The series provoked furious reactions in the Soho bars and pubs, as well as in the boardrooms and St James's clubs: but it was a first-class journalistic idea (and would never have occurred to *Campaign*'s predecessors).

Naturally the twenty-one were not representative of the population, but they represented a fair slice of British intellectual opinion at the time. And it turned out few of them much liked advertising. Twelve were extremely hostile, four were mildly hostile, four saw a few pros buried among lots of cons—but only Peregrine Worsthorne could be said to be enthusiastic about the contributions advertising makes to the economy and to society.

The antipathies ranged from fundamental disapproval of advertising as a phenomenon to individual dislikes of certain of its characteristics. Christopher Mayhew, like Nye Bevan almost two decades earlier, argued that advertising had a wholly corrupting effect on society. Mary Whitehouse said it degraded women. Tribune editor Richard Clements, like Harold Wilson, believed it to be economically wasteful. Many of the twenty-one complained that advertising encourages materialism. As Christopher Mayhew claimed:

> 'Advertising introduces you to the good things of life.' Such was the slogan plugged by the Advertising Association a few years ago. That is to say, the good things of life, according to the Advertising Association, are the things we see advertised, the things we can buy—not honesty, friendship, kindness or good manners; not loyalty, respect for law or sense of duty; but cars, perfumes, chocolates, deodorants, aperients and aperitifs.

The other widespread criticism was that, as Professor John Cohen put it, echoing the consumerist position, advertisements only tell 'half the truth'. Almost all the contributors said they wanted advertisements to give more information, to be more factual, to be more honest.

When the series finished *Campaign* invited J. Walter Thompson chairman Dr John Treasure, and me, to reply. In briefest summary, Treasure responded to Mayhew's argument, while I responded to Professor Cohen's. Treasure pointed out nobody had ever claimed advertising promotes *all* the good things of life—there are numerous areas of life in which advertising is not involved—but for most people the good things in their lives include food, holidays, clothes, comfort, and material possessions—and being able to choose between them. I argued that advertisements could not include all the facts about any product—the very idea is preposterous—and so they provide those positive facts in which advertisers believe consumers will be interested, and consumers are well aware advertisements are biased in favour of the advertiser.

Above all, their essays revealed how the opinions of the critics differed from those of the population at large. Just about every piece of market research on the subject has shown—then as now—that around 80 per cent of the British public believe advertising to be a good thing. A survey at that time, Europe Töday, showed 79 per cent of Britons believed advertising to be informative, while 70 per cent believed it to be essential. During the last half-century the AA has regularly carried out dipstick surveys to gauge the public's attitudes to advertising. The results have been remarkably consistent, and favourable.

It is not uncommon for intellectuals to disagree with the general public, but the intellectuals are usually aware of the conflict. The *Campaign* articles made clear the critics felt their views to be so obviously correct that everyone must surely agree with them. Not so.

Birth Pangs of Planning

In May 1968 one of the most influential British agencies of the twentieth century hung out its shingle: Boase Massimi Pollitt. BMP was a breakaway from a rather sleepy London agency called Pritchard Wood and Partners, owned by the Interpublic Group. Interpublic was the first great international marketing communications holding company and was the brainchild of an American wunderkind called Marion Harper.

Marvel Marion, as he came to be known, was a Yale graduate and was arguably the most innovative advertising empire-builder in history—much of what Saatchi& Saatchi and WPP did later, Marvel did first. Aged 32, Harper became President of one of America's largest agencies, McCann Erikson, in 1948. In 1960 he used McCann as the core from which he spun Interpublic. During the early 1960s Marvel raced round the world gobbling up agencies (including Pritchard Wood and Partners), and other marketing service companies, at faster than one per month. Interpublic swiftly became the world's largest advertising holding company, employing 8,300 people at its peak. But unfortunately Marvel did not suffer from puritan self-restraint. Interpublic bought a fleet of five airplanes, known as the Harper Air Force, and a dude ranch on Long Island for the entertainment of clients. Marvel's personal DC7 boasted a double bed, private library, and sunken bath. Interpublic's overheads rocketed, and its finances snarled up like a Manhattan traffic jam. The company violated its agreements with two New York banks. In November 1967 Chase Manhattan offered Interpublic a lifesaving $10.2 million loan, providing Harper went. The board unanimously voted him out.

Knowing Interpublic to be strapped for cash, Martin Boase and his colleagues in London tried to buy Pritchard Wood. Interpublic refused. Together with partners Gabe Massimi, an American creative director, and Stanley Pollitt, an exceptionally gifted advertising strategist, Boase then yanked the ten most talented staff out of Pritchard Wood, together with Cadbury billings of £350,000—though he probably expected to walk away with a lot more. Boase was as proficient at publicity as Kingsley Manton & Palmer had been—indeed he admits to having learned his skills from them—and the *Sunday Times* hailed BMP as 'the biggest breakaway the advertising business on either side of the Atlantic has ever seen'. This was claptrap, but BMP kept hitting the headlines. To celebrate winning the Cadbury business Boase hired a fleet of chocolate brown Mini Coopers which cruised around central London emblazoned with the letters BMP. The agency appointed as its first chairman the notorious former Tory cabinet minister Ernest Marples because, as Boase later admitted: 'We wanted his notoriety more than his business advice, and the appointment gave us the headlines, even on the electronic ticker tape in Piccadilly Circus.'

Martin Boase, an Oxford graduate who wanted to be an actor and only entered advertising when that ambition failed him, was the most elegant and urbane advertising man of his era. He appears imperturbable: relaxed, unexcitable, seemingly haughty, dry, and practical. His partner Stanley Pollitt, a couple of years older, was his polar opposite. Even their appearances were contradictory—Boase lean and wiry, Pollitt squat and stout. For those who think that to succeed in advertising it is vital to be a snappy dresser, swathed in Armani and/or Dolce & Gabbana, Pollitt was living proof of the opposite. He must have been the scruffiest advertising man of his era—with dishevelled hair, Eric Morecambe specs, cigarette ash down his chest, and scraps of his shirt hanging outside his trousers long before it became chic. Improbably, he had wanted to be a barrister, though he was a god-awful, inarticulate presenter who often turned his back on his audience while speaking. But he was a sharp analyst, with a forensic intellect. A compulsive smoker and drinker, Stanley would be in the pub with the agency tipplers every evening while Martin was wining and dining clients at London's smartest eateries. Like Hobson and Metcalf they were never close friends—indeed they hardly got on at all. In the early days of BMP the senior staff feared their personal antipathy might destroy the infant agency. This never came near to happening.

Before the breakaway, Gabe Massimi had been imported into Pritchard Wood because the agency was in dire need of creative revitalization. To revitalize the creativity of a large, torpid agency is tough, bordering on the impossible—though many people (including me) have had a go. Problems permeate the agency like blurred letters in an old stick of rock. The creative staff are unlikely to be top flight and will have to be changed; the clients will not have appointed the agency because of its creative output and are unlikely to welcome 'difficult' new work; the agency's executives will not be used to fighting for creative work which clients feel unsure about—they are far more likely to tug their forelocks and offer to do the work again pronto. The entire ethos of the organization will be built on pragmatism rather than principle. Martin Boase—Pritchard Wood's Managing Director—was unable to find a creative director in London able and willing to take on the Herculean revitalizing task. So he flew to America and brought back Gabe Massimi. And Massimi made a fairly good fist of it, so he became a partner in the new agency.

From the start BMP espoused a new system of campaign development called 'account planning'. Today most advertising people believe Stanley Pollitt and BMP invented account planning. Consequently, in its 1993 Silver Jubilee list of the 50 most important people in British advertising, *Campaign* placed Pollitt in third spot, only just behind Colin Millward and Charles Saatchi. Pollitt's contribution was unarguably seminal. But account planning started almost simultaneously at BMP and JWT—albeit in slightly different forms. Stanley Pollitt had launched his account planning system at Prichard Wood, before BMP started, though he hijacked the name from JWT, who thought of it first. In any event it is a lousy name as it does not describe the system—but nobody has ever thought of a better one, so it has stuck.

It is also a lousy name because advertising campaigns have always been 'planned'. During the 1930s and after the war leading agencies had what they called 'marketing departments', which analysed market trends, market research, competitive activity, and other key market data before preparing campaign plans for the creative and media departments to execute.

This was provided as a 'free' service to their clients. Few advertisers had marketing departments of their own, so the advertisers accepted the agencies' analytical reports with gratitude. As advertisers built up their own specialist marketing departments in the 1960s, they stopped relying on their agencies for this input.

More importantly, as the new breed of client marketing specialists extended their territorial powers, they began to draw up inflexible rules, disciplines, and evaluation systems for their advertising. These were usually based on simplistic research tools, the best known being 'Day After Recall' (DAR), used by Procter & Gamble, the world's largest advertiser. (Unilever's rulebook, which does not rely on DAR but is equally mechanistic, is called UPGA—'Unilever Plan for Great Advertising'.) DAR involves interviewing a sample of viewers the day after a new commercial is first transmitted, and quantifying the percentage who remember it. With the accumulation of data over time, it becomes possible to benchmark each new commercial against its predecessors. If its recall is worse than average, the new commercial will be taken off air and either tweaked or ditched. DAR is the basis of 'tracking studies', today's standard means of monitoring campaigns (Ch. 7, 'On the Track'). But it cannot be carried out until after a commercial has been made and transmitted.

Account planning is carried out while campaigns are being developed. At JWT account planning focuses on the brand itself; at BMP it focuses on the advertisements. But in practice the account planning process is similar at both agencies. An account planner—an analytical researcher—is assigned to every client. The account planner is not a backroom boffin, as researchers in agencies had previously been, but represents the agency to the client up-front, jointly with the account executive. Together the planner and the executive develop and define the objectives of any new campaign: what are its aims and targets, how will it achieve them? The account planner's part in this is to analyse all the available data: sales trends, past research, competitive activity, marketing reports, and the like. This is similar to the work the earlier agency marketing departments had carried out. The difference is that once the objectives of the campaign have been set, and been agreed with the client, the creative team will get to work, and the account planner will personally carry out focus groups on their creative ideas, as they take shape. (At JWT this was felt to lack objectivity—it does—and the pilot research is generally carried out by independent specialists.) These research probes are at the heart of the system, as they provide feedback to the creators while the campaign is in gestation. Account planning is a continuous circular system: define the campaign objectives, create rough advertisements, research them, create revised advertisements, re-research them, re-revise the creative work... until the advertisement meets the originally defined objectives.

Account planning neatly bridges the schism between the two Johnnies, Hobson and Pearce. Hobson tested numerous creative ideas against each other, selected the one which came out best and pressed ahead with it, not worrying too much about how it was executed. This means the public, effectively, chooses the advertising idea. Pearce selected the best creative idea on judgement and then executed it superbly without bothering to test it. This means the agency selects the advertising idea, which allows for greater innovation and daring. Under account planning the best creative idea is still initially selected on judgement—which allows for the innovation and daring—but it is then checked out in research and either ditched or refined, again and again, with the cooperation of the creators, until the public's responses show it to be right. Naturally all this takes time and costs the agency a good deal of money.

JWT's first head of account planning was Stephen King, who later wrote in his fine paper 'The Anatomy of Account Planning' (1989):

> The rush by other agencies to follow our lead was muted. For several years nothing at all seemed to happen. By 1979 only six other agencies in the top 20 had planning departments.

No doubt this was partly due to its cost, and partly due to the embedded hostility of many creative directors to research, explored below. But there was another objection to account planning, which I embraced for many years, I now think wrongly. I believed it suited the contrasting personalities of Messrs Boase and Pollitt,[1] but in general it degraded the role of account executives, turning them into old-fashioned glad-handers. Account planners, I argued, were superfluous. Account executives should themselves be able to analyse, and plan, and carry out focus groups, as well as to buy clients lunch. Well yes, but some people are better at the one, others at the other. And as the sheer volume of marketing and research data exploded in the 1970s, dealing with it all began to demand full-time specialists. So Adam Smith's specialization of labour triumphed. Eventually account planning spread, first in Britain and then around the world. In October 1978 British account planners launched their own professional body, the Account Planners Group (APG), which had 490 members within 5 years.

---

[1] See Charles Channon on agency philosophies, page 68.

A characteristically stylish, sophisticated—and irretrievably dated—Ashley Havinden early 1950s advertisement for Daks slacks.

The first commercial ever transmitted on British television, for Gibbs SR on September 22 1955. 'I look on it now as an illustrated lecture'—copywriter Brian Palmer.

Those involved were frankly astonished at how well sales responded to the anthropoids' salesmanship. Reproduced with kind permission of unilever. Brooke Bond and PG Tips are registered trademarks.

The Milk slogan came from the client and was initially resisted by the agency's creative department—as clients' creative ideas almost always are.

Around the 1960s there were numerous generic campaigns, like those for eggs and milk. Today generic campaigns are uncommon, as they seldom, if ever, succeed.

YOU'RE NEVER ALONE WITH A

STRAND

The moment you handle the packet you know. This is a different cigarette. Flip top pack. Sleek. Smart. Modern. No loose bits in the pocket. New Strand.

The moment you touch the cigarette you know. This is a different cigarette. Rounder. Firmer. Perfectly made – perfectly packed. New Strand.

The moment you draw you know. Taste all there. So smooth. So cool. Rich Virginia tobacco and millefil tipped. New Strand.

The moment you offer them you know. They're wanted. They're expected. They're absolutely *right*. New Strand.

The cigarette of the moment

MILLEFIL TIPPED

3½ for twenty
(1/7 for ten)

MADE BY W. D. & H. O. WILLS   STR 10C

'It sank without trace. The most memorable campaign since the War and it failed in only one thing. It just didn't sell the product. Otherwise it was perfect'—copywriter John May.

The manufacturers, and the ITA, were neither unaware of, nor blasé about, the public's antipathy to detergent commercials. But they worked.

Oxo's Katie & Philip campaign demonstrated the astonishing durability of strong advertising ideas.

Rather than appoint an agency, for many years Labour preferred to work with committed, unpaid volunteers.

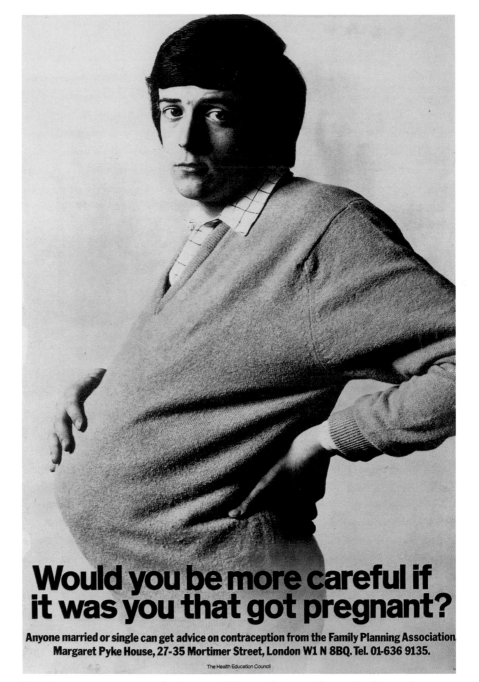

Would you be more careful if it was you that got pregnant?

Anyone married or single can get advice on contraception from the Family Planning Association. Margaret Pyke House, 27-35 Mortimer Street, London W1 N 8BQ. Tel. 01-636 9135.

The Health Education Council

The Pregnant Man won Charles Saatchi's creative consultancy kudos and publicity well before Saatchi & Saatchi was launched.

The great benefit of account planning, both to agency and to client, is that it eliminates dud ideas early on, and it identifies avoidable gaffes and clangers buried within good ideas, so they can be changed before the creative work is presented to the client. Better still, if the agency is presenting an extraordinary or groundbreaking new idea, which a client might find difficult to swallow, both sides will know a modicum of market research has already established the idea has some substance. From the agency's point of view account planning is the greatest sales aid ever invented. It is also, from the agency's point of view, a great benefit to have the research carried out by people involved with, and sympathetic to, the creative ideas—though exactly how involved and how sympathetic has been one of the bones of contention between BMP and JWT, and remains so among different agencies still.

Naturally the entire process will only work if the creators accept the feedback from the planners' research. This is a minefield. There are over 400 articles in the WARC databank concerned with creativity and research, and just about all that deal with creative people's attitudes to research show them to be antagonistic. A small UK study by researcher Sue Burden in 2003 revealed that the kindest responses to research she found among creative people were neutral ('Research is...something you tolerate'), while others were downright negative ('Research is a no-win for us, we can only lose'). A more recent study ('How Do Advertising Creative Directors Perceive Research?', Mark Chong, 2006—admittedly written from outside the UK) reported:

> Past research indicates that creative practitioners have systematically ignored research for a number of reasons...they assert that the creative nature of developing advertisements is fundamentally at odds with the methodical, 'scientific' nature of research, and doubt that the two can be fully reconciled.

Chong goes on to quote an international agency creative director who states bluntly: 'Respect in the creative community for research is zero.' Account planning does not eradicate these problems. But by forcing the researcher/ planner to work closely with the creative team, it ameliorates them.

No campaign development system is perfect, and account planning is no exception. Based on focus groups, it provides only broad-brush data— 'soft' data as it is often called; it works far better for television commercials and for visually striking executions than for long copy advertisements; it is far warmer towards likeable and humorous advertisements than towards more pushy advertisements (and this goes some way towards explaining the particular flavour of British advertising in the late 1970s and thereafter); it does not measure memorability; and it fails to integrate advertisements within the entire spectrum of marketing communications. Despite these caveats, account planning is the least worst means of campaign development yet devised.

* * *

For various reasons, some personal, Gabe Massimi's stay at BMP was not a happy one. In September 1971 he returned to America. However he endowed the agency with a wonderful legacy. When he left BMP, John Webster, an art director he had employed at Pritchard Wood, took over as creative director. Like Colin Millward, Webster had wanted to be a painter. A reticent man, he dressed unexceptionally and did not push himself forward. He disliked meetings—particularly client meetings, though he mellowed over the years—and was a creative director who led by example rather than by the detailed management of others. An enthusiastic but rather hopeless cricketer and golfer, he was the antithesis of the tantrum-and-temper creative man. But he turned out to be one of Britain's outstanding creative directors. More importantly, he was able to rub along almost effortlessly with Pollitt's innovative account planning system. It is largely because of the international fame garnered by Webster's prolific creative output, all based on account planning, that the world eventually followed BMP's leadership rather than JWT's. It was BMP's creative success which popularized Pollitt's system.

As Martin Boase said at John Webster's memorial service in April 2006:

> People often wondered at John's resilience in coping with the rejection or modification of his advertising ideas which was implicit in the use of focus group testing as part of the whole account planning project. But this was to fail to understand where John stood in relation to his work. He was far more interested in real people's response to his ideas than the reaction of those in the hothouse world of advertising.

I am not sure this is quite right. Webster wanted both 'real people' and the 'hothouse world of advertising' to love his work in equal measure. His campaigns were popular and populist, never pretentious, never clever-clever—but his office was strewn with all the trophies he had won, for every visitor to see.

None of this means, nor did Boase say, that Webster enjoyed being told his work had been rejected or needed modification. But his imagination was extraordinarily fertile. I wrote in his *Guardian* obituary:

John could not have worked the account planning system so effectively had he not been immensely fecund . . . Only somebody as imaginative as he could repeatedly come up with fresh ideas, until they found exactly the right one for the job. And only somebody that talented has the modesty and confidence to accept the research's criticisms of their work in progress . . . And because he believed they would be more effective, he wanted to create advertisements which people liked and would welcome into their homes.

(Much the same could be said about Jeremy Bullmore, who was the creative director implementing the account planning system at JWT.)

BMP's creativity, together with its account planning, helped the agency grow rapidly in the 1970s, though its growth was not nearly as rapid as Hobson's and CDP's had been a decade earlier, nor nearly so rapid as its own PR suggested. Nonetheless it floated successfully on the London stock market in 1983, when its prospectus stated:

The main new element introduced into its structure by BMP was called the account planner. The planner brings not simply research, but also the use of data, into every stage of advertising development as a third partner for the account handler and the creative team.

That was a heartfelt salute to Stanley Pollitt. But by then Pollitt had died, in May 1979, aged 49, celebrating Margaret Thatcher's electoral success with more good cheer than his ample bulk could cope with.

In his first years at BMP, John Webster worked with a succession of top-class copywriters. Later he worked alone, which suited him fine. He both had the ideas and wrote the copy—usually minimal, as his triumphs were almost all on television rather than in print. He then took immense pains over the filming, often altering the script at the shoot, to the chagrin of agency managers and clients alike.

Webster was creative director of BMP for 35 years. Over those years his creations included:

- Cresta Bear ('It's frothy man')
- Colt 45 ('Never bolt a Colt')
- Coty L'Aimant ('Do you speak L'Aimant?')
- Courage Tavern ('It's what your right arm's for')
- Courage Best ('Gertcha')
- Guardian ('Points of view')
- Hofmeister Lager ('Follow the Bear')
- John Smith's ('Arkwright')
- Kia Ora ('We all adore a Kia Ora')

- St Ivel ('Prize Guys')
- Smash Martians ('For mash get Smash')
- Sony ('John Cleese Robot')
- Sugar Puffs ('Tell 'em about the honey, Mummy')
- TicTac Mints ('The two flavoured mint')
- Unigate Humphreys ('Watch out ...')
- Walker's Crisps ('No More Mr Nice Guy')

These were in equal measure loved by the British public and festooned with statuettes at creative festivals throughout the world. John Webster's work alone might well have been sufficient to enhance Britain's burgeoning global creative reputation in the 1970s. But there was much more.

Maggots in Bucketshops

On New Year's Day 1970 a chirpy 27-year-old media-buyer called Paul Green had a seemingly trivial idea he thought might net him a few quid. His idea unwittingly spawned the fissure which finally killed off full-service agencies, and split the creation of advertisements from the buying of media space and time. Many identify it as the most important structural development in the British advertising industry during the last century— and it was another direct consequence of commercial television.

But when Paul Green, previously a media group head at the Garland-Compton agency, opened Media Buying Services (MBS), his company and the others that followed were sneeringly called 'bucketshops'. In subsequent years the derided bucketshops snatched all the media-buying away from the traditional agencies, and in doing so massively enhanced the status and skills of the media-buyers.

As a result of the fissure, what will hereafter be called 'creative agencies' (as they are now generally called) emerged. Creative agencies focus exclusively on the planning, origination, and execution of advertisements. 'Media agencies', as the bucketshops came to be called, focus exclusively on the planning and buying of advertising space and time, in all media.

Independent media-buyers—bucketshops—were far from a new phenomenon. As early as 1819 a David Robertson, calling himself an 'Advertising Agent', announced in the *Edinburgh Evening Courant* that he sold space on commission 'without extra expense to the advertisers'. By the end of the nineteenth century many 'advertising agents' did nothing but sell space, often on commissions as low as 1 per cent. Before 1914 the R. F. White agency handled all government space buying, for $2\frac{1}{2}$ per cent commission. Meanwhile weak publications would 'bribe' agents by paying commissions of up to 30 per cent if they brought in business. In Philadelphia in 1842 Volney B. Palmer opened what most Americans insist, wrongly, was the first advertising agency—improbably named 'Real Estate and Coal Office'. Palmer too acted simply as a space seller on commission. Other American agencies soon sprang up which did the same, and have continued to trade in small towns across the country ever since. In France, led by Gilbert Gross, the founder of Carat, media-buying as a separate operation had been growing in importance since the early 1960s. But in Britain the agency commission system had clamped media-buying and advertisement creation together like a vice.

Naturally media paid commissions to agencies because they believed it to be in their own interests—for several very sound reasons. The commission system motivated agencies to sell more advertising space to their clients. The media liked that. Agencies guaranteed their clients' payments, and coughed up even when their clients defaulted. The media liked that, too. As one American magazine publisher said in praise of J. Walter Thompson himself:

> I guess J. Walter has made mistakes in extending credits along with the rest of them. But when that happened, he never came round to see us. We got our pay in real money, even when he didn't get his.

The agencies did all the financial dogsbodying for the media, and as there were tens of thousands of advertisers, but only five hundred or so recognized agencies in Britain, including the tiny ones, the media only had to deal with five hundred or so customers each month, rather than with tens of thousands. And the media liked that.

After 1941, the recognition system also required the agencies to create the advertisements, and commission payments encouraged them to produce effective campaigns. The more effective their advertisements, the more advertisers advertised. The media certainly liked that. And most media want advertisements to enhance the appearance of their publications, and later, their broadcasts. By recognizing only professionally competent agencies, the media knew they would be supplied with proficiently prepared advertisements, on time and to the right specifications. They liked that, too.

The agencies liked it all every bit as much, because the closed-shop recognition cartel provided them with handsome profits. Though it was not surreptitious, the entire system was, in a way, a genteel conspiracy to rip off advertisers.

But what pleased the media most perhaps was that the recognition system gave them—both in reality, and to an even greater extent perceptually—greater leverage, greater power in the advertising process. Yes, agencies were appointed by, and paid by, advertisers. But they could not trade if the media refused to recognize them. The agencies, patrolling the border between advertisers and media, were in thrall to both—instead of being solely in thrall to the advertisers. It was a nimble manoeuvre by the media, and for decades advertisers put up with it.

All in all then, the media got excellent value for the commissions they paid agencies. And Paul Green initially had no intention at all of fighting the recognition/commission system. Green's idea was simply to pitch MBS at large agencies as an extra resource, a kind of safety valve—rather like a creative consultancy, which took on overflow creative work when an agency was stumped, or had so much work it couldn't cope. Green foresaw similar situations occurring in television buying, his personal area of expertise. His plan was for large agencies to subcontract overflow television buying to MBS, and to pay MBS a small percentage of the commissions they received from the television companies. This would not break the large agencies' recognition contracts, as it would not involve them rebating commission to advertisers. The media would be unable to object. They had long accepted that recognized agencies could buy in services—like creative services—from outside. So why should they not buy in media services? The recognized agencies would still be the media's financial guarantor. 'We'll solely be working on behalf of recognised agencies,' Green wisely announced at the MBS launch. His plan sounded wholly logical. But it flopped. As he later wrote:

> Everybody we saw listened attentively and politely but more than once I had the distinct impression they were thinking 'this guy's crazy'.

Instead something completely different happened. New small agencies and creative consultancies, which had little or no media expertise of their own, started to use MBS for television buying. If they were recognized, these agencies could, and did, buy print space. But by 1970 television buying had become infinitely more complex than print buying. Big advertisers and big agencies got the plum spots. The newer, and smaller, shops could not compete, and so could not offer their clients good television value. This put them at a serious competitive disadvantage. (The television companies have always fervently denied they offer better spots to bigger clients—but not everybody has ever been convinced by their fervour.)

MBS began to buy television time for the smaller agencies. Green bought cannily, negotiated hard, and remained flexible till the last minute in order to pick up cheap unsold time—hence the bucketshop moniker. The television companies were unfazed. They had never been as convinced of the virtues of the recognition system as the print publishers, and they were eager to expand their client base by bringing in new, small advertisers—even if they did not always offer them the very best deals. (Particularly if they did not offer them the very best deals: broadcasters always need to off-load their low-rating commercial breaks, a phenomenon to which there is no exact equivalent in print media.) So the incoming MBS advertisers from the smaller agencies were warmly welcomed.

By autumn 1972 Green was going strong. But he was still frozen out by the print media. He decided his only way forward was to seek formal agency recognition for MBS, even though he provided no creative services. The television broadcasters, with everything to gain and with the new, anti-monopolistic Independent Broadcasting Authority breathing down their necks, granted recognition to MBS in 1973. The print media then saw themselves losing smaller advertisers to television. Reluctantly, they offered MBS recognition a year later. Green had driven a coach and horses through the agency recognition system. The way was now open for specialist media agencies to gallop through.

There was no shortage of contenders. Senior media men—and later women—were champing at the bit to leave the traditional agencies, where they were treated as second-class citizens. In traditional agencies the account executives and the creative practitioners were top dogs. Media-buying was seen as arithmetical drudgery and tough-arsed negotiation which could be carried out—should be carried out—by street-fighters. Graduates seldom worked in media-buying departments. Paul Green says: 'We were called media maggots—the media department started where the carpet stopped.' At new client presentations, the media recommendations would be left till last, and scurried through when the creative presenters overran their time. Sometimes this meant the media presentations were completely omitted. Media maven Simon Marquis—most unusually, then, a Cambridge graduate—had worked all night to prepare his presentation to a prospective client, but was unable to present it as the creative people had droned on endlessly before him, and the client then rushed away. Happily, despite this galling setback, Marquis went on to become chairman of Zenith Media.

Leaving such rudeness and condescension behind was deeply attractive to top media guys. It was also deeply attractive because they knew agency media departments were highly profitable, and so specialist media agencies would be highly profitable. Television expenditures were by then sufficiently large to offer bulk-buying opportunities which generated sizeable profits on narrow margins—so the media specialists could compete with their former employers by offering advertisers highly attractive low-cost buying deals.

By 1976 there were 12 independent media agencies in London, handling 4 per cent of all UK advertising expenditure. Much more crucially, that year saw the extension of the Restrictive Trades Practices Act to cover service industries. Now the historic pan-industry agency recognition agreements would have to be registered with—and approved by—the Office of Fair Trading. The traditional agencies accepted the game was up. The recognition system was obsolete. All contractual references to commissions, rebating, and other similar recognition qualifications would have to be dropped. The print media did not fight. From January 1979 contracts between agencies and media had to be negotiated on an individual rather than pan-industry basis. For the specialist media independents, the flood gates were now wide open. In 1982 they formed their own trade body, the Association of Media Independents. To join the AMI a member had to be:

- a corporation in the business of media-buying
- of sound financial and professional standing
- independent of an advertising agency, an advertiser, or a media owner.

The last requirement was the most significant—at least in terms of the industry's structure. By 1980 there were 29 AMI members, handling 13 per cent of all UK advertising. Advertisers of the size and calibre of Bass, Carreras Rothmans, Commercial Union, Dalgety, Gillette, GUS, Hotpoint, Reckitt & Colman, United Biscuits, and Whitbread were employing their services. By now many of London's star media men—including John Ayling, John Billett, Chris Ingram, David Reich, Allan Rich, and Mike Yershon—had quit traditional agencies to set up their own shops.

Axe-grinding arguments about the pros and cons of splitting media-buying from advertisement creation sent hot sparks flying among advertisers, agency people, in the trade press, and in national business papers. The battle was real, tempers flared. John Ayling recalls being personally vilified and abused by full-service agency people. But I do not think anyone realized quite how fundamental the outcome of the battle would be.

The Bogle Inheritance

Masochistic to a fault, in 1974 the advertising industry invited Shirley Williams to be key speaker at its AA conference in Brighton. Prime Minister Harold Wilson had just put Williams in charge of his new Ministry of

Prices and Consumer Protection, and Wilson viewed advertising as an outright enemy of consumer protection. Scuttlebutt has it that until just before the conference Williams had no idea what she was going to say. In desperation she called her civil servants together for a powwow. They suggested she should give the advertising industry a tongue lashing, and threaten it with legislative controls if it didn't stop being so dishonest. This would win her popularity with both the Prime Minister and her party, and she could then get back to the truly troubling part of her ministerial portfolio—prices, which were flying into orbit, fuelled by oil-price inflation. The scuttlebutt has an appealing 'Yes, Minister' ring of truth about it, and the speech Williams gave was indeed mostly devoted to an attack on advertising—but for fuelling inflation, not for being dishonest. She ended, 'Democracy itself can be threatened by a fear about the stability of the currency'—but proffered no suggestions as to what the advertising industry should or could do about this. She hardly mentioned dishonest—or even simply misleading—advertisements at all. Within the advertising industry Shirley Williams's speech is nowadays believed to have been the progenitor of advertising self-regulation. It was not.

The following day the fusillade began. John Methven, Director-General of the new Office of Fair Trading, fleshed out Williams's words, admitting he had 'rewritten [his speech] between 6.00 and 9.00 this morning', which provides circumstantial evidence in support of the scuttlebutt. Possibly Williams and Methven had agreed to play soft cop–hard cop, because the Director-General's speech was far tougher than hers. Methven, a lawyer who had worked for ICI for 17 years, politely phrased his criticisms as questions, but pulled no punches.

Methven began by saying voluntary regulation—he peremptorily rejected the expression 'self-regulation'—would only work if people knew about it, and he claimed neither the public nor businesses knew about the Advertising Standards Authority. He gave examples of misleading pricing, which his OFT was about to outlaw because the advertising industry had dragged its feet and failed to do so. He accepted that not all print advertisements could be pre-vetted, but he felt many more should be. He reminded the audience many aspects of advertising were already controlled by statute in Britain, but added that in other countries statutory controls went much further. Perhaps they should go much further here? He argued the Code of Advertising Practice Committee, which draws up the codes, should contain lay members. Above all he called for an increase in the ASA's funding, as it was clear the ASA could not do an effective job with its tiny annual budget of £50,000 and its tiny staff of nine. It was an impressive broadside.

Campaign headlined its three-page report on the AA conference 'Bad News For Admen'. The admen concurred. The agencies already knew there was a lack of confidence in the veracity of advertising, even within the industry itself. In 1972 a private IPA survey of advertisers had revealed that two-thirds of them felt advertisements include 'invalid or misleading claims', while only one-third believed that 'in general, advertisements present a true picture of the product advertised.' So the industry knew it must respond to Methven swiftly. George Bogle, Director of Government and Industry Affairs at Reed Holdings, and an awesomely persuasive Yorkshire Scotsman, shouldered the task of putting together a new self-regulatory system which would defuse Methven's attack.

Bogle persuaded advertisers to stump up a levy of 0.1 per cent on all their non-broadcast expenditure: £1 for every £1,000 spent. (Broadcast advertising was regulated under statute by the IBA—a point deftly made by Methven when he was insisting on the viability of statutory controls.) The new levy would raise about £350,000 annually. It would be collected by a body to be called the Advertising Standards Board of Finance (ASBOF). Payment of the levy would be voluntary, and ASBOF would not know which advertisers were or were not paying up, nor how much they paid—so individual advertisers would be unable to exert financial pressure on the ASA. The ASBOF board would represent all parts of the non-broadcast sector—advertisers, agencies, and all print, outdoor, and cinema media. The commitment of the media was crucial, as they would have to police the system and refuse to carry advertisements the ASA banned. To meet Methven's concern regarding the public's low awareness of the ASA, the media committed themselves to publicize it by providing free advertising.

The advertising industry would have no influence whatsoever over ASA decisions. The decisions of ASA Council—an independent chairman, eight lay members, and four advertising members who were there to advise on advertising technicalities—would be supreme. Apart from providing and monitoring its funds, ASBOF's only involvement with the ASA would be to appoint its independent chairman, and it would be required to consult the relevant government department before doing so. Thereafter ASBOF would not be able to fire the ASA chairman without the agreement of the ASA Council, so the advertising industry could not force a chairman to toe its line.

With impressive speed, Bogle cleared these quite complicated proposals with all concerned. ASBOF came into being on 1 January 1975—just 7 months after the AA Brighton conference—with Bogle as its founder chairman. He remained chairman until 1990. In 1975–6, its first year under ASBOF, the ASA increased its staff from 9 to 27. It spent £157,704 on advertising, which was supplemented by £228,000 of free space, donated as promised by the print media. The effects of this £385,000 campaign were immediate. The number of complaints received by the ASA jumped eight-fold, from 516 in 1974–5 to 4,086 the following year, and public awareness of the ASA climbed from 17 per cent before the campaign—it had not been quite as minimal as Methven claimed—to 28 per cent afterwards.

The entire funding process is built on trust and commitment. For over three decades the level of advertiser compliance could only be estimated. Now more robust computer data show that over 80 per cent of all expenditure liable to the 0.1 per cent levy pays the levy. No attempt is made to collect the 0.1 per cent from tiny advertisers or media, as the income would not be justify the cost of collection. The high compliance level strongly suggests no major advertiser in Britain fails to chip in.

The self-regulatory system offers benefits to both consumers and advertisers. For consumers it is fair, fast—the average complaint turnaround time is now less than 30 days—and free. (It used to be said a complaint costs only the price of a postage stamp—today more than two-thirds of complaints come by email, so bear no cost at all.) The Codes are applied in the spirit as well as the letter, which provides consumers with a level of protection the law could not match.

Advertisers do not fund the system out of altruism. They believe it increases the public's trust in advertising, and therefore increases the effectiveness of their campaigns. It avoids lengthy and expensive court cases, common in other countries. Indeed for advertisers, as for the public, it is fair, fast, and free—apart from the cost of the levy, which now exceeds £250,000 per year for the largest advertisers.

In 1976 Gordon Borrie took over from John Methven as OFT Director-General. The following year the OFT undertook a review of the effectiveness of the ASA, which had by then been operating in its restructured form for some three years. In November 1978 the OFT published a *Review of the UK self-regulatory system of advertising control*. This dealt in detail with the possibility of converting the ASA to a statutory body with statutory powers, and said (paragraph 6.6):

We see serious objections to this approach. First, it would be likely to seriously weaken the industry's commitment to maintain and finance self-regulation. At present the industry spends a considerable amount of money and executives' time on making its system work; the presence of a statutory body would be likely to make all this seem less worthwhile. Second, the combination of a diminution in

> the industry's involvement in the system and the creation of a statutory body could lead to the Code being interpreted in an excessively legalistic fashion. The strength of a self-regulatory system lies in participants' willingness to observe the spirit of rules which they themselves have had a hand in drawing up . . . The general object-ive of transforming the ASA into a statutory authority would be to increase the protection of the public interest. We are inclined to believe that this objective may be better achieved in practice, if not in theory, by a self-regulatory system which is kept on its toes by its vulnerability to criticism, both public and official.

The OFT Review was no whitewash. It criticized the ASA for not dealing with complaints sufficiently quickly; it felt the ASA should itself do more monitoring of advertisements (instead of relying entirely on consumers' complaints); and it recommended there should be statutory powers to deal with persistent or uncooperative offenders. In fact the ASA had already accepted the need to carry out more monitoring, and it accepted that statutory backup powers would be no bad thing (these were then insti-tuted). But the ASA feared that to expedite its decisions might well lead to miscarriages of justice. In 1978 the Secretary of State for Prices and Con-sumer Protection was Roy Hattersley, who had taken over from Shirley Williams. Hattersley, no friend of advertising, accepted the OFT Review's conclusions.

On 1 January 2000, Gordon Borrie, now Lord Borrie QC, became the ASA's eighth chairman.

There is no known example of an advertiser trying to put pressure on the ASA. In a *Guardian* interview on 31 December 1990, when he was retiring as chairman of the ASA and was about to become chairman of the new Press Complaints Commission, Lord McGregor of Durris said:

> Nobody in the advertising industry has ever attempted to influence me about a decision the ASA has taken or might take. There have been rows. People have said 'Look, the decision you're taking is costing us a tremendous amount of money'. That is legitimate. But I have never been subject to any illicit pressure from the industry.

This situation still pertains. However, as McGregor revealed in the same interview, the actions of politicians have been less innocuous. When Nigel Lawson was Chancellor of the Exchequer he objected to a Brymon Airways advertisement which jokingly depicted him 'fleeing the country'. The ASA rejected his complaint, whereupon Lord McGregor was summoned by Law-son's friend Lord Young of Graffham. The government would not continue to support self-regulation, Young threatened, if the ASA did not observe proper standards. McGregor and the ASA stood their ground. No more was heard. It was, said Lord McGregor, his experience at the uncompromising

ASA that got him the job at the PCC, as control of the press was widely felt to need toughening up.

The self-regulatory system devised by George Bogle in 1974–5 has remained in place ever since, though there have naturally been modifications. In January 1992 direct mail was successfully integrated into the system—though many thought it could not be. At the end of the century internet and telephony advertising were also brought into the fold. In April 1999 an Independent Reviewer was appointed, to handle appeals against ASA adjudications. The Reviewer cannot overturn an ASA adjudication, but can call upon the ASA to review any adjudication he thinks should be reconsidered. The ASA Council retains paramount power, and makes the final decision.

One of self-regulation's great strengths is that it can tackle issues of taste and decency more sensitively than the law. Indeed the system is arguably too sensitive. Conventional wisdom has it that advertising oozes with sex, but the reality is that nipples have only once been seen, briefly, in a commercial, for Neutralia shower gel in 1994 (made, predictably, by a naughty French agency in Paris).

Even in print advertising nudes are exceptionally rare in British advertisements, while the sex act is as unknown as condoms in a nunnery. The same is true of crime and violence. Compared with the programmes and editorial which surround them, advertisements portray a peaceful, sanitized world: an unreal world. Moreover the divergence between the wholesome world of advertising and the unpleasant realities of modern society increases with every year that passes.

During the lifetime of the ASA just seventeen advertisers have attempted to overturn its adjudications, in the courts. Only one of those has succeeded, in 1989, and that was on a technicality.

The HAT Fits

At almost exactly the same time as Williams and Methven were berating the advertising industry in Brighton, Brian Smith was taking a diametrically opposite view in London. Smith, an Associate Director of Everetts, a medium-sized, rather unadventurous London agency, sent a paper to both the Advertising Association and the IPA outlining an ambitious scheme which first became an obsession for him, and then a crusade. He was concerned that Britain's advertising history was not being recorded, or preserved, or celebrated, as it deserved to be.

Smith wanted to launch an exhibition of British advertising, and esti-mated he needed £50,000 to mount it, but was unable to raise the where-withal—particularly in the febrile economic circumstances prevailing. Neither the AA nor the IPA felt able to help. Undaunted, in December 1975 Smith set up a committee of about a dozen advertising and marketing people—all fairly senior, but none of them at the top of the tree—and registered a new charity: 'The History of Advertising Trust' (HAT).

Under Brian Smith's chairmanship, the HAT committee explored several other possibilities, as well as his proposed exhibition. The committee launched *The Journal of Advertising History*—an authoritative publication which came out sporadically during 1977–88, but eventually folded for want of a sponsor. They began running historical research projects, indexing all the extant historical material, and holding regular seminars for those 'with a special interest in the history of advertising'. They recruited HAT members, who paid a subscription of £5 a year. Above all, they focused on the production of a book, a history, and retained Professor Terry Nevett to write it. Nevett's book was published jointly by HAT and Heinemann in February 1982, its cost underwritten by Saatchi & Saatchi.

Slowly more prominent figures joined Smith's little band. In 1978 Lord Barnetson, chairman of United Newspapers and Reuters, became HAT's first president. Barnetson was followed by Dr John Treasure, former chair-man of J. Walter Thompson and an industry leader. Ron Miller, sales director of London Weekend Television and an awe-inspiring fundraiser, signed up, as did David Bernstein and Archie Pitcher, two senior agency men. Despite widespread scepticism money began to flow in, but only at the rate of £10,000 a year. Smith kept his exhibition plan simmering for over a decade but it never materialized. Nor did its successor plan for a 'Museum of Advertising'—a 'Museum without Walls'. But an advertising archive began to be built. In 1987 ex-journalist Michael Cudlipp, who had been involved with the Trust since the early 1980s, took over its running. This was a key appointment. With Cudlipp at the helm, in 1989 annual income for the first time exceeded £100,000, and though it dropped sharply during the next two depressed years, the Trust survived. To cut costs, in September 1990 Cudlipp moved the archive to Raveningham, Norfolk, where it has remained ever since, growing in size unstoppably.

In 2001 HAT celebrated its twenty-fifth birthday. By then its archive contained more than 2 million pieces of advertising, dating from the late eighteenth century onwards. It held the archives of a raft of major agencies and advertisers, storing both printed and broadcast material, original artwork, books, research, and operational records. Today HAT is used by students, historians, libraries and countless other non-profit organizations at little or no cost to themselves—and is extensively consulted by agencies, marketers, and journalists, who pay the going rate. HAT now earns approximately 70 per cent of its income from its trading activities. Today it holds 3 million pieces of advertising, and is the largest advertising archive, anywhere.

Without HAT, writing this book would have been a great deal tougher, but when it was first mooted I was one of the sceptics who thought it a barmy idea, and I said so publicly. Happily, I have lived to eat my words. HAT succeeded because a lot of good people believed British advertising was of sufficient quality to be well worth preserving.

University Challenges

The Advertising Association was formed to promote and protect advertising. It has sought to achieve these twin objectives in many ways. Over the years news stories like 'AA to appoint Public Relations Officer to tell public about benefits of advertising—active antagonism springs from lack of understanding' (*Advertisers' Weekly*, 29 November 1951) have been common. Frequently the AA's ambitious plans have been dashed for want of cash—as happened in 1951.

But one long-term stratagem has achieved considerable, if unquantifiable, success. After 1975, the restructuring of the ASA did not silence advertising's antagonists—but it strengthened advertising's hand in rebutting their attacks. By the late 1970s, with the ASA soundly established following the OFT review, the AA decided the best way forward was to meet the critics in person, in private, and to debate the issues which concerned them off-the-record, face-to-face. Subsequently the AA began to hold annual seminars at Peterhouse, Cambridge, at which controversial issues could be discussed in camera. Some 40–50 delegates would be invited. They would be drawn from leaders of the advertising industry; from leading figures outside advertising—usually hostile—who have a particular interest in the subject under discussion; plus relevant politicians, civil servants, and lobbyists, from both the UK and Europe.

The sessions are held under Chatham House confidentiality rules, allowing unrestricted, and often heated, discussion. The role of the chair is paramount. Seminar chairmen usually come from outside advertising, and have included Claus Moser, Peter Preston, Anthony Sampson, Mary Warnock, Katherine Whitehorn, Charles Wintour—and Shirley Williams.

The meetings became known as 'Peterhouse Seminars', though a few of them were held at other venues. The subjects discussed were naturally felt to be particularly salient, and particularly contentious, at the time:

1979   The Social and Moral Questions about Advertising
1980   Advertising to Children
1981   Advertising and Alcohol Abuse
1982   Advertising, Competition, and the Economy
1983   The Freedom of Commercial Communication
1984   Educating Young Consumers
1985   The Influence of Advertising on Policies and Attitudes
1986   Sponsorship
1987   The Portrayal of People in Advertisements
1988   Financial Advertising
1989   No Seminar
1990   Advertising and the Environment
1991   Alcohol Advertising
1992   Advertising and Children
1993   Advertising: Information or Persuasion
1994   Food Advertising and Public Health
1995   No Seminar
1996   The Rights and Responsibilities of Advertising in Society
1997   How Effective is Advertising Self-Regulation and Could it be Improved?
1998   No Seminar
1999   Advertising Regulation and its Future
2000   Internet Advertising and E-Commerce
2001   No Seminar
2002   Consumer Advertising of Prescription Medicines
2003   Alcohol Advertising
2004   The Context Of Advertising
2005   Self-Regulation in New Media

Peterhouse seminars are not intended to reach conclusions, less still to determine future courses of action—though they sometimes do both. They are intended to help advertising people and their antagonists better understand each others' points of view: to build bridges. Each side knows where the other is coming from, but many of those present come from neither side, which restrains the adversaries from being too foolishly dogmatic. The intellectual level of debate—and dispute—is generally high, and most who attend usually feel the issues have been explored openly, objectively, and in depth.

The political, social, and economic outcomes, if any, cannot be measured. But one specific, if off-piste, outcome occurred in 1993 when the Peterhouse seminar spurred Tim Ambler, a Senior Research Fellow at London Business School, to produce an analysis of all the extant academic literature concerning the effects of advertising. In July 1995, together with Demetrios Vakratsas, a Post-Doctoral Fellow at LBS, Ambler produced a report titled 'Advertising Effects: A Taxonomy and Review of the Literature'. This defined nine different academic models of the effects of advertising on the individual. It cited 201 opinion and research papers, and it has never been superseded. Overall the Ambler and Vakratsas report shows, as we shall see again when dealing with the IPA Effectiveness Awards (and as the unsuccessful search for the Golden Key foretold) there is no single explanation or determinant of advertisings' effects.

Sex Rears its Erotic Head, Maybe

One subject no Peterhouse seminar ever bothered with is sex. The ASA, it is generally felt, handles this smutty subject adequately enough. But in 1975 sex in advertising reared its erotic head with the publication in Britain of a wonderfully whacky book called *Subliminal Seduction*, by Professor Wilson Bryan Key of the University of Western Ontario. *Subliminal Seduction* became a worldwide bestseller, and is still occasionally quoted as a serious text.

To give you a flavour of the book, here is Professor Key describing a Gilbey's Gin advertisement:

> Let your eyes concentrate momentarily upon the third ice cube from the top. Can you see an E formed in the ice cube?... The second ice cube from the top is also interesting... in the silhouette formed by the lime slice is the letter S... Now look at the bottom ice cube... If the X does not immediately appear, try looking away momentarily, then back quickly. You have just consciously perceived your first subliminal SEX... Incredulous though you may be at this point, these subliminal SEXes are today an integral part of modern American life... But there is much more to the Gilbey's ad. Could there be a face in the top ice cube?... The ice cube face appears to be peering down on the ice cube SEX... Look behind the X... the bottle and cap reflections could be interpreted as a man's legs and partially erect genitalia... Take several deep breaths, there is *much more to come*, if you'll pardon the expression.

Come now Professor, you don't need to explain your dirty jokes. If we can turn a bottle cap into partially erect genitalia, we can surely see a puerile pubic pun when it's shot at us?

> At the top is a drop of water which could represent the clitoris . . . the still open vagina is where the discharged penis has been . . . coitus interruptus has just occurred . . . in various parts of the advertisement are three women and two men . . . the subliminal promise to anyone buying Gilbey's Gin is a good-old-fashioned sexual orgy.

That sure is a penetrating USP, Professor. But what's so old-fashioned about a good sexual orgy?

Hold hard, the Professor has not yet reached his climax.

> They might embed the word FUCK or SUCK at an even deeper subliminal level. Not only have the taboo four letter-words proved effective in manipulating mass audiences but other words, with taboo implications, have also been demonstrated to possess subliminal power. Words such as shot (shit), whose (whore), pints (penis), and cult (cunt) can evoke strong demonstrable emotional reactions . . . The word tastes is frequently used in ad copy. Change one letter and the word becomes testes. Twenty-six advertisements in a recent issue of Life magazine used the word come in the copy.

By Jove! That must be why political campaigns keep referring to elections, and why retailers insist on using the word price. I've noticed the word rum keeps appearing in rum advertisements, too. Just change one letter and—in a flash—all will be revealed.

How do advertisers do all this? The Professor knows:

> Every major advertising agency has at least one embedding technician in its art department. The technique is taught at most commercial art schools.

Professor Key's book, like Vance Packard's before it, resonated with that sizeable sector of the public who believe sex constantly perks up in advertising, and that sex will sell anything. Both are twaddle. Unless you can spot coitus interruptus embedded in ice cubes there is, as mentioned earlier, almost no sex in advertising. There are mildly sexy advertisements for perfumes and cosmetics, for fashion and lingerie—all products where a little eroticism hardly comes amiss. Before the rules were tightened up in the 1970s, alcohol advertisers sometimes implied drinking enhances sex, but there has been none of that for more than thirty years. There are advertisements with sexy overtones for a few other products: Cadbury's Flake, Club Med . . . but there aren't many. When an ice cream (Haagen-Dazs) had the temerity to use playful but innocuous sexy images the attendant flurry of nudge-nudge, wink-wink publicity beggared belief. This could not have happened if raunchy advertising was common as muck. It would be astonishing if sex were entirely absent from advertising.

But sexy advertisements for supermarkets, for household cleaners, for electronic equipment, for medicines, for financial services? Hardly.

In Scandinavia and continental Europe there are many more blatant references to sex and sexuality in advertisements, but the British claim they do not like sex dragged into campaigns irrelevantly. (At least, that is what they say in surveys.) About one fifth of the complaints the ASA receives concern taste and decency and these—added to the surveys, and the somewhat conservative views of the ASA Council—ensure British advertisements veer towards the prudish rather than the prurient.

The industry believes its stance on sexy advertising to be one of enlightened self interest. This is because overt sex offends many people—even Neutralia's minimal nipple show prompted 309 complaints within days. And hard though it may be for the ever-randy to accept, as sexologists well know, for many people sex is not that important. Unsurprisingly, this becomes increasingly true as people grow older. And in Britain more than 40 per cent of consumer spending is by the over 50s. They aren't all celibate, but lust is perhaps not constantly uppermost in their minds.

Sex sells some products, to some people, sometimes. But not that many products, nor to that many people, nor that often. Most lewdly sexy magazines, programmes, and films are highly popular—with small minorities. And most advertising is aimed at larger groups.

As for 'subliminal' advertising, which so exercised Professor Wilson Bryan Key's disturbed psyche that he used the word in the title of his book, it does not exist. It never existed. The researcher James Vicary confessed in 1962 that his much-publicized 1957 experiment, in which he claimed to have discovered the existence of subliminal advertising, was faked: a crummy hoax. Despite his confession, many people remained anxious about its use throughout the second half of the twentieth century.

The Dirty Digger Digs In

During the 1970s the share of advertising secured by each of the main media sectors hardly changed, but then it was not a decade of media upheaval—though there were two key developments in print media at its start, and two key industrial disputes at its close.

In the press, as the 1960s closed Roy Thomson's epoch receded, and the rise of Rupert Murdoch began. During the 1970s the Australian newspaper tycoon inherited from the Canadian the role of true grit in Britain's newspaper publishing oyster. Both men came to Britain after building media empires in their own countries, both were of Scottish ancestry, and both proved themselves remarkable print publishers, with multi-media interests and skills. But Thomson was at heart an inspired advertising vendor—editorial was the 'news hole'—whereas Murdoch, Oxford educated and from a publishing family, paid close attention to editorial—whether or not it contained any news.

Murdoch's blitzkrieg on the British press began early in 1969, when he defeated the colourful but crooked Czech-born entrepreneur Robert Maxwell in a scuffle for the *News of the World*. Having pocketed the *News of the World*, later that year Murdoch bought the loss-making *Sun* from the Mirror Group. His down payment was a paltry £50,000, the Mirror Group being desperate to be rid of the millstone. On 17 November 1969 he relaunched *The Sun* as a tabloid, aiming it straight at the heart of the *Daily Mirror*. Murdoch's *Sun* was largely depoliticized, sexed up, and dumbed down. And the paper began to advertise heavily on television with brash, quick-fire, hurry-hurry commercials—jam-packed with celebrity sex scoops and promotional offers. To quote a wisely anonymous *Campaign* commentator in June 1970:

> The Sun could not have got more into its commercial if it tried –and it probably did . . . in a dizzy overpacked production, badly acted, seven subjects stumbled over each other in breathless succession, in an amateur slapped together style . . . even the announcer was gasping when he got to the end.

During its first five years under Murdoch *The Sun* commercials were produced by Hobson Bates—who else?—and were further proof that advertising effectiveness comes in coats of many colours. Likeable the commercials were not; award-winning they most certainly were not; successful they manifestly were.

From a struggling circulation of 800,000 *The Sun*'s daily sales vaulted to almost 2 million in 12 months. For advertisers a powerful new mass medium had been born. Prompted by its commercials, it was now universally called 'The SoarAway *Sun*' (and prompted by Auberon Waugh in *Private Eye*, Rupert Murdoch was now universally called 'The Dirty Digger'). As *The Sun* soared away, the *Daily Mirror* inevitably slipped downward. In 1976 the readership of *The Sun* overtook the *Mirror*'s: it was now Britain's most widely read daily paper, particularly among the 15–24s. In 1978 its circulation overtook the *Mirror*'s—readership changes often precede circulation changes—with daily sales of 3,930,554 against the *Mirror*'s 3,778,038.[2]

---

[2] Circulation and readership figures often get confused. Put simply, the circulation of a publication is the average number of copies it sells per issue. The readership is the (much

A few years later, at a private Ted Bates lunch in New York, Murdoch was asked what his relaunch strategy for *The Sun* had been. His purchase of the *News of the World*, he replied, had convinced him the veneer of Victorian puritanism which the British then affected was less than paper thin. But British national dailies—seduced by the historic success of the campaigning left-wing *Daily Mirror*, and by publishers' personal predilection for political influence—had clung to the belief that the British were only interested in sex on Sundays, and wanted hard-core politics during the week. He had simply shifted the *News of the World*'s Sunday style across to a daily. Unsurprisingly, the daily soon enjoyed the same sort of sales success as the Sunday. (Just as Roy Thomson's *Sunday Times* had for a while been 'The Only One With Colour', *The Sun* for a while was 'The Only One With Nipples'.)[3]

Murdoch's strategy, it is worth noting, was editorially based, rather than commercially based, though naturally the two are entwined. The Soar-Away *Sun*'s first editor Larry Lamb described the paper's almost disastrous first night of publication, in his book *Sunrise* (1989):

> I had a gut feeling that there could be merit in its very crudeness; that there could be lurking in those 48 amateurish pages the kind of rawness, the kind of life and vigour which had for so long been lacking in the complacent deep-piled corridors of Fleet Street.

At about the same time, another feral cat in the publishing jungle had come to a similar conclusion: the British veneer of Victorian puritanism was less than paper thin, and life and vigour had been lacking in...women's magazines. But this time the approach would be far from crude and amateurish.

In February 1972, the National Magazine Company launched the UK edition of *Cosmopolitan*. Already a huge success in the USA, *Cosmopolitan* was aimed at a species it dubbed the *Cosmo* Girl. *Cosmo* Girl, said the magazine's first UK editor Joyce Hopkirk, was 'Liberated, smart, but above all interested in sex—so un-British!' *Cosmopolitan* was *Playboy* for women. Until then British women's magazines had been all knitting patterns, sensible blancmange recipes, and adoring pictures of the Royal family. *Cosmo* was shamelessly raunchy—though the much heralded male nude Paul du Feu, briefly Germaine Greer's husband, did not appear until

larger) average number of people who read each issue. The Audit Bureau of Circulation provides the former figures, various surveys provide the latter.

[3] Lest this appears to contradict my earlier point about the popularity of sexy media, note that even at its peak *The Sun* was bought by fewer than 10% of the adult population—a considerable number, but still a distant 90% from everyone.

the second issue, and even then he had his vital parts hidden by a pot plant to keep out of trouble. Despite Paul's absence, *Cosmo*'s first issue was a sell-out in 24 hours. But unlike the *Sun*, *Cosmo* was stylish and classy, and appealed to stylish and classy advertisers—helped by powerful American international brands, which steadfastly followed the magazine across the Atlantic (and doubtless picked up some first-rate advertising deals in return for their loyalty). *Cosmopolitan* cracked open a new young, female market sector—highly attractive to many advertisers—and it was soon followed by a slew of me-too imitators, but held onto its leadership for over three decades.

Not to be outdone, at the end of the decade the maverick right-wing multi-millionaire Sir James Goldsmith decided he too could be a successful magazine publisher. He launched a British version of *Time* magazine, and called it *Now!* It achieved impressive initial sales of 410,000. But sales slumped to 119,705 in less than two years. Then! Goldsmith threw in the towel, his vanity publishing escapade having cost him £6 million—proving that in magazine publishing, as elsewhere, the size of your pocket matters but it isn't everything.

Following the economic turmoil engendered by the earlier galloping inflation, the 1970s ended with two industrial disputes of considerable long-term significance. In 1978 Times Newspapers—still then owned by Roy Thomson—clashed with the Fleet Street printing unions over the introduction of computer typesetting. Marmaduke Hussey, Thomson's top-drawer chairman, closed Times Newspapers on 1 December 1978. He expected the unions to suffer 'a short, sharp shock' and cave in within weeks. Instead the unions held out for almost a year. When Times Newspapers eventually resumed publication on 13 November 1979, the strike had cost Thomson almost £40 million. Hussey fell on his sword. Then there was more trouble. In August 1980 *Times* journalists went on strike for a 21 per cent pay rise. This was too much, in every sense. A dispirited Thomson sold Times Newspapers to Rupert Murdoch in January 1981 for £12 million. Murdoch was determined such disruptions should never recur. And by then Margaret Thatcher had become Prime Minister—with a little help from *The Sun*.

Over at ITV management–union relations were faring no better. In July 1979 the principal union in independent television, the ACTT, demanded a salary increase of 25 per cent for its members and rejected an offer of 9 per cent. A series of one-day lightning strikes ensued. In response the television companies closed down the entire network, at 6 pm on 10 August 1979. As with Times Newspapers, the television companies believed the dispute would be settled swiftly. Well it was settled faster than the *Times* stoppage, but it was ITV's longest ever strike, continuing for 11 weeks. The companies lost between £90 million and £100 million in advertising revenue, and agencies lost over £13 million in fees and commissions.

But the strike provided a unique opportunity to assess television advertising's effect on sales. Major agency D'Arcy-MacManus & Masius carefully analysed the consumer sales of 96 grocery brands, which had advertised on ITV in 1978 during exactly the same 11 weeks as they were unable to advertise during the 1979 strike. On average the 96 brands lost 4.5 per cent sales during the 1979 strike. The more heavily advertised brands lost still more, 8.7 per cent, while the less heavily advertised brands lost only 2.0 per cent. The 96 brands came from 26 product fields. Total sales of these product fields fell 2.0 per cent. Again the more heavily advertised fields fell more (2.7%) than the lightly advertised fields (1.0%). The key results were statistically significant at the 90 per cent level or above. The study concluded that for every £1 not spent on television advertising, on average each brand lost £2.80 immediate sales—and almost certainly more over subsequent weeks and months, which would normally have benefited from advertising's lag-effect.

There has been no other comparable study, but at the end of the 1970s quantifying the exact effects of advertising made a great leap forward, under the aegis of the IPA.

Star-Spangled Britain

During the 1970s a starry galaxy of British campaigns twinkled and sparkled, were ubiquitously liked and admired, won countless international awards, and remain—several decades later—highly regarded and fondly remembered by everyone who saw them. These were the campaigns which built the creative supremacy of British advertising throughout the world.

Here is my own selection of terrific British advertisements and campaigns from the 1970s, which many still recall with affection, or admiration, or both. (Alphabetical order, with agency and launch date):

- Benson & Hedges: Surrealism (CDP: 1977)
- Campari: Luton Airport (JWT: 1976)
- COI Seat Belts: Clunk! Click! (Masius + Y&R: 1971)
- Conservative Party: Labour isn't Working (Saatchi: 1978)
- Courage Best: Gertcha (BMP: 1979)
- Cresta Bear: It's frothy man (BMP: 1973)

- Fiat Strada (CDP: 1979)
- Health Education: Pregnant man (Cramer Saatchi: 1970)
- Heineken: Refreshes the Parts (CDP: 1973)
- Sugar Puffs: Honey Monster (BMP: 1976)
- Hovis: Boy on a Bike (CDP: 1975)
- John Smith's Bitter: Arkwright (BMP: 1979)
- Perrier: Eau-la-la (LPE/Burnett: 1978)
- Smash: Martians (BMP: 1973)
- Smirnoff: The effect is shattering (Y&R: 1970)
- Unigate: There's a Humphrey about (BMP: 1974)
- White Horse: You can take a White Horse anywhere (KMP: 1970)

Impressive though the accomplishment of long-term memorability is—for something as ephemeral as an advertisement—it is not an essential component of advertising creativity. Here is another bundle of 1970s campaigns and advertisements which are less well remembered by people outside of the industry, but were almost equally terrific:

- Barker & Dobson: Victory V Magritte (BMP: 1979)
- Birds Eye Foods: various (CDP: 1974)
- Central Office of Information: Army Officers (CDP: 1975)
- Dubonnet: S'il vous plait (Dorland: 1973)
- Guinness: various (JWT: 1970)
- John Harvey: Cockburn's Port (CDP: 1974)
- Olympus Cameras: David Bailey (CDP: 1978)
- Parker Pens: various (CDP: 1977)
- Pepsi Cola: Lipsmackinthirstquenchin (BMP: 1978)
- St Ivel Prize Guys: (BMP: 1975)
- TicTac: Why flick a mint? (BMP: 1974)
- Wall's: I'm meaty. Fry me (CDP: 1977)
- White Horse:[4] Scotch on the Rocks (FCO: 1979)

At first sight these advertisements and campaigns have little in common. They appeared in different media, and employed a profusion of styles, tones, and techniques—cartoon and live action, seriousness and humour, realism and fantasy, nostalgia and modernity, puns and narratives, voice-overs and lip-synch, essentially verbal and essentially visual ideas, straightforward USPs and oblique innuendos. But all of them share three less obvious characteristics.

---

[4] The White Horse account had moved from Kinsley Manton and Palmer to the new French Cruttenden Osborne agency—a KMP breakaway.

First, none of them comes from the sock-it-to-'em, loud-mouthed-salesman school of advertising. Second, all of them flatter the consumers' intelligence—or, at least assume the viewer or reader has some intelligence, implicitly accepting David Ogilvy's dictum 'The consumer is not a moron, she is your wife.' Third, all are truly innovative—though some are no more than up-to-the-minute expressions of traditional advertising themes.

During the 1960s Britain had already started to collect a fair number of creative trophies at the annual Cannes Festival, then the unchallenged worldwide arbiter of advertising creativity. (The festival was sometimes held in Venice until the 1980s.) In 1970 Britain did well at Cannes, but was outpaced by the USA, which picked up more awards. And like *Advertisers' Weekly* before it, *Campaign* felt it necessary to express its disappointment. The same happened in 1971. But in 1972 British and American agencies took home an equal number of television Gold Lions (4 apiece), and Britain won the cinema Grand Prix. The next year Britain won more awards than any other country, though most of these were Silvers.

Then the Gold rush started. In 1974 Britain collected 18 Gold and Silver Lions, plus the Palme D'Or. In 1975 our swag of gongs led to the *Campaign* headline 'Venice Goes British'. Come 1976 the *Campaign* headline was 'Britain Sweeps The Board'. We had pocketed the Palme D'Or plus 10 of the 19 Gold Lions. In that year BMP alone bagged 5 Gold Lions. In 1977 it was 'Britain Comes Out Best Again', with the Grand Prix for television and another 6 Gold Lions. 1978 was no different: 'Britain Picks Up Top Honours With Style', having won the Grand Prix for both television and cinema—a rare occurrence—and garnered a massive 80 Gold, Silver, and Bronze Lions. Then, after 5 years at the top, in 1979 and 1980 Britain dropped back. In 1979 the best *Campaign* could manage was 'British agencies and production companies do well' (2 Gold Lions), followed in 1980 by a humbling 'Britain Slips Back in Race for Honours'. In 1981 the British made a come back—'Britain Comes Out Best at Cannes', with more Gold and Silver Lions than any other country, and our creative leadership continued during the first half of the new decade, when Britain collected 45 Gold Lions against America's 23. But never again would Britain enjoy a five-year winning streak comparable with that of the mid-1970s.

Why was British advertising so creatively outstanding in the 1970s? The time was right and the circumstances were propitious. Fifteen years after the launch of commercial television, British advertising had both the skill and the confidence to push new ideas and techniques to the limit, and to build on the British taste for humorous, laid-back advertising. Television increased the authority and influence of art directors—no longer mere visualizers—which changed the style and tone of advertisements. The art directors, many of them from the new art schools, tended to be less cerebral then the copywriters, more empathetic, and much of the televisual humour was inherently visual. At the same time the domination of household cleanser advertising was ebbing and new advertisers—less constrained by advertising dogma—were emerging. Many of these new advertisers were British: they had great faith in British creativity, and were willing to back their own judgements. The growing threat from retailers' own brands (pages 229–30) may have driven the marketers in manufacturing companies—consciously or subconsciously—to seek more creative campaigns, to differentiate their brands excitingly from those of the retailers' workaday low price offerings. And, particularly at BMP, account planning was already helping to 'sell' innovative creative work to clients. But above all there was a phalanx of amazing talent in London—art directors and writers in agencies, independent film directors and freelance photographers—all ready and willing to take advantage of these developments, backed by several agency managements who were sure Gold Lions were the fastest track to gold-lined bank accounts.

Breaking News: Advertising Works!

The zealous enthusiasm for creative awards was not, however, embraced universally. Indeed it created its own backlash.

Many top agency people, who were not innately hostile to creative awards, nonetheless feared agencies' obsession with awards was running amok. Chris Hawes, later an outstanding IPA President, was especially concerned that the publicity garnered by creative awards was beginning to damage—even to trivialize—advertising in the eyes of advertisers. He felt the balance between creativity and effectiveness had swung altogether too far towards creativity. D&AD's cachet in creative departments had taken control: never mind the sales results, behold the Yellow Pencils. To quote Jeremy Bullmore, talking about those years, and echoing John Metcalfe's earlier sentiments:

> The backlash to the creative awards was that people in agencies were losing their compass bearings, and doing work designed just to win awards.

Left to fester, this would inevitably lead to a drop in advertising effectiveness. This in turn would inevitably lead to advertisers slashing their budgets. The agencies were committing hari-kiri. None of this thinking was new. Not only

Metcalfe but many of the foremost advertising men—including Rosser Reeves and David Ogilvy—have inveighed against the pernicious effects of creative awards.

At the same time, toward the end of the 1970s, a group of leading British researchers and planners, led by Dr Simon Broadbent, were growing anxious about an overlapping problem: many advertisers and agency people still believed the sales effects of advertising were not measurable. This was increasingly worrying, because financial systems in client companies were growing increasingly sophisticated. Top financial managers in client companies were growing increasingly powerful, and a new phrase—'cost effectiveness'—had become the mantra of the day. The finance directors wanted their companies' advertising spends to be proved cost effective—on the balance sheet, not at awards dinners.

Broadbent, with an Oxford first and a PhD from London, found all this exasperating. He began his career in industry. He then moved to Leo Burnett UK, becoming Media Director and later Research Director. For a spell he worked for Burnett in Chicago. Advertising evaluation had made more progress in America than it had in Britain. In 1961 the Association of National Advertisers—the advertisers, not the agencies—had published a highly influential short book called *Defining Advertising Goals For Measured Advertising Results* (*DAGMAR*), which has since been repeatedly republished and updated. *DAGMAR* set out clear procedures for measuring advertising effectiveness, stressing that it was essential to specify the measurement criteria, and the means of evaluation to be used, before the campaign begins.

Broadbent himself belonged to the Hobson school: he was a business consultant rather than a words-and-pictures man. Exceptionally numerate, many felt him an academic at heart, not least because he did not suffer fools at all gladly. Slender and intense, he seemed to work hard at smiling to stop himself scowling. He wrote prolifically, and influentially, and when he died quite suddenly in 2002 he was described, with justice, as 'a global legend in media research'. Naturally he knew all about *DAGMAR*.

To foster agencies' interest in measuring advertising effectiveness Broadbent decided to take a leaf out of the creative book. He proposed the IPA should develop an awards scheme of its own, a scheme which would honour only those campaigns which could prove they had been effective. The American Marketing Association had been running an effectiveness awards scheme called the EFFIES since 1969. But the EFFIES were, and are, run by advertisers. The IPA scheme would be run by agencies—that was its point. Moreover Broadbent wanted the IPA scheme to be more rigorous than the EFFIES. IPA entries would need to reveal detailed sales results (indexed for confidentiality if necessary), and would be judged by eminent businessmen and academics, as well as by market researchers and leading agency people. In Broadbent's awards, the creativity of the advertisements would play no part whatsoever.

When Broadbent asked the IPA to sponsor his scheme he found himself pushing at an open door. Many other agency chiefs, it transpired, were worried about the seemingly inexorable impact of creative awards. In 1979 the IPA Council agreed to Broadbent's proposals. In March 1980 UK management and trade magazines carried an unusual advertisement. It offered prizes worth £16,000 in a competition:

ADVERTISING WORKS
AND WE'RE GOING TO PROVE IT

In the advertising business we all know that the ultimate test of any advertising campaign is the sales result to which it contributes. Sadly this hard truth is not always acknowledged outside the agency world where the accountability of advertising is held in some doubt.

The Institute of Practitioners in Advertising is now setting out to remedy this situation with a unique competitive award scheme that will be based solely on the assessment of the *effects* of advertising campaigns in any media. It will aim to achieve three things:

1. A better understanding of the crucial role advertising plays in marketing.
2. Closer analysis of advertising effectiveness and improved methods of evaluation.
3. A clear demonstration that advertising can be proven to work, against measurable criteria.

The winning entries will be the ones that convince the judges of the contribution made by a particular campaign in its marketing context.

Entries would be detailed case histories, and would have to be signed off by clients. The data which entries would be required to contain were stated as:

- Business background.
- Marketing and advertising objectives.
- Description of the campaign, including creative and media strategies: it is not essential to show the executions, but they should be described (this may be supplemented by audio-visual material but the description should be sufficient without it).

- Campaign evaluation.
- Conclusions on the success or otherwise of the campaign, on the way the advertising worked and the methods used.

(The reference to 'describing' the campaign, and the lack of any need for 'audio-visual material' subjugates the advertisements to being mere tools in the marketing process—pure John Hobson, anathema to John Pearce.)

Much emphasis was placed on the entries being written clearly and persuasively. The scheme has never disguised its polemical aims. There were four. The awards aimed to persuade doubters and cynics that advertising is effective and measurable; to persuade advertisers that agencies are serious about sales results; to persuade agencies that producing effective advertising can be good for their reputations; and to encourage best practice in campaign planning and evaluation.

The four aims have been achieved triumphantly. Today, nobody who knows a jot about advertising questions whether it works. Some advertisers are still suspicious about agencies' creative self-indulgence, but such suspicions are far less prevalent than they were a couple of decades ago. All the leading UK agencies have entered for IPA Awards, have boasted when they have won, and have improved their reputations in consequence. And agency staff are now far more knowledgeable about campaign planning and evaluation than they used to be, and about how to go about it properly (and have no excuse for not doing so).

Competition entries are now almost always written by account planners. Without account planning the IPA Effectiveness Awards might well have flopped: the two have become wedded inextricably. For account planners, collecting an IPA Effectiveness Award is a badge of honour, as exalted as collecting a D&AD Yellow Pencil is for creative people. The key role of planners probably explains why, in the awards' first decade, BMP and JWT showed all other agencies a clean pair of heels, winning 21 IPA awards and commendations apiece. No other agency came close, though Saatchi & Saatchi won a creditable 9 awards, putting it in third place. Collett Dickenson Pearce, unsurprisingly, was far behind, entering only half a dozen times and gaining 4 commendations but no awards.

Since 1980 some 1,000 case histories have been entered. In aggregate they provide a rich library of data about different brands and markets—large and small, consumer and industrial, national and regional. The 400 winning and commended papers are publicly available from the IPA databank, the World Advertising Research Center website, and in book form. They comprise the largest, most comprehensive and authoritative collection of successful advertising case histories available anywhere.

The scheme has its weaknesses. Almost by definition, only highly effective campaigns are entered, and many effective campaigns are not highly effective. Indeed the scheme falls into the trap of encouraging people to think campaigns are either effective or ineffective. This is untrue. The effectiveness of campaigns is inherently gradated: a campaign may lift sales a little, or quite a lot, or hugely. In each case the advertising has had an effect, but the outcomes are quite different. Many campaigns, particularly for long-established brands, are intended simply to preserve the status quo: to keep sales ticking over. But keeping sales ticking over would not be sufficient to win an award. Another lacuna: the awards generally report sales or market share outcomes, and the key test of any advertising is not merely whether it increases sales, but whether the profit resulting from the additional sales more than covers the cost of the campaign. This is what advertisers' finance directors need to know—the campaign's cost effectiveness. The IPA encourages entrants to report on cost effectiveness, but they seldom do in any detail. And finally, the awards may suggest there are only a handful of effective campaigns each year (the winners), whereas in reality there are hundreds of thousands of effective campaigns, little and large, running all the time.

Above all, the IPA papers have once again shown advertising works in a cornucopia of ways. In 1997 I commissioned an independent researcher to analyse all 650 entries since the start (at that time): the winners and the losers. It transpired that most campaigns aim to achieve several results simultaneously. A campaign might aim to increase sales, to increase retail distribution, to increase awareness, to increase profitability, to change the brand's image, to generate product trial or to build repeat usage, to change the consumer profile—any or many of these. Every campaign achieves, and is almost always intended to achieve, several outcomes. The researcher showed that on average, each campaign had 2.5 stated objectives.

Does advertising add value? Does it support price premiums? Or does it lead to lower prices? Does it build awareness? Does it provide information? Does it change images? Does it expand markets? Or does it only promote brands? Does it act immediately? Or is it invariably a long-term investment? The IPA entries show a campaign will sometimes do one of those things, sometimes several, occasionally many of them at once. So when somebody asks 'What is the purpose of the advertising?' the answer should almost always be 'How long have you got?'

The strengths of the IPA Awards far outweigh the weaknesses, which is why they have flourished and been copied in other countries and in other industries. Since 1980 there have been modifications and refinements, but the underlying character of the competition remains intact, and winning an IPA Effectiveness Award remains as prestigious as it has ever been. The fundamental importance of sales effectiveness regained lost ground.

Bunch of Five

During the 1970s there were so many excellent campaigns it is difficult to choose which to highlight. Everyone would make a different selection. Here are my five.

First, Smirnoff. Smirnoff was launched in Britain by International Distillers and Vintners (IDV) in 1953. The spirits market was then dominated by whisky and gin, both of which were predominantly drunk by the old. Until 1962 Smirnoff was virtually the only vodka available in Britain, and its Russian origins smacked of firewater. Not many British drinkers like firewater. So until the early 1960s Smirnoff was advertised as ideal with mixers (drinking it with mixers would mask its putative fieriness). Sales grew slowly. With the arrival of Vladivar and Cossack in the 1960s, vodka began to take off among the young, and Smirnoff's market share fell. In 1970 IDV moved to ensure Smirnoff's long-term dominance of the market. It asked its agency Young & Rubicam to create a campaign which would fulfil the following rather pedestrian, jargonized brief:

Key Consumer Benefit
Smirnoff, unlike other high profile drink brands targeted to young consumers, does not just follow the latest trends and fashions, but breaks the rules and conventions in an individualistic, stylish and confident manner.

Advertising proposition
  Smirnoff sets the pace.

Brand personality
  • Individualistic
  • Confident
  • Stylish
  • Witty and irreverent

Target audience
  • C1C2 men and women
  • Age 18–30

- Drinkers and non-drinkers of vodka
- Style and fashion conscious (like to be one step ahead)
- Enjoy drinking and socialising

IDV stressed the brand's Russian origins should be played down, both because of the firewater connotations and because the Smirnoff family had fled Russia after the 1917 revolution, taking its business with it.

At that time the drink companies had voluntarily embargoed advertising spirits on the box, so using television was not an option. Y&R copywriter John Bacon and art director David Tree were given the task of turning the insipid brief into delectable advertising in print and on posters. For several weeks they laboured in vain, trying to compare the excitement of Smirnoff with the lacklustre taste of other drinks. This proved too negative. Then David Tree noticed, serendipitously, a magazine pin-up on the office wall and quipped to John Bacon, 'If we get stuck, we can always say "I was a boring housewife in Southgate until ...".' (Tree lived in Southgate.) Instantly they realized they had the answer.

The campaign slogan was 'The Effect is Shattering', which exploited vodka's reputation for potency without spelling it out. Each advertisement in the campaign would reveal how Smirnoff had transformed somebody's humdrum life into one of glamour and excitement. This is a well-worn advertising theme. Its most famous rendition was the campaign for Maidenform bras created by the New York agency Norman Craig Kummel in 1949, which ran for 20 years. Maidenform transformed every wearer's humdrum life into one of glamour and excitement, albeit in her dreams. Dressed only in her underwear, and loving it, a Maidenform girl would say: 'I dreamed I was a social butterfly in my Maidenform bra,' or 'I dreamed I went to blazes in my Maidenform bra.' NCK boss Norman B Norman was a keen disciple of Dr Ernest Dichter and of motivation research.

The early, draft, Smirnoff advertisements proved too sexy. The first showed a couple who might (or might not) have been misbehaving, and even before it appeared it was vetoed by London Transport—notoriously prudish about the advertising it will accept. Y&R's second effort showed a nude blonde on horseback. This was vetoed by IDV even before it reached London Transport. Y&R tried harder. The advertisements grew subtler, and leapt several notches up the creative ladder. Innuendo was all that was needed: research showed drinkers got the message without difficulty.

There followed a series of exquisitely photographed fantasy advertisements, including:

- 'Accountancy was my life until I discovered Smirnoff'
- 'It was the 8.29 every morning until I discovered Smirnoff'
- 'I was the mainstay of the Public Library until I discovered Smirnoff'
- 'I'd set my sights on a day-trip to Calais until I discovered Smirnoff'
- 'I never saw further than the boy next door until I discovered Smirnoff'

The brand's origins were deftly implied by displaying the apparently Russian label, without mentioning it. For Smirnoff the campaign was indeed shattering. After years of relative stagnation, sales tripled (Table 6).

The campaign made vodka chic. Within a decade vodka had overtaken gin in popularity. And Smirnoff held onto around 50 per cent of the market, despite being more expensive than its leading competitors.

But equally shatteringly, from Smirnoff's point of view, in 1975 the Advertising Standards Authority—under pressure from the government—pulled the plug on the campaign. In 1975 the alcohol advertising rules were tightened. No longer could an advertisement target the young, nor 'claim or suggest that any drink can contribute towards sexual success', nor claim that a drink might beget 'social success or acceptance'. For Smirnoff and Y&R, a landmark campaign had run its course.

Table 6. Smirnoff sales (index basis, 1970 = 100)

	Sales
1970	100
1972	148
1974	229
1976	307

Source: IPA Effectiveness Award Paper, 1990.

The similarities between the Smirnoff case history and my next thumbnail case history, CDP's campaign for the UK launch of Heineken, are almost uncanny. Smirnoff popularized a small-selling foreign drink and helped transform British drinking habits. So did Heineken. Both attained their aims with the help of inspired advertising. Both were based on slogans—'The Effect Is Shattering' and 'Refreshes The Parts Other Beers Cannot Reach'—which swiftly entered the vernacular, and have never quite left it.

The Smirnoff case history above was mostly culled from two IPA Effectiveness Awards papers, exemplifying how the awards opened up advertising to public scrutiny. The Heineken campaign was never entered for an IPA Award. This probably reflects CDP's lack of commitment to the competition. Consequently much of the Heineken story is anecdotal. *Thirsty Work* (1983), a history of the first ten years of the campaign, by Peter Mayle, is great fun but nimbly avoids providing the reader with any meaningful data. Fortunately the story has been fleshed out for me by Anthony Simonds-Gooding, who was Marketing Director of Whitbread Brewers and was responsible for Heineken's marketing and advertising at the time.

Anthony Simonds-Gooding is one of a small number of advertisers who in recent years have closely followed the advertising agency game, and personally know many of the players. In this respect he is something of a throw-back. Until the 1970s, most large companies employed advertising specialists whose sole job was to manage the company's advertising. They had their own professional body, the Incorporated Advertising Management Association (IAMA), which was founded in 1932. At its peak in the late 1950s IAMA had 600 members. An important part of its members' expertise was to know precisely what was going on in the agency world. So they diligently visited agencies, and attended agency cocktail parties, and—especially—accepted agency lunch and dinner invitations. This onerous work helped them keep their fingers on agencies' pulses.

It all started to change during the 1960s, when advertising specialists were superseded by marketing specialists, and advertising came within the compass of this new breed. For the marketing specialists, advertising was (and still is) but part of their holistic role. Marketing managers are responsible for every aspect of their brand—product formulation, price, packaging, public relations, and promotions through to manufacture, media-buying, market research, and much more. Important though advertising is, they have neither the time nor the inclination to stay closely in touch with every advertising agency in town. Even getting them to an agency lunch requires long-term planning (and nowadays some primly refuse all offers of entertainment). Apart from marketing executives, the only client people who now regularly deal with agencies are media specialists and—much to the agencies' chagrin—commercial purchasing managers, often called procurement managers, who negotiate the agencies' contracts. Most advertisers now know so little about the agency game they use outside consultants when switching their accounts. In the days of IAMA, such consultants did not exist. Now IAMA does not exist.

Anthony Simonds-Gooding, though a thoroughgoing marketing man, has always been an advertising agency groupie. Coming from a military family he joined the Royal Navy, then left the service to become a marketing trainee at Unilever. He stayed at Unilever for 13 years, moved to Whitbread in 1973 as Marketing Director, and rose to become the brewer's Group Managing Director. His previously stable career then jumped hither and thither. In 1985 he went to Saatchi & Saatchi, where he was chairman and chief executive of their worldwide marketing services network for two frantic years, before leaving to become chief executive of the ill-fated British Satellite Broadcasting company, which proved a disaster. He then switched jobs some more before belatedly becoming chairman of D&AD, and quite a successful artist.

Arriving at Whitbread from Unilever, Simonds-Gooding was given an almost free hand to market Heineken as he pleased. The brewing company had just acquired Heineken's UK licence, and its sales were small beer: it was a minor brand in a minor market. Traditional British ales accounted for more 80 per cent of beer sales.

At CDP the account executive handling Whitbread's business was Frank Lowe, another of British advertising's movers and shakers at the end of the twentieth century, to whom we will return. Simonds-Gooding and Lowe had first met at Lintas, where they shared an office. Owned by Unilever, Lintas was a rare (and not particularly successful) attempt by a major advertiser to set up its own advertising agency. Simonds-Gooding had been seconded to Lintas to learn about advertising as part of his Unilever marketing training. Frank Lowe had been employed by Lintas to polish up its unremittingly bland image—a task which proved beyond even the power of his resplendent pink suits.[5] Lowe soon left Lintas for CDP, where he found himself teamed up with Simonds-Gooding again, but now as agency executive and client. At CDP Lowe swopped his pink suits for smart-casual sports gear, and sometimes strolled round the offices carrying a cricket bat.

Whitbread research had revealed that while ale drinkers talked about flavour, lager drinkers talked about refreshment. To lager drinkers the taste was relatively unimportant: they simply wanted a refreshing drink. The competitive lagers were fighting turf wars, pressing home Unique Selling Propositions which focused either on their countries of origin or on their superlative ingredients. The USPs were indeed Unique, and may even have been Propositions, but were not Selling—a common failing of poor USP campaigns. Whitbread and CDP decided to make a pre-emptive category claim for Heineken—to capture 'refreshment' and to attach it to their brand. The creative brief for the new campaign apparently comprised just two words: 'Heineken' and 'Refreshment'—a refreshing improvement on the Smirnoff brief's gobbledegook.

---

[5] Lowe's pink suits were just one of many attempts to enliven the Unilever agency. Other attempts were more radical, but equally unsuccessful.

It was agreed the word 'lager' should be outlawed, as the image of lager was feminine and weak. Heineken would be a beer. And as with Smirnoff, its foreign heritage could be implied but not trumpeted: this was what the competitive European brands were already doing, to little effect. Most of all, Simonds-Gooding insisted the Heineken campaign should have 'legs'—it had to be able to run and run, as he foresaw that building a major lager brand would take years. Though television could not be used by spirits it could be used by beers, and would be the key medium.

The two-word brief was given to copywriter Terry Lovelock and art director Vernon Howe. Like the Smirnoff creative team, they too found the nut hard to crack. But they were probably in no hurry. As Gallaher's Peter Wilson pointed out, CDP liked to take its time. Lovelock and Howe spent weeks getting nowhere—at least nowhere beyond the local eateries for inspirational and ever-lengthening lunches. To show they were working themselves to a frazzle they papered their office wall with scamps—scribbles of ideas for advertisements, none of which was much good. Then Howe had to go to Morocco to shoot a Ford commercial, and Lovelock cadged a flight ticket to accompany him. On hearing this Frank Lowe furiously ordered them not to return without a Heineken campaign. In Marrakesh they wallowed in the luxury of Winston Churchill's beloved La Mamounia hotel, and at 3 o'clock one night Lovelock suddenly awoke and wrote two lines: 'Heineken is now refreshing all parts' and 'Heineken refreshes the parts other beers cannot reach.'[6] He preferred the second. Though intrinsically meaningless it said refreshment, it said beer, and it hinted at unsuspected extra strength: perfect. He roughed out some commercials which embodied the line.

By now Simonds-Gooding was growing tetchy about the time CDP was taking. He was about to fly with Lowe, and a party of other CDP clients, on a freebie to Leningrad (St Petersburg), on Aeroflot, to see the impressionists in the Hermitage. Lowe presented Lovelock's ideas to him in flight. This was bizarre. Normally important campaigns are presented in grand agency boardrooms, with fanfares of trumpets, suitable histrionics, and reams of enthusiastic charts. But Lowe and Simonds-Gooding were old mates.

Moreover Simonds-Gooding was intent on introducing Whitbread to a new advertising culture. This would avoid new campaigns being first presented to the most junior marketing staff, and then progressing up the company's hierarchical ladder (the Unilever system, employed by

---

[6] Lewis Carroll wrote, 'Sometimes an idea comes at night, when I have to get up and strike a light to write it down.'

most large companies). Simonds-Gooding believed this type of approvals regime sentences creativity to death by a thousand improvements. Throughout the Heineken campaign's life he would personally agree new ideas with Lowe and instruct his subordinates to carry them out. As one of Lowe's senior subordinates told me:

> Frank would come back from playing tennis with Simonds-Gooding, hand me a Heineken script and say 'It's approved, get going'. My oppos at Whitbread got the same treatment from Simonds-Gooding. So we played the game the way the two bosses wanted it played. Then Frank would constantly interfere because his attention to detail is manic.

Excellent though this may be as a way to get good advertising, it is no way to train or motivate good subordinates.

Starting as he meant to go on, Simonds-Gooding bought Terry Lovelock's idea in mid-air. He saw immediately that it could be developed and would run indefinitely. The idea was polished up a little and shown to the Whitbread board and to Freddie Heineken, owner of the brand. They bought it too. As with Strand, all this was done on hunch, with no research: another consequence both of the Simonds-Gooding–Lowe relationship and of Heineken's minimal importance to Whitbread. When market research was eventually carried out on the first three Heineken commercials, advertising folklore has it that the results were completely negative, but Simonds-Gooding and Lowe pressed on regardless. For creative people this is an attractive tale as it emphasizes the importance of judgement and courage, and minimizes the importance of research. But it is only partially true.

The research, which comprised a few focus groups, rejected the 'Refreshes the Parts' slogan because it was not 'proper' beer advertising, a response Simonds-Gooding and Lowe ignored. But by then they had sold the campaign to the top brewery managers in Britain and Holland, and had already lashed out the cost of making three commercials. To have eaten humble pie and trashed them all would have been tricky. Fortunately, two of the commercials came out of the research much better than the third, so the third bit the dust. But in their Unilever days, even small scale negative research would probably have been sufficient to raze the entire campaign. Lowe and Simonds-Gooding had the bottle to keep going.

'Refreshes The Parts' now began a triumphant 22-year run—that certainly is legs. When the Australian lagers arrived in the 1980s, Heineken's European provenance was emphasized by Victor Borge's gently comedic voice-overs—a tad misleadingly, as Borge was Danish (the home of quality lager) while Heineken was Dutch. 'Only Heineken Can Do This' was added to the 'Refreshes The Parts' slogan, to make it more competitive. The campaign did not end until drinkers deserted relatively weak lagers (like Heineken) and switched to stronger lagers (like Stella Artois—whose advertising also came from the Lowe–Simonds-Gooding stable).

During the long campaign the Heineken commercials were superbly directed by a pool of celebrated film makers, including Bob Brooks, Ross Cramer, Hugh Hudson, Alan Parker, Paul Weiland, and art director Vernon Howe himself. Almost as memorable as the commercials were the billboards. Each visualized the 'Refreshes The Parts' concept with instantly accessible wit, sometimes mirroring the commercials, sometimes not. And the television and posters were in turn backed up with cartoon advertisements in the press which swiftly interpreted current news and sporting events, as seen through Heineken's refreshing eyes. CDP were briefed to present newsy cartoons whenever inspiration struck them, and the ideas would (or would not) be approved instantly. CDP mythology has it that the agency occasionally ran its newsy cartoons without client approval, if no Whitbread personnel were on hand. This sounds apocryphal. For an agency to run an advertisement which has not been signed off by the advertiser is ludicrously risky, however close the relationship. In any event, the newsy Heineken advertisements flowed thick and fast. Among them were cartoons based on the World Cup, the London Marathon, the Cup Final and the Grand National, the first night of The King and I, Carl Andre's pile of bricks at the Tate Gallery, the end of the Times Newspaper industrial dispute, Charles and Diana's engagement, and the attempted mating of two Chinese pandas. All of them—because their subjects were so current—repeatedly refreshed the refreshment campaign over the years.

Sales responded handsomely. At that time the brewers sold their own beers in the tied pubs they owned, and Whitbread owned far fewer pubs than its major competitors. Nonetheless Heineken's sales grew strongly in Whitbread's tied houses. More importantly, licensed supermarkets were grabbing a sizeable share of lager sales, and in supermarkets—where the shoppers could freely choose—Heineken soon outsold its competitors. Despite the results of those first group discussions, 'Refreshes The Parts' became one of Britain's best known and best loved beer campaigns, itself parodied by cartoonists, comedians—and other advertisers.

When planning this book I intended to nominate 'Refreshes The Parts' as my 'British Campaign of the Century'. I dropped the idea as being too catchpenny, and too simplistic. Nonetheless 'Refreshes The Parts' has many qualities which would justify the accolade. It helped switch the public's beer drinking from ale to lager; its pre-emptive 'refreshment' strategy was completely right; it worked equally well in all three prime media—television, print, and posters—which gave it maximum flexibility, coverage, and impact; its verbal and visual messages were integrated perfectly; it ran without faltering for over twenty years, constantly refreshing itself; just about every execution was top-notch; it obtained universal awareness and, as far as I can tell, universal approbation; it is quintessentially British—witty, understated, literally meaningless but totally comprehensible. And although, as with Smirnoff, it is based on one of the corniest advertising ideas—'this product will briefly transform your life'—it managed to mock the idea while exploiting it. All of this would surely have made it a worthy winner.[7]

Like Heineken, the CDP Benson & Hedges King Size 'Surrealist' campaign, launched in 1977, might well have won my personal, albeit nonexistent, campaign of the century trophy. It broke every advertising rule ever penned—and succeeded. American advertising people still find this inexplicable. Again, the campaign was never entered for an IPA Effectiveness Award. Doubtless this too reflects CDP's lukewarm attitude to these awards. But additionally, in this case, by the late 1970s cigarette manufacturers were intent on keeping their marketing out of the public eye. The last thing they wanted was to promote the effectiveness of their advertising publicly.

Gallaher launched B&H King Size in 1961. Gallaher was the second largest British cigarette manufacturer, and king size cigarettes were still a minority taste. Previously John Pearce had turned down a cigarette account offered to him by John Player & Sons, a much larger advertiser than Gallaher. Turning down business from John Player was brave to the point of foolhardiness, especially as CDP's finances were decidedly ropy at the time. But Pearce felt in his bones that the Player's brand was dead in the water, while B&H King Size was destined for great things. He was right about both.

---

[7] Though I rejected the idea of nominating a 'British Campaign of the Century', in 1999 *Campaign*'s 'Best of the Century' jury suffered no such inhibition, and unanimously appointed John Webster's Cadbury Smash Martians its own campaign of the century. Its citation stated that—in addition to the campaign's manifest creativity—the Martians had been hugely sales effective. Smash has indeed been instant mash brand leader ever since the Martians landed on our screens, and although they have been exiled to Mars several times, they have rocketed back to earth twice, in 1992 and 1999. My personal reservation about the Smash Martians, lovable and memorable though they were, is that they emphasize the artificial, tinny nature of instant mash. This was confirmed when I briefly worked with Dornay Foods, producers of Yeoman instant mash. Dornay research showed consumers were well aware instant mash was easy to make—the Martians' message—but were not that keen on the taste. It may, or may not, be significant that Smash's agency BMP, which has entered almost all its famous campaigns for IPA Effectiveness Awards, and won lots—never entered the Martians.

For the first 15 years B&H King Size advertising was built around the brand's iconic gold pack, using the slogan 'Pure Gold from Benson & Hedges'. The advertisements were stylish, opulent, and delightfully photographed—wittily implying in a variety of unlikely and sometimes hilarious situations that the pack was made of real, 22-carat metallic gold. The commitment of the agency to the campaign, and of the client to the agency, were total. Peter Wilson, of Gallaher, later said:

> We let CDP develop the executions. We didn't interfere. There was the occasional discussion as to whether a particular ad should appear, but fundamentally CDP won the right from us to develop and run the ads. We signed them off of course, but we knew CDP were the experts and we were not. We didn't want to buy a dog and do the barking ourselves. That's a fairly rare situation in advertising and it's a situation that has to be earned by the agency.

'Fairly rare' here is one of the great understatements of advertising history. To give an agency such clout is all but unknown (though David Ogilvy claims he obtained the same licence once—from a minuscule advertiser). CDP attained similar relationships with several of its clients. No doubt such advertisers gravitated towards CDP, and CDP gravitated towards such advertisers. As well as the John Player assignment, Pearce turned away other advertisers he knew his agency would be unable to work with. Occasionally he foolishly accepted clients who could not put up with CDP's intransigence (as the clients saw it) and the relationship soon faltered. Pearce would then mischievously provide the departing client with a list of more flexible agencies that might be more congenial.

The B&H King Size 'Pure Gold' advertisements bagged creative trophies by the score; the excellence of the executions could not be faulted. But classy though it was, the campaign was not, in my view, all that original. It was superb but not groundbreaking. The wit and style did not quite transmute an ordinary idea—a gold pack might be real metallic gold—into radical advertising. Still, B&H King Size sales grew strongly. By 1975 B&H King Size was the sixth most popular brand in Britain, and was brand leader in the king size sector. The brands which outsold it were smaller and cheaper. Despite this success, research shows B&H King Size had begun to lose smokers in the early 1970s. The 'Pure Gold' campaign was apparently running out of puff—though neither Gallaher nor CDP have ever admitted as much. In any case the ASA delivered another deadly blow. When the rules governing cigarette advertising were tightened, yet again, the ASA decided the 'Pure Gold' campaign was unacceptably aspirational.

Ever since its launch, B&H King Size had been sold to trendy young smokers as being fashionable and chic. This was now banned. Its USP remained its gold pack—a Unique Proposition which had proved to be a Selling Proposition. A new campaign based on the gold pack was needed, a campaign which would both appeal to the trendy smokers and be acceptable under the stringent new ASA rules. Frank Lowe claims he then decided: 'We had to do something nobody will understand, because if they don't understand it they won't be able to object to it.'

This poisoned chalice of a brief was handed to Alan Waldie, one of CDP's most talented art directors. The brief inherently suggested a visual rather than verbal campaign—though nobody could have guessed how far that writ would run. Again, and understandably, Waldie took his time, wrestling with the brief—as he commonly did—in the nearby Carpenter's Arms. He says:

> I can't remember the time scale. I was thinking, worrying, working...the pressure was on me...days drifted into weeks.

Eventually the Carpenter's Arms weaved its magic, and Waldie was ready to present his ideas to CDP management. As he describes it:

> Silence descended on the room as they gazed at some totally incomprehensible layouts of birdcages, mouseholes, eggs, sardines. No message, no words at all. Unified only by a solitary gold pack.

Gallaher bought the campaign on sight. Once again there was no market research. Once again the client had accepted CDP's judgement. Gallaher's only recorded response was to insist the campaign should use 'great art direction, great photography, and spare no expense'. This is not an injunction any agency—and especially not CDP—would wish to disobey. The top-flight photographers used included Brian Duffy, Adrian Flowers, and David Montgomery. There was no electronic or digital retouching then: sets and props were built with meticulous care, and the photographers used every trick they knew, no matter how long it took, no matter how much it cost. Hugh Hudson's utterly bewildering 'Iguana' cinema commercial, replete with a swimming pool in the desert, sardine cans, and Battersea Power station, was shot in Arizona, and entered the *Guinness Book of Records* at that time as the most expensive commercial ever made.

To Waldie's mouse holes and sardine cans would soon be added a gilded chameleon, a hard working colony of ants, the Pyramids, plaster ducks flying over a mantelpiece, 3,500 golden bees, a shadowy hotel lobby, an electric plug, a mystifying red jacket on a coat hook, a deluge of pouring cigarettes, and lots of other unfathomable stuff. In all there were 90 different executions. None contained a single explicatory word—the cigarette deluge did not even include a pack. The only words on show were the statutory government anti-smoking health warnings. (This was the bizarre era when the cigarette companies spent hundreds of millions of pounds warning the public not to use their products.)

Though the advertisements lacked words, and sometimes packs, from the moment they appeared the public intuitively knew they were for B&H King Size. And from the moment they appeared they were dubbed 'surreal'—as they loosely resembled the surreal paintings of Rene Magritte (who himself created several tobacco advertisements during 1932–6).

Benson & Hedges were not the first to run advertisements without a brand name or pack. John Gilroy had done the same for Guinness in the 1930s, when his animal posters had grown so well-known they needed no identification. Nor were Benson & Hedges the first to use surreal images. In addition to Magritte's own work, the year before the B&H King Size campaign broke, fashion photographer Guy Bourdain had taken Dali-esque photographs for a Charles Jourdain shoe campaign in France. Sometimes the footwear was the star of the advertisement, sometimes it was so hidden as to create a game of hunt the slipper. Alan Waldie would assuredly have known about the Charles Jourdain campaign—but he took his surrealism much further. The Bourdain photographs exuded sexiness and glamour, which enhanced the Jourdain shoes. The B&H King Size advertisements bordered on the distasteful. How could mouse holes, chameleons, ants, bees, and ghastly plaster ducks enhance the image of an expensive, fashionable brand? Why would anyone be tempted to smoke cigarettes resembling oily tinned sardines, or an electric plug?

The truth is, nobody knows. Among advertising people, the accepted dogma is the campaign so intrigued the public it involved them in the advertising process—and they loved it: they enjoyed the mystery, enjoyed the puzzles. Decoding them flattered people, made them feel sophisticated. Well maybe. In subsequent years people have often quizzed me about the campaign—though I had nothing to do with it. What did the advertisements mean? What were they getting at? What deep subconscious tricks were they playing? I wish I knew. Nobody has ever suggested the images meant anything, were getting at anything, were playing any deep subconscious tricks at all. They simply drew attention to the unsaid Pure Gold message in a spellbinding way. The public involvement must have been comparable to that for Strand. But the outcome was as triumphant as Strand's was disastrous.

B&H King Size began a prolonged sales rise. In *Inside Collett Dickenson Pearce*, John Ritchie claims that by 1980 the brand's share of the UK cigarette market exceeded 20 per cent. This may be a tiny exaggeration. Ritchie, who handled the Gallaher account at CDP, is an inveterate enthusiast. But by 1983 B&H King Size was certainly overall market leader, with an 18 per cent share of all smokers, Moreover in 1985 the brand's advertising was thought to be eye-catching (by 74% of the public), up-to-date (by 67%), different (by 64%), interesting (by 57%), and clever (by 56%). When the public were asked to name the 'best' cigarette, B&H King Size was way ahead of all others. It was not until 1990, when its market share had grown to 24 per cent, that it first reached a plateau, then slipped back.

These results might well have won B&H King Size an IPA Effectiveness Award—had the case history been entered. Unarguably they show the surrealist campaign—whatever the hell it meant—was a triumph, in sales as well as creative terms.

Yet it failed to have much creative influence. In the early 1980s many commentators—me included—believed B&H King Size had broken the mould of traditional advertising forever. Not so. With just a handful of exceptions, surrealism crept back into its mouse hole. Advertisements returned to their previous, relatively rational and comprehensible, formats—from which of course, 99.99 per cent had never departed.

Unlike Smirnoff, Heineken, and Benson & Hedges, it is debatable whether my next campaign has any right to be included in this brief selection of 1970s campaigns. It was scrappy, and achieved little or nothing for the advertiser. But it included one of the most famous British posters of all time, and this achieved a great deal for the agency which created it. I am referring to the 'Labour Isn't Working' poster, and Margaret Thatcher's 1979 general election campaign.

Harold MacMillan's triumphant 1959 election campaign had left the Labour party bruised, and impressed, but unwilling to go the whole hog and appoint its own advertising agency. Instead, in 1963 Labour put together a voluntary, unpaid group of advertising and market research professionals to produce their campaign for the 1964 election. This was based on the slogan 'LET'S GO With Labour and We'll Get Things Done.' The voters did as they were bid. Meanwhile the Tories had ditched Colman Prentis & Varley—which had lost many of its best people—and in subsequent years moved to a succession of agencies, none of which produced anything especially memorable. Having won in 1964, Labour stuck to its voluntary group formula for some time afterwards but they produced nothing especially memorable either.

With the election of Margaret Thatcher as Tory leader in February 1975 the Tories were ready for—desperate for—a change. Thatcher appointed Gordon Reece her Director of Communications, and for the first three years Reece concentrated on improving her personal presentation. He taught her oratory, persuaded her to change her hairstyle and her clothes, and to lower her voice. Later, the belief that Saatchi & Saatchi had repackaged Mrs Thatcher became almost unshakeable—a misapprehension the Saatchi brothers were far too busy to contradict.

In 1978 Reece decided the Tories needed a new advertising agency. He wanted an agency that was young and hungry, willing to work its butt off, but large enough to provide the resources necessary to handle a major political campaign—an agency that was highly creative, and was British. These being the criteria, Reece said, Saatchi & Saatchi virtually picked itself. Saatchi and Saatchi was then 8 years old, and immensely successful. Reece phoned and asked to come and see Charles Saatchi. 'Come this morning,' Charles replied. When he got there Charles refused to see him. Instead Maurice saw him. Well if he hadn't seen one Saatchi, at least he'd seen another.

That afternoon Charles Saatchi telephoned Tim Bell, on holiday in Barbados. Bell, who was now number two (or three) to the brothers—and often foolishly called 'the third brother'—had been a young media-buyer at CPV and knew how much turmoil a political account can create. He also knew recent Tory agencies had gained no kudos from handling the party's account and, worst of all, he knew he would be thrown in at the deep end, as neither Charles nor Maurice handled clients themselves. From Barbados, Bell argued forcibly the account should be rejected. The brothers ignored him. By the time he returned to London, Saatchi & Saatchi was the Tory agency. Fortunately, by then Bell had changed his mind. He threw himself into his new task with characteristic gusto and soon became Mrs Thatcher's favourite adman. Unlike the Saatchi brothers, who were then hardly interested in politics, Bell was a committed Tory.

Saatchi's first work for the Tories was a Party Political Broadcast (PPB). Britain forbids paid-for political advertising on television and radio—instead political parties are offered limited free time in which to transmit their own 'political broadcasts'. These are not subject to ITA, ASA, or any other vetting. PPBs generally get small audiences. To overcome this Saatchi's ran 'teaser' advertisements on the morning of their first PPB, claiming people who missed television at 9 o'clock that evening would regret it for the rest of their lives. (Perhaps it was as well the ASA has no jurisdiction over election advertising.)

The PPB showed everything in Britain going backwards—people walking backwards over Waterloo Bridge, Stephenson's Rocket steaming backwards, the Comet (the world's first jetliner) landing in reverse, climbers backing down Mount Everest, and so on. The voice over intoned:

> This country was once the finest nation on earth. We were famous for our freedom, justice and fair play. Our inventions brought the world out of the Middle Ages to industrial prosperity. Today we are famous for discouraging people from getting to the top. Famous for not rewarding, skill, talent and effort. Britain is going backwards.

In the final sequence, photogenic Tory grandee Michael Heseltine—Maurice Saatchi's former boss at Haymarket Publishing—said:

> Backwards or forwards? We can't go on as we are. Don't just hope for a better life—vote for one.

Though there is no evidence the PPB shifted the electorate's voting intentions, it raised the profile of Saatchi & Saatchi and put the wind up Labour. Edward Booth-Clibborn, then chairman of D&AD and of Labour's voluntary group, sent a private memorandum on 4 April 1978 to Prime Minister James Callaghan:

> Saatchi & Saatchi are not only London's fastest-growing and most successful agency in financial terms, they are also a force to be reckoned with in the execution of the work they undertake.

Callaghan appears to have been unmoved, but the Saatchi team was now hard at work. Large-scale quantitative and small-scale qualitative research was carried out. Marketing and political jargon intermingled. A group flew off to America to study campaigning methods there. (A pedagogic transatlantic trip is now *de rigueur* for all advertising people working on political campaigns.)

Despite this frenetic activity, the opinion polls showed Labour was recovering, having been way behind the Tories since 1976. Callaghan was expected to call the election in October 1978, and throughout that year the Tory lead shrank. Worried, the Tories planned a poster campaign to re-establish their earlier impetus. In June 1978 Tim Bell presented some poster ideas to Gordon Reece, one of which was headlined 'Labour Isn't Working'. This showed a dole queue snaking out of an unemployment office, with the slogan (in much smaller type) 'Britain's Better Off with the Tories'. 'That's a wonderful ad,' Reece said immediately. Bell presented it to Mrs Thatcher, who simply said 'Wonderful!' Nonetheless the poster almost fell by the wayside. The Tory top brass was nervous about the word 'Labour' being in much larger type than the word 'Tories'. Voters, they feared, would think it was a Labour poster. It almost never ran.

In the event it appeared on just 20 sites in August 1978, on a budget of about £50,000. And it might well have passed unnoticed, but when it appeared Labour leaders hit the roof. Unwisely ignoring David Windlesham's advice after the 1959 election, Denis Healey and other Labour leaders vilified the poster. They claimed the dole queue was made up of Saatchi staff. Bell denied it. They were not unemployed, he admitted, but neither were they Saatchi staff: they were Young Conservatives from South Hendon. This inane dispute put the poster onto every television newscast. Bell estimated it gained £5 million-worth of free publicity (though such estimates are always self-serving claptrap). Tory Party treasurer Lord Thorneycroft later opined that the poster had 'effectively won the election for the Conservatives'. That was claptrap too. During August 1978 Gallup Poll's Labour lead of 4 per cent never wavered.

The real outcome of the poster, if any, is that in September 1978 James Callaghan decided against holding the election the following month—as had been universally expected. He postponed it until April 1979. This was probably a mistake, as the nation's economic situation worsened and there was recurrent union strife. Echoing Shakespeare, that winter was dubbed 'The Winter of Discontent'. So the delay may possibly have cost Labour the election. But that claim too is unsubstantiated. The polls in early winter do show Labour support falling, but its position strengthened as the election came closer.

Neither the Tories nor Labour spent a huge sum on their campaigns. The Tories spent a total of £1.5 million on all forms of advertising (press, posters, and cinema). Saatchi claimed their use of cinema advertising was startlingly original—presumably unaware S. H. Benson had employed cinema advertising for the Tories 44 years earlier in 1935. Labour spent £610,000. In real terms, less was spent in 1979 than had been spent in 1964.

The Tory advertisements which followed 'Labour Isn't Working' said:

'Edukashun Isn't wurking'—chalked by a child on a blackboard.
'Britain Isn't Getting Any Better', showing a hospital queue.
'1984: What would Britain be like after another five years of Labour government?'
'Cheer Up! The Conservatives are Coming'

and there was a T-shirt paying clumsy homage to Smirnoff:

'I thought "On The Rocks" was a drink 'til I discovered Labour Government.'

Except for 'Labour Isn't Working', none of this mishmash left much of a footprint in the sands of time.

But when it comes to election campaigns, it is not the taking part which matters, it is the winning. In May 1979 there was a 5.2 per cent swing to the Tories, which buried Labour. Not since 1931 had Labour seen its share of the vote sink so low. The Tory triumph was ascribed by many to its advertising—a conclusion with which Saatchi & Saatchi did not disagree. But a more considered analysis was provided by the psephologist Professor Ivor Crewe, in his paper 'Why the Conservatives Won', in which the Saatchi advertising is not once mentioned. Instead Crewe writes:

> In any explanation of the Conservative victory one should not underestimate the importance of that most basic of political feelings—after...five years of economic decline, it was time to give 'the other lot' a chance again.

What then does political advertising achieve? The Tories were well ahead in the polls from 1976 onwards, and their popularity dipped during the course of the 1978–9 campaign. From this you might deduce, if you so wished, that political advertising is counterproductive—a view which has been argued by Professor Howard R. Penniman. This seems to me perverse.

There are two basic differences between political and commercial advertising which make the effects of political advertising well nigh impossible to measure. First its discontinuity, and second, the minuscule swings which decide most elections.

Commercial advertisers can and do test their campaigns by stopping advertising in regions of the country, for measured periods—and they expect sizeable sales variances to result. Such controlled experiments are not possible in politics. Were a party to carry out such an experiment during an election—which would be brave to the point of idiocy—who can say whether the results would be repeatable five years later, in completely different circumstances? The likelihood is they would not.

So nobody knows, nobody can know, exactly what election advertising achieves. In Professor Hilde Himmelweit's classic longitudinal study *How Voters Decide* (1985) the word 'advertising' does not appear. The only possibly relevant test I have discovered was carried out in Illinois in 1972. Reporting this test Lynda Lee Kaid begins her paper: 'No classic study of voting behaviour has found political advertising an important determinant of voter decisions.' But her report to some extent contradicts this finding. In the 1972 test newspaper advertisements appear to have swayed approximately 3 per cent of voters from one candidate to another. (There was no broadcast advertising.) But it was a long time ago, it was a local election, turnout was low, and Illinois is not Britain.

So the chances are that advertising encourages a small number of voters to switch sides. It also helps activate the party's activists, and bolsters the support of waverers. Moreover, as I discovered when I helped run the Social Democratic Party's minuscule advertising budget in the early 1980s, voters have come to expect parties to advertise, and they feel any party which does not do so is not really trying. But all these effects are trifling. In an election like that of 1979, when the outcome was a landslide, the advertising was a waste of money. But in a tightly fought election like 1992, when every vote counted, the advertising may well have mattered. So political advertising probably makes a difference to the outcome of an election occasionally—but usually does not. And if the SDP/Liberal Alliance had had more cash to spend on advertising in 1983, when Labour nudged it into third place by a tiny margin, the Alliance might instead have nudged Labour into third place—and the political history of Britain would have been altered forever![8]

My fifth 1970s thumbnail case history is Clunk! Click!, which promoted seat belts. It was never a great award-winner, but like OXO's Katie & Philip campaign it achieved massive public awareness and was much respected within the industry. It exemplifies how governments increasingly used advertising for social engineering during the latter half of the twentieth century. Governments had previously used advertising for recruitment and propaganda in wartime, and to help deal with crises—like water shortages—but by the end of the twentieth century governments had come to use advertising routinely to help combat social problems, and successive governments became the largest advertisers in the country. Governments have used advertising to combat drunken driving, to curb the spread of AIDS, to deter drug taking, to reduce smoking, to encourage crime prevention measures, to minimize the number of accidental fires, to promote blood donations, and for a host of other socially beneficial objectives. The intended outcome of many of these campaigns, in addition to their social benefits, is to save money for the exchequer, and thereby for taxpayers, by reducing the burden of costs to the National Health Service, the police, and the other emergency services. In other words they are intended—like commercial campaigns—to pay off.

[8] The electoral success of the SDP did however prove it is possible for a major British political party to be established—though not perhaps ultimately to win power—with almost no advertising at all.

But they have not been universally welcome. In 1988 Dr Digby Anderson, Director of the Social Affairs Unit, published a polemic titled 'The Megaphone Solution' in which he argued that such campaigns cost a lot but achieve precious little—that they are mere flag-waving, designed to persuade the public the government is doing something about socially intractable problems it has no idea how to solve. At that time around £100 million annually was being spent on government campaigns, and Anderson's polemic immediately prompted parliamentary questions. What was the £100 million achieving? Ironically this happened during Mrs Thatcher's administration, and Thatcher had come to power in 1979 promising to save taxpayers' money by slashing government advertising. (Churchill had promised the same in 1951.) When in opposition Thatcher believed, like many others, that government advertising often has a hidden agenda—that it is deliberately boosted before elections, when the flag-waving is intended to win votes. The evidence for this is scant. If it happens at all it is minimal, and has a less than minimal effect on voters.

Digby Anderson argued that whereas businesses know whether or not their advertising works because they can easily see its effect on sales—something of a simplification—there is no equivalent measurement of the effectiveness of government campaigns. Who knows, he asked, whether drink-drive advertising really stops drivers drinking, or whether the anti-AIDS campaign really curtailed the spread of AIDS?

Almost all government advertising is coordinated by the Central Office of Information (COI), working in harness with the ministerial department sponsoring the campaign. The COI was set up in 1945 by Attlee's Labour government, which believed the state had a responsibility to tell the public what it was doing, and why. Since 1945, successive governments have judged, correctly, that ministries and departments have relatively little advertising expertise, and need a specialist operation—the COI—to help and guide them. This does not always lead to affable relationships between the ministerial departments and the COI, and agencies working for the government need to keep their wits about them when dealing, as they have to, with both. But the COI has generally encouraged high creative standards, and winning business from the COI is an honourable accolade for an agency. The COI handles all government communications—not just advertising—and it has a sizeable market research department. It uses research assiduously to validate its campaigns whenever possible; more assiduously than many businesses.

The story of road safety advertising starts a decade before Clunk! Click!. The first concerted road safety campaign came not from the government, but from the advertising industry itself. It was planned and organized by the IPA, and ran in July–August 1962. This timing was chosen both because summer is the peak driving season, and because the media made no charge for the campaign, and they are happier to give away free advertising when demand is low—that is, during the summer holidays. In fact the media were not ungenerous. ITV, national and provincial newspapers, consumer and trade magazines, posters, the cinema, and even Radio Luxembourg donated free space and time. Direct marketing and door-to-door distributors also mailed and distributed leaflets without charge.

Major advertisers chipped in, and the advertisements were created under the auspices of the IPA, with IPA agencies raising £10,000 towards their production costs. The campaign slogan, which was claimed to have been based on research, was all-embracing but rather feeble: 'REMEMBER! Road Accidents can be caused by people like you.' A panoply of celebrities appeared in the advertisements, all unpaid, including: Acker Bilk, Lord Boothby, Bud Flanagan, Jimmy Greaves, Margaret Lockwood, Cliff Richard, and Peter Sellers. The campaign was endorsed by the Royal Society for the Prevention of Accidents (ROSPA) and by the Minister of Transport, Ernest Marples. It was launched in a blaze of publicity at The Waldorf Hotel on 6 July 1962.

With an advertising message so vague, it would have been astonishing if the campaign had any quantifiable effects on accident rates, and no attempt was made to measure them. However, two separate post-campaign surveys showed public awareness of the campaign reached 'approximately 80 per cent'. This was deemed a great success, but the advertising industry was disheartened that only 8 per cent of the public realized it had run the campaign pro bono. I think it was the first, last, and only public service campaign sponsored by the entire advertising industry, working for nothing.

The first government road safety campaigns ran in 1964 and 1967 (the year the breathalyser was introduced) and were targeted at drunken driving. Both campaigns helped convince the public it was unacceptable to drink and drive, but the conviction was soon forgotten when the campaigns ended. In 1967 the government published a White Paper: 'Road Safety—A Fresh Approach' (Cmnd 3339). The White Paper promised a three-year publicity blitz aimed at cutting road accidents. This was an entirely novel idea: there was no precedent anywhere in the world for such a sustained road safety campaign.

The first decision to be taken was its focus—which types of accident were to be targeted? Having considered the options, three topics were selected:

1. Seat belt wearing
2. Dangerous overtaking and right-turning
3. Pedestrian safety

Commercials for each subject were produced, and the campaign—which combined all three—began in May 1968, principally on television. The attempt to cover so many issues in one campaign was widely criticized, but the government responded that as the different commercials were unified by a single pay-off line—'You *know* it makes sense'—the advertisements would reinforce each other. This sounds unlikely. On completion the campaign was evaluated by research. The seat belt advertising, on which most had been spent, had failed completely. During the campaign belt wearing fell by almost 25 per cent! The dangerous overtaking advertising was hardly more successful, as 'incorrect overtaking' also increased, even though drivers claimed their propensity to overtake had been reduced. The pedestrian advertising did not change pedestrians' awareness of traffic dangers one iota.

Unfortunately the second year's campaign was already underway before these results became available. (Given how disappointing they were, the government may not have exactly rushed to publish them.) However, in the light of the results the campaigns were belatedly adjusted. Less was spent on seat belts and overtaking, and the pedestrian advertising was focused on children. Further changes were made throughout 1969 and 1970. During this time the Ministry of Transport was closed down, and responsibility for road safety was transferred to the new Department of the Environment. In autumn 1970 the DOE reviewed the results. The optimists' conclusion was that the campaigns had heightened public awareness of road safety; the pessimists' conclusion was that casualty rates had not been reduced at all. It was decided three new, separate, campaigns should be tested:

1. A national campaign on child safety
2. A London and South-East campaign on overtaking
3. A North-East campaign on seat belts.

The child safety campaign was aimed at parents and promoted a newly launched 'Green Cross Code'. The overtaking campaign featured TV personality Shaw Taylor, and it claimed overtaking 'was a trip into the unknown'. The seat belt campaign also featured Shaw Taylor and aimed to inculcate the seat belt habit by encouraging drivers to belt up as they entered their car—as the door shut 'Klunk!' the belt went 'Klick!'. All three campaigns ran in summer 1971.

This time casualties were carefully measured. In summary the results were:

1. The Green Cross advertising reduced child casualties by 11 per cent, and the reduction was greatest among 5–9-year-olds, at whom the campaign had been aimed (via their parents). A cost benefit analysis showed the campaign had paid for itself. But the Green Cross Code skidded into trouble with the National Association of Road Safety Instructors, which claimed it was dangerously misleading.
2. The overtaking campaign produced no measurable reduction in accidents or casualties.
3. The seat belt campaign was much the most successful of the three, almost doubling belt wearing among both drivers and front-seat passengers. The increase occurred immediately the campaign started, and was sustained throughout its duration. Moreover drivers' attitudes to belting up improved significantly, even among those who did not bother.

The decision was taken to drive the seat belt campaign forward. In 1972, following a change of advertising agency, Shaw Taylor was replaced by Jimmy Savile; and Klunk-Klick was replaced by Clunk! Click!. The commercials were made more shocking: so much so that three of the six new ones were banned during children's programmes. But the fundamentals of the campaign remained the same. In summer 1972 the Jimmy Savile commercials were tested in two television areas, Granada and Yorkshire TV. Belt wearing increased to the same level as it had previously done in the North East.

Following the two area tests, Clunk! Click! went national in the summer of 1973. Beforehand, about 14 per cent of drivers across the country wore belts. After the summer campaign this rose to 32.4 per cent of drivers, and 36.5 per cent of front-seat passengers. But once again, when the campaigns stopped, belt wearing dropped. This eventually convinced the government seat belt legislation would be essential, as running repeated advertising campaigns proved inefficient and costly. But fortunately the campaigns persuaded even recalcitrant drivers that belt wearing was beneficial, so the government felt confident it could be made obligatory without drivers rebelling *en masse*. In 1983 front seat belt wearing was made compulsory.

The anti-drink-driving advertising, which began in earnest in 1976, can similarly be shown to have contributed significantly to the long-term U-turn in public attitudes to drunken driving. Both these campaigns—and many others since—refute Dr Digby Anderson's concerns and antipathies. The experimental testing and retesting of road safety campaigns, though long-winded and initially rather cack-handed, was an exemplary way to approach complex social engineering issues. Not all government advertising is successful. But neither is all commercial advertising.

The World's Favourite Agency?

Saatchi & Saatchi was not a breakaway. It started with no business other than it brought from Cramer Saatchi, particularly the Health Education Council. It grew faster and larger than any British agency in history—probably faster and larger than any agency, anywhere, ever. It was an advertising and business phenomenon, about which four books by journalists have already been published.[9]

In addition, a welter of features, articles, and news stories has been published all over the world. Few companies can have generated so much global publicity in so short a time.

Saatchi & Saatchi dominated British advertising in various ways for nearly 30 years. How did it achieve so much so quickly, and how did it affect the rest of British advertising?

Three heavy-duty strands wind through the story. The remarkable relationship between the two brothers; Charles Saatchi's manic love affair with, and instinct for, publicity; and Maurice Saatchi's diffident but relentless salesmanship. Naturally there were other factors of great importance—their driving ambition; Charles's creativity; Maurice's business acumen; their ability to spot a trend and leap onto it; their financial impudence; their elastic integrity; their ability to identify and employ talented people (though this was not one of their greatest strengths, as they employed a lot of duds in senior positions too); their workaholic energy; and their luck. But most of those second-layer talents are shared by many other business people. The three heavy-duty strands made them unique.

The bones of the story are well-known. Charles and Maurice Saatchi come from an Iraqi Jewish North London family. Having left school aged 17 in 1960, Charles began working for a small advertising agency which he hated and soon left. After a spell of unemployment he got a job with the London office of the American agency Benton & Bowles, where he first worked with John Hegarty and then teamed up with Ross Cramer. Cramer was 5 years older, and an established art director. Ross and Charles hit it off

---

[9] Philip Kleinman, *The Saatchi & Saatchi Story* (1987); Ivan Fallon, *The Brothers* (1988); Alison Fendley, *Saatchi & Saatchi: The Inside Story* (1995); Kevin Goldman, *Conflicting Accounts: The Creation and Crash of the Saatchi & Saatchi Advertising Empire* (1997). I have used the Fallon and Goldman books extensively as sources.

and moved as a team, from B&B to CDP, in 1966. Leaving CDP after two years, they set up their own creative consultancy. Soon they were producing famous, high-profile campaigns—which Charles publicized with inspired skill.

Maurice, 3 years younger, had won a place at the London School of Economics, where he gained both the Sociology Prize and a First. LSE wanted him to become an academic but he wanted to be a businessman. On graduation he joined the Haymarket Publishing Company, owned and run by Michael Heseltine, one of the brightest young Tory MPs, and his partner Lindsay Masters. Maurice was their personal assistant. He was instrumental in planning the launch of *Campaign*, and did everything from researching new publishing ideas to selling space—at which he swiftly became proficient.

From the vantage point of his creative consultancy, what Charles saw of other agencies did not impress him. He knew he could do better. By early 1970 he itched to open his own shop. Maurice agreed to join him. The agency was to be called Saatchi Cramer Saatchi, but Cramer pulled out as he wanted to make films. Charles and Maurice decided to go it alone, with some of the Cramer Saatchi team, including the exceptionally talented art director John Hegarty, who took over Cramer's role as Charles's partner (though he was never as close to Charles), and Jeremy Sinclair, who became the Saatchi creative director—a role Charles himself shunned.

Initially Charles wanted the agency to employ no account executives: he believed they impeded great creative work, and they hadn't been needed at Cramer Saatchi. (Small advertising agencies often dispense with account executives—and they remain small.) However, from the start Charles wanted a media-buying specialist on staff. At CDP he had learned that creating advertisements and buying media were the two— and the only two—quintessential agency functions. On the media side he approached Paul Green, who was said to be the best in town. Green was about to join the embryo Saatchi agency when he decided to set up MBS instead. As second choice the brothers hired Tim Bell, who was then Media Director at Geers Gross. For Charles and Maurice, being spurned by Paul Green proved the first of many blessings in disguise.

Needing £25,000 capital, the brothers raised it via Lindsay Masters— Maurice's ex-boss at Haymarket—who set up an investment consortium with the fashion designer Mary Quant. Michael Heseltine wanted to join the consortium but had just become a government minister, which barred him. Though Masters acted in a private capacity, these intimate links with Haymarket—and through Haymarket with *Campaign*—would pay off a thousand-fold in the years to come. The start-up agency comprised seven highly talented creative people, plus Maurice and Tim Bell. The creative people were seduced by Charles's manifest flair and by his bullying perfectionism—qualities akin to those of Colin Millward, one of Charles's heroes. Charles and Maurice each owned 40 per cent of the company, the Quant consortium 15 per cent, and the remaining 5 per cent was split between John Hegarty, Tim Bell, and another excellent art director, Ron Collins. From the start Maurice had his eye on floating the agency on the London stock market after five years. In 1970 this was not a radical idea. Lots of other agencies had recently floated.

The agency was launched with what came to be recognized as typical Saatchi chutzpah. On Sunday 13 September 1970 a full-page advertisement appeared in the *Sunday Times*. It cost £6,000, almost a quarter of the agency's capital. The headline was 'Why I think it's time for a new kind of advertising.' Unusually for an advertisement, it had a byline saying it had been written by Jeremy Sinclair. This was untrue. It had been written by Robert Heller, the editor of Haymarket's *Management Today* magazine and a highly respected business journalist. The original intention was that it should be bylined with Heller's name, but Heller got cold feet. A bemused Jeremy Sinclair, who had had nothing to do with the advertisement, was promptly bylined as author.

The advertisement declared Saatchi & Saatchi would not accept the normal 15 per cent agency media commission. Instead clients would be charged 22 per cent. But they would save the extra 7 per cent because Saatchi & Saatchi would buy media more cheaply than any other agency—the Paul Green/Tim Bell role—and produce more effective campaigns. In a still traditional, conservative industry, this was a bomb blast. Nobody had ever asked clients to pay almost 50 per cent above the going rate. Whether any clients ever did so is a moot point. The advertisement declared there would be no account executives—'the middle-men between the advertiser and the people who are paid to create the ads'. Within a year the agency had employed six account executives, doing precisely the job the advertisement had roundly condemned. The advertisement promised the agency would focus on sales, not on images or brand awareness—'images and brand awareness are meaningless if they fail to achieve greater turnover: the test is cash in the till.' Even in 1970 this was old hat. But the advertisement's hard-hitting, radical tone—and the 22 per cent—stunned the advertising world. People started talking about Saatchi & Saatchi.

One of Charles Saatchi's enduring traits is a dislike of the limelight. He ducks being photographed, almost never talks 'on the record' and so can rarely be quoted. This provides him with the aura of mystery those who shun the limelight frequently acquire. The more reticent they are, the more the media try to hunt them down. By avoiding personal publicity Charles became a maestro at getting publicity, both for himself and for anything he is publicizing—first his agency, today his art. He is naturally withdrawn, does not make friends easily, avoids making speeches, rarely accepts social invitations from anyone except intimates. He seldom met Saatchi & Saatchi staff, or clients, once the agency got going. He has a notoriously short fuse. Stories about his temper tantrums are legion, and mostly fanciful. They range from his predilection for throwing agency chairs to attacking a parking warden who gave him a ticket, accusing the functionary of blatant anti-semitism. Those who worked at Saatchi & Saatchi in the early days say Charles assiduously fostered his intemperate image, well aware that to the outside world tantrums equal creativity. But they also feared his anger. One told me 'You'd be scared of going to work in the morning if you knew Charles was in a rage. His face would be menacingly close to yours within minutes.'

Still, in the early days he was capable of grabbing the limelight when it suited him. The week before Saatchi & Saatchi was launched he gave a far from anonymous interview to *Campaign* claiming—fictitiously—his new agency already had £1 million billings. Throughout his career he has courted journalists assiduously—though not by taking them to lunch, as others do. Back at Cramer Saatchi he would learn agencies' secrets, as consultants often do, and leak them to *Campaign*, to ingratiate himself with the journalists. When Saatchi & Saatchi got going he kept his ear to the ground for newsworthy titbits. Occasionally he passed stories to the nationals, especially the *Sunday Times*. In return, the journalists told him about other agencies' unhappy clients, and published puffy stuff about Saatchi & Saatchi.

With the agency launched, the skills Maurice had acquired at Haymarket blossomed. While working for Heseltine and Masters, Maurice had learned to make financial projections for new magazines. Now he made financial projections for the new agency. He had sold advertising space by making 25 cold-calls a day. Now he sold his advertising agency by making 25 cold-calls a day. Being a new agency with a funny name, getting through to prospective clients was tough. But when my secretary went to work for him she was taught to phone prospective clients and ask for them by Christian name 'sounding as much like a sultry mistress as I could—never saying why I was calling, just saying it was very personal—the clients' secretaries always put me through. Then I'd say,

"Mr Smith, I have Maurice Saatchi for you," and I'd click the call through to Maurice before Mr Smith could ring off.' Irritating, but ingenious. Maurice's remorseless focus on new business infused the whole agency. Saatchi & Saatchi never took its foot off the new business accelerator for an instant.

Maurice's projections showed the agency could not achieve a public flotation in five years by organic growth alone. Organic growth—winning new clients and building them up—would be vital, but would be insufficient. If the brothers were to reach their goal, they would need—like Marion Harper, Carl Brunning, and the Kimpher Group before them—to go on a buying spree. The first acquisition, curiously, was a tiny property company called Brogan Developers, in 1972. Then the brothers bought Mitchells, one of the country's oldest agencies, founded in 1836, and a Manchester shop called E. G. Dawes, which they merged with their own Manchester office, set up to handle the nearby Great Universal Stores business they had won. Next they bought two London agencies: Notley Advertising and George J. Smith. Notley was an excellent buy, from which they learned a lot, but G. J. Smith lost them £90,000 at a time when the UK economy was dire, and they could ill afford it. Never daunted by disasters, the brothers ploughed on. Even when the final disaster came at Saatchi & Saatchi, and they were forced out, they still ploughed on.

By now Maurice was writing to agencies throughout the country, offering to buy them. He even approached my small shop. I responded warmly but greedily. I wanted 10 per cent of Saatchi & Saatchi. Maurice politely told me to shove off. When agency chiefs met at parties they cheerfully swopped Maurice's letters. Having learned from the G. J. Smith debacle, he would offer little cash up-front, but a generous 'earn-out' paid in instalments, based on the attainment of future profits. Maurice did not invent this earn-out system, as is sometimes claimed, but he used it skilfully. Every agency he bought at this stage was absorbed into Saatchi & Saatchi, which was unusual. Even more unusually, Maurice boasted that nobody was ever fired after a Saatchi acquisition. This negated one of the main financial benefits of buying and merging agencies, the reduction of overheads—to whit, staff. But Maurice was farsighted enough to know he would need to go on buying agencies, and nobody would sell to him if word spread that he decimated his purchases.

Meanwhile Saatchi & Saatchi was winning clients and creative awards, and Charles vigorously publicized its successes—most real, some less so. With Maurice running the finances and the acquisitions, and Charles running the creative department, together with Jeremy Sinclair, Tim Bell managed the agency and grew increasingly powerful. He was clever, charming, and a masterful presenter. Things were bright and beautiful. Unexpectedly, in 1975 the brothers were approached by Compton UK Partners, the agency group which in 1972 had floated on the stock market via the reverse takeover of Birmingham Crematorium (complete with grisly bone-crusher).

Compton UK was still controlled by its New York parent Compton Advertising Incorporated, which held 49 per cent of its shares. But Compton UK was sick. This was partly because the UK's economy was sick, but mainly because the company itself was ailing. The group's London agency, Garland-Compton, had an undistinguished creative reputation and was winning no new business. Among its clients were major advertisers like Procter & Gamble and Rowntree, but its billings were static and its profits falling. Chairman Kenneth Gill had concluded the agency needed to revamp itself by gobbling up a small, creative hotshop. This conclusion is frequently reached by large, stagnating, usually American, agencies in London. Sometimes such revamps work, more often they do not. Saatchi & Saatchi was not Compton's first choice. The large, conformist agency felt the two Jewish whizz-kids to be too brash, flash, and vulgar. But when Compton's preferred choices rejected them, in desperation Gill contacted the brothers. What he found impressed him a lot.

Though initially reluctant, the brothers soon came to realize a deal with Compton would be an unmitigated blessing. 'It's a marriage made in heaven,' Maurice told his elder brother. For them, the potential benefits were immeasurable. They would immediately be part of a major international network, as Compton Incorporated owned 20 overseas offices. They would be publicly quoted. They would leap up the agency billings league. The brothers knew they were London's hottest creative shop, but also knew they lacked marketing skills, and so had been unable to attract major packaged goods advertisers. Compton would bring them such advertisers. On the other side, before the deal, Gill consulted his agency's largest clients. They said they would not interfere.

The marriage with Compton may have been made in heaven, but to get there it went through hell. During the negotiations the brothers insisted the new agency be called Saatchi & Saatchi Garland-Compton, though Compton was taking over Saatchi & Saatchi. Kenneth Gill responded by insisting the new agency should occupy the Compton offices in Charlotte Street—important both symbolically and practically, as staff numbers ramped up from 100 (in Saatchi & Saatchi) to 280—quite a hike from the 9 the brothers had started with 5 years earlier. Despite Maurice's belief in holding on to staff, several of Garland-Compton's senior people soon quit—mostly because they were effectively demoted when Saatchi staffers were given the top jobs.

Throughout London advertising people predicted—hoped, prayed—the merger would flop, and the smart-arse brothers would get their comeuppance. The situation was aggravated by Charles's incestuous relationship with *Campaign*. In no uncertain terms, *Campaign* portrayed the deal as a Saatchi takeover. In reality the brothers now owned 36 per cent of the new agency—a hefty slug, but not control. Yet on 26 September 1975 *Campaign's* front page screamed, 'Saatchi swallows up the Compton Group.' In New York, Compton Incorporated went through the roof. In London Kenneth Gill went through the roof. Garland-Compton's staff would have liked to have gone through the roof, as would Garland-Compton's clients—it was not what any of them had been promised. But doubtless Charles was happy. These were just difficulties to be overcome.

And they were. During the following three years the Saatchi team brilliantly exploited the opportunities the merger provided. One of the Garland-Compton casualties was the agency's finance director. His place was taken by a chap named Martin Sorrell. Sorrell was one of the brothers' ace recruitments. New business poured in. Assignments came from Schweppes, Sainsbury, British Leyland, BP, Black & Decker, British Rail, Du Pont, and the Central Office of Information, plus extra business from former Garland-Compton advertisers including Procter & Gamble, United Biscuits, Bristol Myers, and Rowntree—who thus demonstrated they were happy with the merger. But still the brothers could not shake off their capricious image. A survey among 248 of the top 500 advertisers in 1978 showed that when advertisers were asked which agencies were likely to produce highly creative advertising, Saatchi easily led the field, with 84 per cent of advertisers' votes. But when advertisers were asked which agencies produced reliable advertising, JWT remained far out in front, with 82 per cent of advertisers' votes, while Saatchi was in 11th place, with only 46 per cent.

Still, they leapt up the billings table. In 1975 the newly merged agency shot to 4th in the agency league, with £30.5 million billings. Good, but not good enough. Charles was fanatical about reaching the top. He insisted this would bring big business benefits, as no advertiser would be able to ignore Britain's biggest agency when moving his account. But this is nonsense: the ambition was as irrational as it was powerful. Charles employed an assistant whose principal task was to manipulate the published billings figures, as far as possible, to get Saatchi to the top—and ahead of JWT in particular. Charles got his wish. The agency clambered up the league table each year, reaching the pinnacle in 1979, with £67.5 million billings.

In 1978 acquisitions restarted, and in 1979 the brothers came within an ace of buying CDP—one of the few acquisitions in which Charles took a close personal interest. But the deal fell through. As a more than adequate consolation prize, that same year the Tories won the election, which made Saatchi and Saatchi one of the most famous advertising agencies in the world.

While the benefits of fame may be intangible, the benefit of working for the Tories delivered hard cash within a couple of years. John King, the formidable head of British Airways, was one of Mrs Thatcher's favourite businessmen. King was certainly aware of Saatchi's handling of the 1979 election campaign. Though Thatcher may not have been personally involved in the appointment—any such involvement has always been strenuously denied—Saatchi won the BA account, worth £25 million. But Tim Bell was not amused. Though he now held the grand title of Chairman and Chief Executive of Saatchi & Saatchi Compton Worldwide, he had not been consulted about the BA pitch, not least because he personally handled the British Caledonian account, and BCal was BA's leading UK competitor. Bell knew BCal would have to be ditched, and he was furious. A chasm opened up between Bell and the brothers.

For BA the agency came up with the slogan 'The World's Favourite Airline'. Its Spielberg-inspired first commercial, in which Manhattan Island floated loftily through the sky and was talked down by air traffic control at Heathrow, might easily have been an embarrassing shambles, but directed by Richard Loncraine it was breathtaking, and was hailed an international creative triumph. Saatchi's creativity was now established worldwide—though it was built on a typically shaky tripod. Everyone knew Charles Saatchi had created three of the most celebrated advertisements in modern history. Except he hadn't. One: the Health Education Council's Pregnant Man (this was created at Cramer Saatchi by Jeremy Sinclair and Bill Atherton, before Saatchi & Saatchi started). Two: the Tory's 'Labour Isn't Working' poster (this was written by Andrew Rutherford, art directed by Martyn Walsh, and like Labour probably didn't work). And three: British Airways 'Manhattan Island' (written by Rita Dempsey and art directed by Phil Mason). Thus was tiresome reality obfuscated by the Saatchi creative reputation. But would these campaigns have come about without Charles's guiding spirit? Unlikely.

What made the Saatchis run? Whatever the wisdom of hindsight may claim, it is clear the brothers had no idea the way things would turn out. Opportunism, ambition, optimism, and lucky breaks all played their part. But the three entwined heavy-duty strands carried the enterprise forward.

First, the brothers. Charles is a seer, utterly uninterested in management. Maurice executed Charles's seemingly impossible dreams with skill and determination. It was a potent amalgam. But the relationship was not easy. Charles publicly abused, bullied, and humiliated his younger brother— 'How could we have come from the same womb?' was one of his refrains. Maurice rode these below-the-belt punches as nobody but a loving brother would. Within family businesses, family members are often far more brutal to each other than mere colleagues dare to be. Charles goaded Maurice to achieve more and more. Others would have quit. Maurice achieved more and more. Their talents interlocked—and nobody could slide a sheet of tracing paper between them. Despite the rows, their fiery loyalty to each other was uncompromising.

Second was Charles's compulsive love of media coverage. Most top agency people work hard at getting media coverage, it is their form of advertising. But Charles was manic. He phoned *Campaign*'s editor—an ever-changing pageant—almost every day, sometimes two or three times a day, to leak off-the-record stories and manage Saatchi news. He would chat to the editor for hours. He has an exceptional nose for a newsworthy story, real or invented. His flair for news mirrors his flair for advertising.[10] Charles senses what will capture and captivate customers and readers alike. He has a gut-feel for what is hackneyed, what is boring, in news and in advertising (and in art). He stays in the shadows and exploits the news media brilliantly.

Third was Maurice's salesmanship. At school Maurice's cleverness was combined with shyness, and later with diffidence. He is no hail-fellow-well-met glad-hander, but a quietly seductive chap who wins trust and confidence. Iraqi he may be, but his salesmanship is quintessentially British. Thoughtful, diligent, he does his homework, makes his notes, reads his speeches word-for-word. Time and again advertisers pay tribute to him as 'a chap they can rely on', a loyal business advisor. But Maurice is no *soi-disant* academic, like John Hobson or Simon Broadbent. He is a go-getter, a snappy dresser. This too is a rare combination of qualities: a restrained, reflective, high-pressure salesman. But his charm seldom extends to those unlikely to be of use to him. He fails to return their calls, and famously looks over people's shoulders at parties, searching for more influential people to talk to. Not everyone finds this endearing.

---

[10] Several of the greatest advertising men—including Leo Burnett, Charles Havas, Albert Lasker, and Raymond Rubicam—started as journalists before switching to advertising.

As the agency grew larger, one other key factor made Saatchi & Saatchi unique: it had no advertising philosophy. In some ways this was the most crucial factor of all.

Previous agency empire builders fervently believed they had discovered advertising's Golden Key, or Golden Keys: how to create perfect advertising. Each had his own advertising philosophy. The Saatchis had no such pretensions. To quote their 1977 Annual Report:

> *Our approach to advertising*
> . . . the agency does not adopt any 'house style' or 'tone of voice'. We believe that a hard sell is suitable for some situations, mood and imagery for others, humour for others. Our advertising has only one linking factor—it tries to make a single minded proposition 'come alive' in a compelling way.

This is a restatement of Ted Bates's USP philosophy, by then broadly accepted by almost all agencies. The 1977 Annual Report goes on to say the agency has:

> A belief in excellence . . . Our aim in all of our activities is the avoidance of the average and the achievement of the excellent . . . All our standards are set by the 'norm'—whatever that is, there is a better way.

None of this could remotely be called an advertising philosophy. It is motherhood and apple pie. It is so commonplace it would be surprising if Charles Saatchi had bothered to read it. One guesses he left Annual Reports to his brother.

The brothers' oft-quoted leitmotif was 'Nothing is Impossible!'—but this is no agency philosophy either. It is a Boy Scout-ish, ra-ra mantra. It reflected their refreshing vigour, and motivated staff, but it has nothing particularly to do with advertising. The nearest the agency came to an advertising philosophy was its espousal of globalization. After the Compton deal the agency banged the globalization drum to persuade large global advertisers that Saatchi & Saatchi was no longer just a titchy British hotshop, but had a serious multinational network—a network which understood the challenges facing multinational corporations. But globalization is not an advertising philosophy. It is no help in the creation of effective campaigns. On the contrary, many advertising people—including almost certainly the younger Charles Saatchi—are firmly convinced globalization results in less effective campaigns.

Not only did the founders of other mighty agencies have their own credos about advertising, they also tried to define and promulgate them, so their clients and staff could grasp them. Not Charles, nor Maurice. Ivan Fallon writes in *The Brothers*:

Charles has no interest in philosophising or intellectualising about advertisements . . . to the Saatchis advertising is either 'terrific' or 'shit'.

Responses which, while doubtless heartfelt, are hardly philosophical.

Lacking any coherent, constraining convictions (except the importance
of bigness) the agency was able to acquire and integrate a host of other
agencies—agencies which approached the advertising craft in different
ways—without upsetting those agencies' clients. They were able to handle
simultaneously advertising for the Health Education Council and for
Procter & Gamble, for the Tories and for Dixons' shops. They consistently
produced remarkably good work, but little of it was radical. None of this
belittles their massive achievements, but they were not innovators. They
were supreme exploiters of well-trodden paths—living proof of Andrew
Carnegie's famous maxim: 'It's better to be a follower than a pioneer. The
pioneers got scalped.' And when, later, they had a crack at being pioneers,
they got scalped.

6

The Nineteen-Eighties: Brits Buy Up the Business

Bigger Still and Bigger

If the 1970s particularly celebrated British creative triumphs, the 1980s particularly celebrated British financial triumphs. On 2 July 1989 the *New York Times Magazine* devoted its front page to an 8-page feature titled 'BRITS BUY UP THE AD BUSINESS'. The Saatchis and Martin Sorrell's WPP had taken large bites out of the Big Apple.

True, Britain's creativity continued to flower, and much of the 1970s impetus surged on into the 1980s. The first half of the decade introduced the public to Tosh, as in 'Hello Tosh, Gotta Toshiba?'; to J R Hartley endlessly scouring the Yellow Pages for his fishing book; to Lego's much-garlanded Lego 'Kipper' commercial; and to Arkwright, the flat-capped, phlegmatic hero of the John Smith Bitter campaign which ran for nine years. Two excellent campaigns retouched Hollywood: the first for Swan Vestas matches, in which Clark Gable and Jean Harlow among others cosied-up to the iconic matchbox; the second for Holsten Pils, in which Griff Rhys Jones co-starred with Humphrey Bogart, John Wayne, James Cagney, George Raft, and Barbara Stanwyck in a series of brilliantly tricked-up beer commercials. In 1985 the defining commercial at the end of the extended summit of British creativity was for Levi's 501s, when Nick Kamen stripped off to his boxers in a launderette, blissfully oblivious of the other customers, while Marvin Gaye 'Heard It Through The Grapevine'. There was more first-rate stuff to come—but much of it was for campaigns which had started in the 1970s.

The creative agency world was dominated by three creative leaders. David Abbott, at Abbott Mead Vickers, where he became a partner in November 1977; Frank Lowe, who left CDP and launched Lowe Howard-Spink in May 1981; and John Hegarty, who had been one of Charles Saatchi's most talented collaborators and was a founding partner of Bartle Bogle Hegarty in March 1982. Their agencies were spiritual descendants of CDP—directly in one case, indirectly in the other two. Like CDP, Abbott, Lowe, and Hegarty have an innate distaste for vulgar advertising. None of them would want—nor even know how—to produce pushy detergent commercials or Prices-Slashed-Buy-Buy-Buy! retail campaigns, of the kind Saatchi & Saatchi could happily turn its hand to when necessary. But only Lowe's shop matched the initial dynamism of CDP in the 1960s, leaping into the agency league top ten by the end of the 1980s.

Also toward the end of the decade, led by the Butterfield Day Devito Hockney agency, seven new shops opened for business, dubbing them-selves the 'Third-Wave'. The Third-Wave offered the frothy promise of wonderful creativity combined with wonderfully efficient client service—but the wave failed to reach the shore, and within a few years all seven had sunk without trace.

The most momentous agency developments of the 1980s had little or nothing to do with advertising creativity, or even with media-buying. Following a series of massive acquisitions, Saatchi & Saatchi became the world's largest agency. And their ex-finance director Martin Sorrell turned a tiny engineering company called Wire and Plastic Products into an advertising holding company, which zoomed from almost non-existent to humungous in four years. That was how Sorrell found himself, together with his former agency colleagues, on the front page of the *New York Times Magazine* in 1989 'BUYING UP THE AD BUSINESS'.

The most momentous developments in the media world had nothing to do with creativity either. On television, competition to ITV finally arrived in the shape of Channel 4 and TV-am, followed by the UK's first multi-channel broadband cable system, and by Sky TV—which was, astonishingly, hardly noticed at first. Having got the competitive television market they had long begged for, advertisers and agencies promptly grumbled about the fragmen-tation of TV audiences—a problem as mythical as the unicorn. In print media the only change of real significance to advertising was Rupert Mur-doch's relocation of Times Newspapers to Wapping, with the concomitant collapse of the Fleet Street print unions. But there was lots of less substantial hustle and bustle. Robert Maxwell bought the *Daily Mirror*, Conrad Black bought the Telegraph Group, Andreas Whittam-Smith launched

The Independent. And an ex-Robert Sharps media-buyer called David Sullivan launched the *Sunday Sport* because, he said, it was impossible to get really rich working in an advertising agency.

Murdoch's move was a direct consequence of Margaret Thatcher's union-shackling legislation. Thatcher also impacted advertising with another groundbreaking economic change. Out of the blue came a totally new advertising sector: the nationalized industries—being privatized. Privatization on this scale had never before been attempted anywhere in the world. And the subsequent upheaval in the structure of the UK economy could not have happened, at least not in the satisfactory way it did, without advertising.

The 1980s are remembered as the 'me decade', the selfish decade, the greed decade, the Thatcher decade. Pay packets, bonuses, options, and the stock market soared—until Black Monday in October 1987, when US economic troubles triggered a worldwide plunge in shares, beginning the decline that led to the 1989–91 recession. At almost exactly the same time—in one of history's nice ironies—the Berlin Wall fell, largely because people living under the hammer and sickle wanted to share in the largesse of capitalism. Shortly after the Berlin Wall fell, the IPA was invited to Moscow to teach the Russians about Western advertising.

During the 1980s computer graphics, electronic design, and digital retouching grew commonplace: a major innovation, but not one that was British or specific to advertising, though it spawned several innovative campaigns. In most other respects the 1980s reflected consolidation rather than innovation. Having slowly spread to the leading British agencies, account planning began to be recognized and adopted abroad. The IPA Effectiveness Awards gained purchase and built their authoritative reputation. The ASA went from strength to strength. Independent media-buyers became respectable, their share of the media-buying market increased sharply, and the separation of creative from media-buying agencies continued apace.

Throughout the decade advertising expenditure grew strongly (Table 7) and in 1989, before the recession began, it reached 1.53 per cent of the GNP, a level not exceeded until the brief dot.com boom ten years later (when it reached its highest level ever).

Media Mayhem

In November 1980 a new Broadcasting Act extended the life of the Independent Broadcast Authority for a further sixteen years, and paved the

Table 7. Total advertising expenditure as % of GNP

	Expenditure (at current prices) £million	% GNP (at market prices)
1980	2,604	1.12
1982	3,211	1.15
1984	4,188	1.29
1986	5,328	1.38
1988	7,085	1.50
1990	7,946	1.44

Note: From 1980 onwards the Advertising Association included expenditures on Direct Mail advertising within its published data, but the above figures have been adjusted to exclude Direct Mail, to be comparable with the earlier, and later, tables herein.

Source: Advertising Association.

way for the introduction of both Channel 4 and a breakfast channel. The following month the IBA announced a new set of television contracts, to run for eight years. At the regional level these contracts amounted to little more than a shuffling of the cards. But the contract for the new breakfast channel was awarded to TV-am, to start in May 1983. This long lead-time was designed to give the new Channel 4 time to launch in November 1982, and to get established. In May 1981 the government announced plans for the introduction of both satellite and cable television. At last ITV was going to suffer real competition.

Channel 4 had been a battleground. Advertisers wanted a bloodthirsty competitor to ITV. ITV's monopoly power had long made them feel taken for granted, not to say taken for a ride. The ITV companies, predictably, wanted to control the new station, fearing competition would slash their revenues—which, they argued, would mean a concomitant drop in pro-gramme standards. But Home Secretary William Whitelaw dashed both sides' hopes when he stated the government's position at the Royal Tele-vision Society conference in September 1979, saying:

> The conclusion I have reached is that competition for advertising on the two channels would inevitably move towards single-minded concentration on maxi-mising the audience for programmes, with adverse consequences for both of the commercial channels and, before long, for the BBC.

Advertisers and agencies were incensed. ITV was incensed. But the die was cast. The success of the new channel would depend on its ability to attract small, specialized audiences, which could be provided to advertisers inexpensively. Jeremy Isaacs was appointed chief executive of the new channel. ('The job of a lifetime was mine,' Isaacs says in his autobiography *Look Me In The Eye*, 2006.) Isaacs, a pugnacious Jewish Scot, was an experienced and headstrong programme maker who had worked for three commercial television companies and for the BBC. He recruited his own people to the key C4 jobs without consulting anyone else. ('The Board, the Chairman particularly, were furious with me.') He then set about realizing Whitelaw's aim, which he totally shared—'to cater for substantial minorities presently neglected' as he put it. None was a mass audience in itself, but in aggregate they totted up to a worthwhile total. This was sufficiently radical to bring C4 and Isaacs into constant conflict with their detractors. Comedians and cartoonists, politicians and press, invented ludicrous C4 series—'Sisal-weaving in Uzbekistan' or 'Backgammon for lesbians'—as they lambasted the new channel. Isaacs held his ground. Today such minority programming is nothing special. But Isaacs and C4 got there first, and established how well it could be done.

Channel 4 (including the Welsh language fourth channel S4C) began transmitting in November 1982 as planned. Despite the mockery, the launch was soon hailed a success. Within a year C4 had gained 5 per cent of total viewership, and pushed up commercial television's market share commensurately. The launch of C4 was expected to be catastrophic but was a small triumph. The launch of TV-am was expected to be a triumph but was catastrophic.

Together with ex-civil servant and journalist Peter Jay, five of Britain's most celebrated television broadcasters—Anna Ford, David Frost, Robert Kee, Michael Parkinson, and Angela Rippon—set up the TV-am company to apply for the breakfast broadcasting licence, and dazzled the IBA. Having won the contract, TV-am planned to go on air in May 1983, but when they heard the BBC would be starting its breakfast broadcasts ahead of them, TV-am's launch was pulled forward to 1 February. The BBC still beat them to the punch, launching on 17 January.

The TV-am launch generated mountains of publicity, most of it unfavourable. The Famous Five, it seemed, were not a happy bunch. The first viewing figures, published at the end of February, did nothing to cheer them up. The BBC had twice as many viewers as its glamorous competitor. Immediately commentators opined that sensitive British digestions could not wolf down commercials with their corn flakes, and so the project was doomed. Within six weeks internal ructions led to the resignation of the chairman and chief executive Peter Jay. Jay was replaced by the Tory politician Jonathan Aitken. More well-publicised rows ensued, and four weeks later Jonathan Aitken was replaced by his cousin Timothy Aitken. By this time, less than three months after the launch, all the Famous Five who had so dazzled the IBA had followed Peter Jay out the door, Anna Ford and Angela Rippon having been sacked.

A new editor-in-chief from London Weekend Television, Greg Dyke, was appointed at the beginning of May, when the BBC's share of breakfast viewing was 85 per cent, and TV-am's was 15 per cent. Then the recovery began. In July the TV-am audience share reached 32 per cent, and in August it jumped to 52 per cent, helped by Roland Rat, who captured the children's school-holiday audience. At last TV-am was winning larger audiences than the BBC. Advertisers gained confidence and booked time. The British, it transpired, had no difficulty consuming commercials with their corn flakes.

With C4 and TV-am performing well, the pressure was now on the BBC. Why, commentators increasingly asked, is the Corporation forbidden to carry commercials? This had been mooted in 1934 and been powerfully opposed by Lord Reith. Unsurprisingly advertisers and agencies were—and have always been—much in favour of the BBC carrying advertising. It would provide another mass medium, and the competition with the commercial stations would force down advertising costs. Equally unsurprisingly, the commercial stations and all other media have been unremittingly hostile. So far, and happily as far as I am personally concerned, governments of all hues have refused to countenance the notion.

On a smaller scale, 1983 was also a crucial year for the press. In Warrington a regional newspaper publisher, Eddie Shah, decided to install computer printing technology, which would cut costs and numbers employed at his Messenger Group. The unions responded fiercely. The Messenger Group was besieged each night by up to 10,000 furious trade unionists. At first even the police kept away because they were so scared of them. The Messenger Group hired three bouncers, with dogs, to protect its 140 staff—but was told by the police to desist, as the dogs might attack the union pickets. For seven months the battle raged, and a national poll showed 85 per cent of the public backed Shah. Then Shah used Margaret Thatcher's new legislation to sequester the unions' funds. The unions surrendered forthwith.

Watching all this from afar was Rupert Murdoch, who supported Shah throughout. Like Roy Thomson before him, Murdoch was exasperated by the antediluvian British print unions—but unlike Thomson he could do something about it. Camouflaging the truth with phoney rumours of a forthcoming 24-hour newspaper, during 1985 Murdoch's

News International company built a major new production plant in East London. Everyone knew something was afoot, but knew not what. Until the very last moment, only the company's most senior management had any inkling what was really happening.

Seemingly out of the blue, on 23 January 1986 News International transferred its entire newspaper production from its old, union-riddled, 'hot metal' plant near Fleet Street to its new, high-tech computerized plant in Wapping. The unions were first startled, then enraged. Four thousand members of the Society of Graphic and Allied Trades went on strike. They were promptly sacked. They picketed the plant *en masse* to stop distribution of the newspapers, but the Thatcher legislation empowered police to ensure the papers got out and away. In February, in the worst of the violence, police wearing anti-riot gear clashed with several thousand pickets, and people on both sides were badly injured. Production and distribution continued unabated. So did the nightly battles. Several Murdoch journalists defected to the union side. But when union funds were sequestrated, and their cars impounded, they once again capitulated. Murdoch had slashed British newspaper production costs forever.

The way was now open for other publishers to take advantage of his victory. After loss-making decades, national newspapers found themselves on far firmer financial footings. Better still, from the advertisers' point of view, the real cost of press advertising fell every year for the next five years—while television rates rose, until the recession bit hard at the end of 1989.

From having been an industry suffering incessant closures, in the three years after the Wapping move more than half a dozen new national and London newspapers were launched, of which three remain in publication two decades later. In 1986 Andreas Whittam-Smith and two ex-*Daily Telegraph* colleagues launched *The Independent*, a new quality daily which—together with the *Independent on Sunday*—is still with us, despite many vicissitudes which seemed certain to destroy it. That same year David Sullivan launched *Sunday Sport*. It too is still with us.

An Insane Irrelevance?

As has been seen, playing Knock-the-Adman has been a popular intellectual parlour game for as long as admen have existed. Fresh antagonists constantly take potshots, unaware most of their new attacks are shabby old hats. But every so often an antagonist raises criticisms which deserve serious attention.

Professor Raymond Williams's essay 'Advertising: The Magic System' qualifies handsomely. Williams was an influential Marxist academic, social commentator, novelist, and critic, and his essay was published in *Problems in Materialism and Culture* (1980). For Williams, one of the central problems in materialism and culture was advertising.

Sharing the stance of many consumerists, Williams argued that far from being too materialistic, modern advertising is not materialistic enough, because the images with which advertisements surround goods deliberately detract attention from the goods' material specifications: 'If we were sensibly materialist we should find most advertising to be an insane irrelevance.' However, he says—more or less accurately—that in the nineteenth century advertisements were generally factual and informative, except for fraudulent patent medicine and toiletry advertisements, which had already adopted the undesirable practices which later became common. In other words Williams was not attacking all advertising, just most present-day advertisements.

Why, he asked, do advertisements which should be promoting the material benefits of the goods they represent, exploit 'deep feelings of a personal and social kind'? It is because—here he echoes J. K. Galbraith—the concentration of economic power into ever larger units forces these units to make human beings consume more and more, in order for the units to stay operational. At this point he parts company with the consumerists. 'The fundamental choice, in the problems set to us by modern industrial production, is between man as a consumer and man as a user.' He argues that usage is continuous—today we might say sustainable—but consumption is inherently destructive. The emphasis on consumers and consumption rather than on users and usage is an emphasis on destruction, and this emphasis occurs because destruction is necessary to keep the wheels of industry turning. (Quite how we can use liquorice allsorts without consuming them Williams neglects to explain, but we'll let that pass.)

Like Christopher Mayhew (page 99), his central point is that many human needs—'hospitals, schools, quiet'—are out of phase with an industrialized society. So the industrialized society uses advertising to focus attention on its industrial output, and to distract humanity from its non-industrial aspirations. This, he says, is why modern advertisements usurp our sexual and emotional desires, our weaknesses and our fears, attaching them to goods and services. It is akin to the voodoo of the primitive magic man—hence the essay's title: it diverts the tribe towards inessential needs.

On the surface it is a seductive argument. Naturally I think it wrong. ('It must not be assumed', Williams writes, pre-empting me, 'that magicians—in this case advertising agents—disbelieve their own magic.') It is wrong because while the usage of some goods—spectacles, say, or paintings—does not destroy them, the usage of most goods does destroy them, however slowly. And that is as well, because the 'the fundamental choice' is not, as Williams posits it, 'between man as consumer and man as user', but between man as consumer and man as producer (the male chauvinism is his, not mine). Williams correctly says advertising keeps the industrial wheels turning. But if the industrial wheels stopped turning the result would be mass unemployment.

Above all Williams is wrong because, as has been argued in previous chapters, insofar as advertising emphasizes emotional and sexual desires, fears and weaknesses—far less than he supposes—this is not merely because human beings inevitably have emotional relationships with material goods, but because most material goods have no intrinsic value; they are simply means to ends. People do not buy drills because they want drills, they buy drills because they want holes. It is the benefits material goods provide which matter, and these benefits may be emotional, or may be material. But whether you agree or disagree with him, unlike the whacky Professor Wilson Bryan Key's bawdy allegations, Professor Williams' case is neither irrational nor indefensible.

Capitalism for All

Immediately Margaret Thatcher came to power in 1979 Sir Keith Joseph, one of her closest and cleverest colleagues, pledged the government to return nationalized industries to private ownership. Thatcher and her supporters were convinced state owned industries were inherently undesirable—particularly when they were monopolies, as most British nationalized industries were.

Returning publicly owned companies to private ownership was not a new idea. *The Economist* coined the word 'privatization' in 1936, and travel agents Thomas Cook, which had been owned by the state, was privatized in 1972. Nonetheless Sir Keith's pledge was rash. (Though immensely clever, he was often unwise.) Thomas Cook was a small company, easy to sell off. But in 1979 several of the state owned companies were among the largest in Britain. They were—as the Tories rightly claimed—poorly managed, over-staffed, unprofitable or hardly profitable, and had been starved of investment for years as successive governments had milked them. Who would want to buy these lumbering dinosaurs? Not the so-phisticated financial sector, where investors knew they could easily obtain faster, safer, and bigger returns. Nor would privatizations be universally popular. Many of the public, heirs to the 1945–51 Attlee government's legacy, firmly believed public utilities and 'the commanding heights of the economy' ought to be owned by the people, via the state. To them, this was not negotiable. For Thatcher, Joseph, and their cohorts, privatization was not negotiable. It was the only way to modernize British industry, to ensure Britain did not slough into an economic backwater. It had to be done. The public must be persuaded.

The privatizations started tentatively. Between 1980 and the summer of 1984, fourteen relatively small companies were privatized. The largest was Britoil (November 1982) which went for £549 million. The companies were floated in the traditional way, through City institutions, with prospectus advertising in financial publications. However, to minimize public hostil-ity to the sell-offs (and to raise as much money as possible) small investors were urged to buy shares and reap the rewards of capitalism. This too was part of the Thatcher creed. By way of wider share ownership the public—the electorate—would be wedded to the market economy: everyone—every voter—would partake of its fruits. Depending on your political perspective, this can be seen either as cynical electoral manipulation or as economic democracy in action. Doubtless it was a bit of both—but initially it did not work. Some smaller investors applied for the privatiza-tion shares but sold them again within weeks. This was no way to build wider share ownership.

Following Thatcher's post-Falkland war electoral triumph in 1983, her re-elected government decided to attack privatization more forcefully. British Telecommunications would be privatized in 1984. Although only 49 per cent of BT was to be sold off, the sale would be about 8 times larger than Britoil, the previous largest. BT would be by far the biggest privatiza-tion ever: a massive challenge, and a massive risk.

Every flotation, big or small, is a challenge and a risk. The company is valued, and a price is set for the shares. Despite the skill and experience of professional financiers, fixing the value is not a science, it is a matter of hunch and judgement. If investors think the shares have been overvalued they will walk away. Normally the City handles such debacles as quietly as possible. But for a huge government flotation like BT such a failure could not be hidden—and consequently could not contemplated. The BT privatization had to succeed. This could not be achieved in the traditional way, with advertising in financial papers to professional investors. The public would have to buy into the privatization, in a huge way.

The first task was to make the public feel BT was a company worth investing in. This would not be easy. A MORI survey in September 1983 showed the public image of BT was lodged firmly between humdrum and lousy. BT was seen to provide a reasonably good service, but charged too much; was neither polite nor helpful; and was slow to respond when help was needed. BT was thought to spend too little on Research & Development, and was not even attempting to become more efficient. These were not the characteristics of a company in which punters—even unsophisticated punters—would rush to invest their cash.

To groom BT for privatization the government was already investing heavily in capital projects designed to ensure the company could provide the most modern high-tech services—but this had not got through to the public. BT's agency for corporate advertising, Dorland, was briefed to run a campaign—'The Power Behind The Button'—which would communicate BT's technological revolution. BT spent £16 million on the campaign, and within a year BT's image had improved radically (Table 8).

Following the clear success of 'The Power Behind The Button', the government pressed ahead with the BT privatization. Handling this campaign would be tricky, not least because the law controls company flotations tightly. Share prospectus advertising is not permitted on television—and nor is paid-for political advertising. Privatization advertisements could easily be seen to be either share prospectuses, or political advertising

Table 8. Public Image of BT (September 1983 = 100)

	September 1983	August 1984
Use most up-to-date technology	100	140
Provide good service	100	112
Charge too much	100	89
Spend a lot on R&D	100	142
Doing a lot to become efficient	100	143
Polite and helpful	100	116
Essential to Britain's success	100	130
Good value for money	100	125

Source: IPA Effectiveness Awards Paper, 1986.

(or both). Dorland chairman and chief executive Jack Rubins had his work cut out persuading the IBA to allow the privatization campaign to appear on television, which both Dorland and the government believed to be crucial. The flotation was scheduled for November 1984 and would be do or die: there would be no second chance.

But the public felt share ownership to be a prerogative of the affluent. The great majority of the population were savers rather than investors (Table 9).

Table 9. Personal savings and investments (March 1984)

	% of adults 15+
Own stocks and shares	6
Savings in building societies	54
Savings account in a bank	34
Have life insurance policy	44

Source: BMRB Target Group Index, quoted in IPA 1986 paper.

To raise £3,900 million—for the 49 per cent of BT on offer—and to build wider share ownership, it would be necessary roughly to double the number of people who owned shares, from 6 per cent to 12 per cent. To put the £3,900 million into perspective, the private investment sector raised just £1,400 million from all new equity issues, in total, that year. The BT target was daunting, perhaps unachievable. Within the government people got rattled. There were wrangles, fissures, compromises. The *Sunday Times* ran a headline warning 'City Fears BT Disaster'. Dorland feared the City had already decided to oppose the flotation. An especial effort was then put into convincing the City, and financial journalists, the shares would be well worth buying—hard to establish before their price had even been set.

The main media advertising budget was over £11.0 million, and the campaign was to have four phases:

1. An Alert Phase: to create high awareness and communicate the offer was for everyone, not just big investors.
2. A Maintenance Phase: to impart specific information about the offer, and elicit an initial response from those interested.
3. An Action Phase: to ensure people had cash ready, and instil a sense of urgency for the eight days the offer would be open.
4. The Prospectus Phase: to provide the public—particularly first-time investors—with the necessary paperwork to buy the shares.

After research, the selected campaign theme was 'Share In BT's Future' and the advertising was closely supervised by the Dorland creative director Royston Taylor. Taylor had an impressive creative track record, having created the 'Schhh...you know who' campaign for Schweppes while at Mather & Crowther, and created a beautifully nostalgic award-winning Dubonnet campaign at Dorland. His BT advertisements won no creative plaudits, but were straightforward and cleared all the legal hurdles. The campaign saturated the mass media. Additionally a campaign was run in specialist magazines, targeted at intermediaries from whom first-time buyers might seek guidance: bank managers, solicitors, accountants, and financial advisors. No pebble was left unturned.

Public attitudes and awareness were tracked throughout the campaign. By the time the offer opened market research showed 8 per cent of adults—just over 3 million people—claimed they were 'certain to buy BT shares'. In the event 70 per cent of these applied—an unusually accurate result: respondents generally exaggerate when asked to predict their buying intentions, for any product or service. In all 2,141,647 people applied for five times as many shares as were available. Of these 1,373,706 were 'small investors', who applied for 800 shares or fewer. The flotation brought in £3,916 million, and the number of shareholders in Britain nearly doubled. The new shareholders were pleased with their buy, not least because the shares opened at 86 per cent above the flotation price on the first day of trading. Though 450,000 sold their shares within six months, this was a far lower percentage than had sold out after previous privatizations.

The press changed its sceptical tune instantly. *The Observer* described the privatization as 'A national event, a brilliant piece of social engineering', while *The Sun* called it 'A brilliant success'. A new means of transferring the ownership of massive public holdings to a wide—albeit not universal—tranche of the public had been born.

The following year saw the still larger British Gas privatization, applying much the same campaign formula—except that the British Gas advertisements were even more populist, not to say condescending. The British Gas agency was Young & Rubicam, and after testing two alternative approaches a campaign based on the slogan 'If you see Sid, tell him!' was launched, backed with a total marketing budget of £40 million. The slogan quickly passed into common parlance, and was mocked by comedians and cartoonists alike. But research showed the public took it for what it was: an encouragement to tell anyone and everyone about the share offer, as it was an excellent investment opportunity. The enthusiasm aroused by the campaign encouraged the government to set the share price 5p higher than had originally been planned, which brought in an additional £200 million. In total £5,434 million was raised. British Gas received 4.6 million applications, twice as many as BT, and 2.2 million were from first-time investors.

In the following years British Airways, Rolls Royce, British Airports, British Steel, and others were privatized, utterly transforming Britain's economic landscape, just as Margaret Thatcher and Keith Joseph intended. Between 1983 and 1991 the number of shareholders in Britain increased from 4 million to 11 million. By the end of the 1980s the government had raised £37 billion from privatizations, approximately equivalent to the entire public sector deficit in 1992. Not all of the privatizations have since been judged successful—though few people would now choose to return to the times when these great organizations were owned by the state. As economists Bishop, Kay, and Mayer cautiously put it in *Privatization and Economic Performance* (1994):

> One of the most enduring legacies of the 1980s has been the programme of privatizations the Thatcher government put in train . . . even if the UK privatization programme can be faulted in many respects, it has identified the way in which privatizations can be successfully achieved.

Mass, popular advertising was an essential ingredient in the process, though economists do not appear to realize it. Without mass advertising it is inconceivable millions of people would have invested. Without mass advertising the companies could only have been sold (if at all) via the financial markets, to a small number of wealthy and institutional investors—as has happened elsewhere.

Britain's lead has been followed by many other countries. It is another example of British advertising paving the way.

March of the Maggots

Long after the OFT had effectively quashed agency recognition agreements, the small print of the Institute of Practitioners in Advertising Bye Laws continued to insist IPA member agencies must provide both creative and media-buying services. Consequently, despite their growing strength, the media agencies were locked out of the IPA. And consequently again, when the President enforced this bye law, media agency boss Ray Morgan and I were unceremoniously ejected from an IPA Council meeting—despite having both been democratically elected onto the Council by IPA members.

Morgan's new media-buying agency had no creative department, my new creative agency had no media-buying department. The IPA President, a big, burly, clever but bumptious oaf named Bert de Vos,[1] could easily have informed us of the problem before the Council meeting, but he patently wished to make a point. And the point he wished to make was that full-service IPA agencies would have no truck with specialist agencies like ours.

Though many other leading media-buyers had by this time set up media agencies, Ray Morgan's decision to set up his own agency dealt the death blow to full-service agencies. Morgan had been media chief at Benton & Bowles, and was one of London's most highly respected strategic media-buyers. But in 1985 Benton & Bowles merged, globally, with another American-based international agency, D'Arcy-Macmanus (the agency which had carried out the ITV strike analysis). Unfortunately—or as things turned out for him, fortunately—Morgan did not have the style and elan required of a top media man. He lacked presence, was prematurely bald, had a slightly squeaky voice, and was no snappy dresser. None of this should have mattered. But it seemed to. Following the international merger the top job in London went to a D'Arcy man, and he appointed another D'Arcy man as media chief. Morgan was passed over. This was inane. Within weeks Morgan quit and set up Ray Morgan & Partners, taking with him the most talented of the Benton & Bowles media team and most of Benton & Bowles's clients. The head of D'Arcy, who demoted him, was the same Bert de Vos who later banished both him and me from the IPA Council. Of course this may have been a coincidence.

Morgan, a conservative man who was rightly trusted as a straight talker and straight dealer, was a reluctant rebel. This made his conversion to media separatism all the more influential. Once he had quit Benton & Bowles he proselytized for specialist media agencies, and picked up lots of new clients. The march of the maggots was gaining momentum, and the media agencies were gaining in skill and professionalism—bucket shops no longer. Only a couple of the top media men were then graduates: most were street fighters who had left school at 15 or 16 and clawed their ways to the top. But Morgan was a graduate, and went to great lengths to attract and employ graduate trainees. Many who later reached the top in media agencies began their careers working for him.

The media agencies were by now carrying out their own research, developing strategic planning capabilities, and winning a rapidly growing share

---

[1] Normally I concur: *de mortuis nil nisi bonum*. But there are exceptions to every rule.

of the media-buying market. In 1985 they handled 20 per cent of total UK billings, and on Guy Fawkes Day 1985 the largest media independent, TMD, floated on the London stock market. It was already making pre-tax profits of £1.7 million.

The hostility of the traditional agencies to the upstart media independents was understandable. The creation of copy and layouts had originally spun out of the media-buying services offered by the earliest agencies. But once this had happened, agencies—and most advertisers—came to believe the two functions were inseparable. They were essential parts of the same totality: an advertising campaign. The unification of the two functions may have been opportunist but it had survived, it was argued, because it was the most efficient way to produce effective campaigns.

Moreover, and more importantly from their perspective, the traditional agencies made healthy profits from their media-buying operations. They earned interest on the huge cash flows provided by their billings, as advertisers pay their agencies before the agencies pay the media. Above all, their billings effortlessly provided them with the funds necessary to pay both for the creative work and for the media-buying operation, with a handsome margin left for profit. If the media operations broke away, the agencies would only be able to charge their clients fees for creative services—and the agencies knew such fees would not be nearly as bountiful as the billings flow. Thus the traditional agencies were genuinely uncertain whether unbundling their media and creative operations was in their clients' best interests, and were absolutely certain unbundling was not in their own best interests.

But the tide was too strong. The specialist media agencies were buying space and time more cheaply than the traditional agencies, and often more inventively. Canute-like, many traditional agency bosses still tried to resist. Eventually most realized that if you can't beat 'em, you had better join 'em. The only way forward was for the agencies to set up their own media specialists, who would no longer be media independents, but media 'dependants', because they would depend on the parent agency for most of their clients. Ironically, Ray Morgan had instituted exactly such a system in 1974, when he had set up a Benton & Bowles media subsidiary called Mercury. Mercury handled all B&B's clients, plus a small number of non-B&B clients—and it was Mercury's separate existence which made it so easy for him to extract the entire media shooting-match from B&B eleven years later. But in 1974 nobody had followed Morgan's lead.

In August 1988 Saatchi & Saatchi made what was to prove the decisive leap. The idea came from John Perriss, the Saatchi Worldwide Media

Director, who had come into Saatchi via the Compton merger. The Perriss plan was for Saatchi to buy Ray Morgan & Partners, and in quick succession merge his media agency—with his connivance—with the media operations of all the agencies Saatchi already owned, to form much the largest centralized media-buying company in Britain: Zenith. Though in those days the trade press paid little attention to media agencies, the launch of Zenith merited a huge front page *Campaign* splash. The man Bert de Vos had passed over was appointed Zenith's chairman and chief executive. Ray Morgan became a rich man.[2]

By 1990, more than 1500 people were employed in media agencies, and Zenith was billing £521 million, more than double the billings of CIA, the UK's largest wholly independent media agency. Moreover £149 million of Zenith's total came from advertisers unconnected with other parts of the Saatchi empire. This put Saatchi in touch with a host of possible new clients for their creative agencies. The launch of Zenith was one of Saatchi's boldest and most profitable initiatives. Other large agencies had no alternative but to follow suit.

Eventually the IPA accepted media agencies into its fold. The Association of Media Independents expired. By the end of the century there were no creative agencies of any size with in-house media operations. As might be expected of a new commercial sector, during the last decade of the century the media agencies gobbled each other up, forming ever larger and stronger units. Then most of them were gobbled up by the major holding companies—principally Omnicom, WPP, and Interpublic—generating the bulk of their turnover, and a healthy proportion of their profits.

Though they foresaw media agencies were a financial threat, the traditional agencies never foresaw how profoundly their own status would be demeaned by the separation: many have still not come to terms with it. From having had control of total advertising budgets—the costs of space and time, plus the costs of creative work—creative agencies were now only able to charge for their creative work: about 8 per cent of their earlier total billings. So their turnovers plunged to 8 per cent of what they had previously been. The remainder switched into the media agencies.

Worse, the creative agencies ceased to have direct contact with the media themselves, who naturally focused their attentions on their new customers, the media agencies. Today the media hardly know which creative agency is working for which advertiser: they have little need to. This has massively reduced the power of creative agencies. They morphed

[2] In 1991 Morgan quit advertising to become a farmer.

into smaller companies, with small turnovers, and fewer employees—as mentioned above, even the largest employ only a couple of hundred people. Today there is only one creative agency quoted on the stock market.[3] All the bigger, and many of the smaller, creative agencies are owned by the publicly quoted holding companies.

Did the separation of the creative and media-buying functions, into separate companies, increase the overall cost-efficiency of advertising and marketing? There is no way of knowing, but I doubt it. The competitive marketplace decided on the separation, and the marketplace usually makes the right decisions. But in this instance the separation was largely provoked by the way traditional agency managements looked down their noses at media-buying. This was stupid, unnecessary, and would not happen today.

What is certain is that if BMP and JWT had not invented account planning, the role of creative agencies in developing advertisers' marketing strategies could well have shrunk to nil—they would have become, as Cramer Saatchi had been, creative consultancies: groups of creative people realizing their clients' instructions. Account planning has enabled them to continue to have a role in their clients' marketing—but the role has been greatly, probably irreversibly, diminished.

And early in the twenty-first century a media agency boss became president of the IPA.

New Kids on the Block

David Abbott was Britain's pre-eminent twenty-first-century copywriter. In *Campaign*'s collection of the '100 Best Ads of the 20th Century', Abbott has 7 entries, just pipping John Webster who has 6—with no one else in sight. If he wished to use them as doorstops, the trophies and awards Abbott has won at worldwide creative festivals would wedge open most of the agency doors in London.

His career started uncertainly. Leaving Oxford before he graduated, because of his father's early death, Abbott joined Kodak as a junior writer, churning out trade advertisements and literature. He moved to Mather & Crowther, his first agency, and went on to Doyle Dane Bernbach when it opened in London. While there he was seconded to DDB New York, where he came under the influence of Bill Bernbach. His admiration for Bernbach

---

[3] M&C Saatchi.

is all but unqualified, and his stint with DDB New York was the formative influence on his creativity. Returning, he became DDB's Managing Director in London before he was 30. In 1971 he left DDB to become a partner in a small new agency, French Gold Abbott. FGA sparkled then passed away when cracks opened up between the partners. In 1977, to reassure present and prospective clients, Abbott foolishly took a large personal advertisement in the trade press, in which he insisted he was going to remain at FGA. Then he left, to join Peter Mead and Adrian Vickers, who had started their own agency a year earlier. To net him, Mead and Vickers had to offer him a hefty shareholding: he proved well with the price.

Abbott, a tall, striking, and rather shy benevolent despot, had found his perfect partners. Mead (who did not attend university) and Vickers (with whom Abbott had been friendly at Oxford) were highly professional and utterly dissimilar account directors. However, they shared two essential characteristics. Both have the enduring resilience of Duracell bunnies, and both were happy for Abbott to stamp his personality on every aspect of the agency, deferring to him on all creative and most other matters. As John Hegarty put it, 'Abbott's personality runs through AMV like a steel pole.' Together the trio built what became Britain's largest agency. It has a very particular ambience—rather too self-regarding and sugary for many, but utterly committed to the highest quality work. Abbott, a staunch Catholic, is unknown to tantrums but is, quietly, every bit as autocratic as most creative leaders.

Launched in 1977, AMV got into its stride during the early 1980s, building an enviable reputation for thoughtfulness and creativity. It did nothing truly startling, either creatively or managerially. Nor did it have Saatchi & Saatchi's restless ambition. But everything it did, it did superlatively well. In November 1985 AMV floated on the London stock market, and its shares were oversubscribed 30 times. But it was not until 1991, when the American holding company Omnicom bought a 23 per cent stake in the agency and merged it into its international BBDO network, that the new AMV-BBDO agency climbed into Britain's top ten. It then kept climbing, and reached the top of the pile in 1996—where it has now remained for over a decade. In an extremely competitive business, this is no mean feat.

While still at DDB, Abbott won his first D&AD Silver award for a Uniroyal Rain Tyre campaign. Over the next 30 years he wrote award-winning campaigns for the ASTMS trade union ('The Board and I have decided we don't like the colour of your eyes'), the British Medical Association, Books for Children, BT (the Bob Hoskins campaign), Chivas Regal, *The Economist*, Lufthansa, *The Observer*, the RSPCA, Sainsbury's, Volkswagen, Volvo, Wella, and the J. R. Hartley commercial for Yellow Pages. It is a formidable list, in terms both of quality and quantity. In most cases he wrote numerous advertisements during the life of each campaign, usually in collaboration with his long-standing art director partner, Ron Brown.

That Abbott's advertisements are probably less well remembered than John Webster's reflects the differing memorability of press and television. Abbott, the copywriter, was more successful in print media. Webster, the art director, was more successful in visual media. (Though both would no doubt have rejected any such limitation of their talents.) Many of London's brightest and most talented creative people wanted to work for David Abbott, and he was able to pick and choose the best of them. The AMV creative teams both created fine campaigns of their own and contributed to—and won many awards for—Abbott's campaigns, as these progressed over the years.

AMV's strength in print, rather than television, was reflected in the agency's lack of success at Cannes—where television and cinema were dominant—until late in the 1990s. But in 1999, two years after Abbott had handed over the creative reins to his successor Peter Souter, the agency created the remarkable 'Surfers' commercial, for Guinness. Directed by movie director Jonathan Glazer, 'Surfers' is based loosely on Moby Dick and took nine days to shoot in Hawaii. It is, incidentally, a fine example of the account planning process in action. 'Surfers' took a year to come to fruition, while it was repeatedly researched and amended. Its future was often in jeopardy, until creative solutions could be found to problems the planners uncovered. But the outcome was worth it. 'Surfers' was voted by the public 'The best British advertisement ever', in a poll conducted jointly by the *Sunday Times* and Channel 4 in May 2000. (Though 'ever' is a bizarre word here, as nobody under 35 would have remembered any advertisements from before the 1970s.) It won at Cannes and is the only advertisement ever to have scooped up two D&AD Gold awards in the same year.

David Abbott remained agency Chairman until October 1998, but relinquished his management responsibilities in September 1997, to concentrate on copywriting for a select group of the agency's clients. Several of the advertising luminaries interviewed by *Campaign* when he retired described him as a genius. This is probably too big a word for an advertising copywriter, but if anyone deserves it, Abbott does.

* * *

Abbott Mead Vickers snitched no accounts from the partners' previous agencies. It built its business client-by-client, brick-by-brick. The next major new agency 'Ripped £9m out of CDP', as the *Campaign* front page put it on 9 May 1981. This rip-out was the work of the formerly pink-suited Frank Lowe—the CDP man who had sold the Heineken campaign to his friend Anthony Simonds-Gooding on an Aeroflot flight to Leningrad. Lowe set up his new agency with Geoffrey Howard-Spink, then one of CDP's deputy managing directors. Just as Abbott was the driving force at AMV, Lowe was the driving force at Lowe Howard-Spink—Abbott being a creator with substantial management talent, Lowe being a manager with substantial creative talent. Like Abbott, Lowe is a benevolent despot— though perhaps a shade more despotic and less benevolent. He has a volatile temper and has been publicly described as 'terrifying', but this is an epithet with which he might not agree. ('What can I say about being called a complete bastard? I don't think I am,' Lowe meekly averred to *Campaign* in 1993.)

Since the memorable Aeroflot flight, Lowe's career had been chequered. In addition to Whitbread, he built exceptionally close relationships with several other CDP clients, including Birds Eye, Fiat, Parker Pens, and Olympus Cameras. For all those clients CDP created exceptional advertising. Among advertisers who take to him (he is not everyone's half-of-lager) Lowe's influence is mesmeric. His success with so many of CDP's largest clients, together with his personal popularity among the agency's creative staff, soon carried him to the top. John Pearce appointed him managing director when he was 31.

Unusually for a bright alumnus of Westminster School, where he excelled at sport, Lowe did not go to university. He went straight into advertising aged 17—not because it held any particular fascination for him, but because advertising was trendy. Well-spoken, casually modish, he is in many ways a public-school version of the earthy, nail-biting Colin Millward, Lowe's erstwhile CDP hero. Both share a visceral ability to recognize great advertising creativity. Like Millward, Lowe prefers judgement to research, prefers absolutism to pragmatism, prefers fighters to trimmers, prefers unreasonable perfectionists to even-tempered moderates. Though he is a loner rather than a team player, with few if any close friends in advertising, these qualities make Lowe compellingly attractive to many highly talented creative people. Similarly, they make him compellingly attractive to clients who admire his style—like Anthony Simonds-Gooding—but impossible for others, who cannot cope with his unbending and egocentric certitude. In *Campaign*'s Silver Jubilee Issue (1993) Lowe was placed 4th most important man in British advertising of that era—behind only Colin Millward, Charles Saatchi, and Stanley Pollitt—though many would now think that placing a trifle generous to him.

Under Lowe's leadership as managing director, CDP's rapid growth continued, as did the sublime quality of its work. But just when his career seemed to be shining luminously, things went badly awry. In 1978 the Inland Revenue initiated a prosecution of CDP—a public company—for PAYE and staff benefit transgressions, and announced its intention to prosecute John Pearce, Ronald Dickenson, and Frank Lowe personally. Apparently a clerk in the CDP finance department had blown the gaffe. The cases took two years to come to court, but in November 1980 all were found guilty. The company was fined £150,000, while Pearce, Dickenson, and Lowe were fined a total of £15,000. This was no massive, Enron-like skulduggery. The sums involved were paltry, and it seems extraordinary that three businessmen of their calibre should have engaged in such petty scams. But the case proved a tipping point for CDP. It knocked much of the stuffing out of the agency, and shook the staff: their much admired bosses had been cheating (and been caught). For loyal ex-CDP people it remains a sad, sore issue: several I tried to discuss it with simply refused to talk about it, pleading a lack of knowledge, or a lack of memory, or both.

Lowe stepped down from his managing directorship and left CDP—naturally claiming his departure had nothing to do with the tax case. But significantly, he continued to be employed by CDP as a consultant, working with his clients. This awkward arrangement continued until May 1981, by which time the tax case had—outside CDP—blown over.[4]

That was when Lowe and Geoff Howard-Spink announced the launch of their new agency. Lowe does not have Charles Saatchi's deft way with the press. 'I want to build a very special agency,' he announced to *Campaign*, 'I hope that in two or three years we will have as many famous campaigns as CDP.' Well, er, yes. But the flimsiness of these statements was beside the point once Lowe ripped the £9 million Whitbread account out of his former agency—his friendship with Simonds-Gooding still holding fast. Birds Eye and Parker Pens quickly followed, as did several of CDP's top creative people. Unsurprisingly—though Lowe seems to have been surprised—all this left CDP seething and embittered.

By 1982 Lowe Howard-Spink's billings had doubled to £18.4 million, and in August 1983 the partners sold a majority of the agency to Interpublic, the holding company created by Marion Harper. The deal was almost a carbon copy of the first Saatchi deal with Compton. Interpublic owned the

---

[4] John Pearce suffered a fatal heart attack in September 1981, aged 68.

international agency Wasey Campbell-Ewald, which was struggling in London as Compton had been. Though Wasey Campbell-Ewald was twice the size of Lowe Howard-Spink, Lowe gained almost complete control of the newly merged shop, to be called Lowe Howard-Spink Campbell-Ewald (shades of Saatchi & Saatchi Garland-Compton). Frank Lowe became Executive Chairman, and joined the Campbell-Ewald Worldwide board. The merged agency's billings exceeded £50 million. Lowe had bounced back from the ignominy of his court case three years earlier with magnificent panache.

As Lowe had promised in his *Campaign* interview, his new agency's creative output was classy. Its work for Whitbread—particularly for Heineken and Stella Artois—continued with undiminished flair, fully justifying Simonds-Gooding's loyalty. And new clients rolled in, for whom the agency also created famous campaigns, including: Abbey Life, Bergasol, Castella cigars, Chewits, Irn-Bru, JVC, KP snacks, Lloyds Bank, the *Mail on Sunday*, Ovaltine, Reebok, Tesco—perhaps the agency's most important win, retail advertising being about to boom—and Vauxhall cars, which had come with Wasey Campbell-Ewald. Suddenly, to people's surprise, in 1987 Lowe ceded chairmanship of the agency to Geoff Howard-Spink. Lowe wanted, he said, to 'concentrate on corporate and international matters'— hardly his strongest suit. The move was generally interpreted to mean that he wanted to climb the greasy pole within Interpublic. Nonetheless his London agency continued to thrive, and at the end of the decade was 9th largest in Britain, having overtaken his old shop CDP, which had sunk to 11th. Though the quality of Lowe Howard-Spink's work never quite matched that of CDP, Lowe's declared ambition, the speed of its growth assuredly did.

Lowe's corporate and international role was initially a mite nebulous, but towards the end of 1993, Interpublic bought the once hugely successful American creative agency Scali McCabe Sloves, and merged it with Lowe's operation. Lowe's agency now controlled global billings of $2.6 billion, just 12 years after its launch. And in London it was still winning business— it won first Diet Coke in 1993, and then Coca-Cola itself in 1994. It continued to produce fine creative work. Better still, and unlike CDP, it was highly profitable. In both 1993 and 1994 Lowe Howard-Spink topped the UK agency profitability league tables—an exceptional business performance. For Frank Lowe things were getting better and better. More shades of Saatchi & Saatchi, Lowe tried and failed to buy—not a bank (page 208), but his favourite soccer team, Manchester United.

In 1999 Interpublic merged yet another of its worldwide agencies, Ammurati Puris Lintas, into Lowe's operation. What goes around comes around. All previous attempts to invigorate Lintas having failed, the agency where Frank Lowe had shared an office with Simonds-Gooding three decades earlier had been sold by Unilever to Interpublic, had undergone several transmogrifications, and was now part of Lowe's own empire. The new agency was renamed Lowe Lintas—which must surely have given Frank a frisson of pleasure. And Lowe Lintas was the 5th largest agency in the world, which would have pleased him more than a frisson. Like the Saatchis in the 1970s, Frank Lowe looked unstoppable. In 1999 Lowe Lintas in London leapt to 2nd largest agency in Britain, and in January 2000 it was anointed *Campaign*'s Agency of the Year.

Just over a year later, in June 2001, Interpublic announced yet another management reshuffle. Interpublic seems to enjoy management reshuffles, though its shareholders may be less fond of them. This reshuffle would give Lowe further control of two Interpublic global agencies. Lowe was now within sight of the top job at Interpublic. For a Brit to run an American marketing services conglomerate, then the largest in the world, would be an unparalleled feat—in its way more impressive than the success of the Saatchi brothers. The number of Brits who have run major American public companies, in any field, can be counted on the toes of one arse-kicking foot.

Then things fell apart. Interpublic, it transpired, did not plan to promote him. Lowe had gained a reputation for being a reckless spender. He had led Interpublic into sports marketing and motor racing ventures which were disastrous. The headlines said: 'IPG Revamp Sidelines Frank Lowe.' Lowe's rise to power at Interpublic was over. His personality, it was said, had finally got under the skin of Interpublic's leaders. Like Icarus, he had flown too close to the sun. The Lintas name disappeared, and Frank Lowe became chairman of Lowe and Partners Worldwide: his personal fiefdom, with no other name on the door. In 2003 he parted company with Interpublic—launching a new agency in London called, whimsically, The Red Brick Road, not long afterwards.

* * *

If Abbott Mead Vickers and Lowe Howard-Spink were driven by Abbott and Lowe respectively, Bartle Bogle Hegarty—the third of this trio of highly creative 1980s agencies—was that surprisingly rare advertising phenomenon, an agency driven by a triumvirate of equals. The three partners were equal in shareholdings, equal in clout, equal in mutual respect. Still more remarkably they liked each other, and continued to work together for nearly 20 years, until Bartle retired—and even then Bogle and Hegarty went on working together. They worked as a harmonious team, in which each played his own game.

John Hegarty, son of an Irish labourer, had worked his way into Hornsey Art School. Like Millward and Webster, Hegarty had originally wanted to be a painter.[5] Instead he became a creative director in the David Abbott mould—absolutely firm and resolute, but slow to anger—though unlike Abbott he rarely involves himself in general management. BBH was run by Bartle and Bogle. Bartle had been a marketing executive at Cadbury Schweppes, where he worked closely with BMP, and so knew the ins-and-outs of account planning. At BBH he ran the account planning department, following Stanley Pollitt dogma, but less dogmatically. Bogle, the son of ASA builder George Bogle, had wanted to be a lawyer but fluffed it, and started in advertising as an account executive.

BBH was the offspring of a French agency always called TBWA. It is always called TBWA because its full name is Tragos, Bonnange, Weisendanger and Arjoldi—the partners being a Greek-American, a Frenchman, a Swiss, and a German. This quartet decided to set up a European-based international agency, and having started in Paris in 1970 they traipsed over to London in 1973. But they were strapped for cash. So instead of buying a London agency TBWA recruited half a dozen young advertising chaps and offered them the chance to launch an agency themselves, with small personal shareholdings in the venture. This was an extraordinary long-shot, as the half-dozen were relative strangers to each other. Fortunately for TBWA—or perhaps it was brilliant judgement on their part—five of the six got on well (and the sixth soon left). John Bartle, Nigel Bogle, and John Hegarty got on particularly well. Bartle and Bogle became TBWA's joint managing directors, Hegarty was creative director.

TBWA London quickly began to win business. Slight, attractive, and extremely likeable, Hegarty—who was knighted for his services to advertising in 2007—proved to be a wonderful salesman of creative work. Long after the three had left TBWA, Bill Tragos—deliberately belittling Hegarty's creativity—claimed salesmanship was his greatest talent, saying: 'John is a salesman at heart, and very few people can stand up and sell advertising as well as he can.' Yes, but as Charles Saatchi had long before recognized, he

[5] In the past many copywriters yearned to be serious novelists, but that is no longer so true. Instead, it seems, many art directors yearn to be serious painters.

is pretty damn good at creating advertisements too. Bartle is unusually numerate, and analyses marketing data with insight and originality. Bogle is diligent, retiring—not to say taciturn—and has manifest integrity. They were an impressive young trio. TBWA blossomed. In 1980 *Campaign* decided to anoint an annual 'Agency of the Year', and its first anointment was TBWA. But T, B, W, and A seem to have been miffed by their British progeny's runaway success. The London shop became the group's flagship agency, but the Londoners received little kudos from their parent company. Reluctantly, they decided to quit and launch their own shop. They took no TBWA clients with them, because they still felt TBWA was 'their' agency. TBWA had, to quote Bogle, given them the chance to learn how to launch an agency at other people's expense. Now they would turn the trick for themselves.

Bartle Bogle Hegarty has never claimed to have a unique approach to advertising. Like AMV—the agency they most resemble—they are supreme craftsmen. Everything they do they do superbly. But they made one bold and rare decision at the start. Under no circumstances would they undertake speculative campaigns for new client pitches. From time immemorial agencies have bitched about having to pitch for new clients, with speculative campaigns. BBH turned the bitching into action.

While at TBWA the three of them had become convinced speculative new business campaigns were a monstrous waste of time and money: they have to be created quickly, with minimal agency–client collaboration, and are presented in wholly artificial circumstances. They interrupt work for existing clients and are almost never used. Like short-order cooking they are underdone and synthetic. Even though the policy stopped them pitching for government accounts, as the COI used to insist on speculative creative pitches, BBH stuck to its guns.

Today most agencies have improved the pitch process by holding 'tissue meetings' before making the final speculative presentation. Tissue meetings resemble what BBH has been doing all along. At tissue meetings the agency presents its work-in-progress to the prospective client, sketching out the directions in which its thoughts are travelling. There may be several tissue meetings, which—as a helpful by-product—allow advertisers and agencies to get to know each other better. The tissue meetings will (or anyway should) stop the agency finally presenting work that is grievously off-track. But the selection procedure will still finish with a full-blown speculative creative presentation—except at BBH.

Starting with no clients, for BBH to refuse to do speculative pitches was a risky strategy. However, the trio's already high reputation at TBWA—plus

Hegarty's famed salesmanship—ensured clients came to their new agency swiftly, starting with Levi's Europe, which they won from McCann Erickson four months after opening. The creative awards followed swiftly too. By the end of the decade BBH had won business from and created award-winning campaigns for: Audi ('Vorsprung Durch Teknik'), the Brewers' Society, BT, Buxton Mineral Water, Derwent Valley Foods, Dunlopillo, Golden Shred Marmalade, Haagen Dazs, *The Independent*, K Shoes, Levi's (most famously the 'I Heard It Through The Grapevine' launderette commercial for 501s), Pretty Polly, Puma, Dr White Tampons, and Speedo. During the mid-1990s BBH's annual bag of Cannes awards rivalled John Webster's. (As the Cannes festival grew it gave away more awards with each passing year, making comparisons difficult.) By most reckonings BBH was the world's most successful agency at Cannes during the 1990s—further fuelling Britain's reputation as world leader in advertising creativity.

Structurally, BBH's most innovative thinking has revolved around its international operation, which was developed in the twenty-first century. Bogle claims the partners always knew they would one day strive to build an international agency—they had been indoctrinated by Tragos, Bonnange, Weisendanger, and Arjoldi. To pursue their international vision they eventually sold 49 per cent of BBH to the American multinational Leo Burnett for £25 million. (Burnett is now part of the French holding company Publicis, the fourth largest holding group in the world behind Ominicom, WPP, and Interpublic.) Employing a hub-and-spoke structure, BBH opened offices in four cities—New York, Sao Paulo, Singapore, and Tokyo. The first of these manages their business in North America, the second in South America, the third and fourth in Asia Pacific, while London deals with Europe. They use the much larger Burnett network to handle things locally—but the strategy and the campaigns emanate from the BBH hubs. Having only four BBH offices has enabled them to fill the key positions in each with trained and trusted staff from BBH London. This was a radical approach to international agency management, which sceptics said would never work. It has.

Despite its reputation and superb creative work, BBH grew quite slowly. In its early years it lost several accounts quite soon after winning them. So for many years it yo-yoed up and down the agency league, not reaching the top ten until almost 25 years after its launch. In part this may be a price it paid for refusing to make speculative creative presentations, which denied it the opportunity to pitch for many advertisers who demand them. In any event—taking the diametrically opposite point of view to

Charles Saatchi—BBH claims it never wants to be the biggest, or even nearly biggest, agency in Britain.

BBH thinks of itself as a small, challenger agency: renegade rather than establishment. It likes to believe that when everyone else zigs, it zags. Its symbol is a black sheep, surrounded by white ones. Not growing too big has been the dream of many agencies. David Ogilvy, late in life, said one of his main regrets was having allowed his agency to get too big. But for an advertising agency standing still is not an option. An agency (or any business) which does not grow cannot provide opportunities for its best young people. Worse, if an agency does not regularly win new clients its staff—and its existing clients—begin to wonder what is wrong. In the agency game, floodlit by *Campaign*'s annual assessment of agency success, this can quickly turn to disaster.

The Supercharged Supermarket Trolley-Maker

By the beginning of the twenty-first century WPP chief executive Martin Sorrell was the most powerful advertising man in Britain, and in July 2000 *Fortune* magazine claimed he was the 'biggest adman in the world' (an unkind allusion to his diminutive 5' 6½" height; at school he was nick-named 'titch'). But he was not, and has never been, an advertising man. Still, the description was not wholly inappropriate, as his empire includes four of the world's largest agency networks: J. Walter Thompson, Ogilvy & Mather, Young & Rubicam, and Grey. Today WPP employs 100,000 people in 2,000 offices in 106 countries, and annually pumps some £70 billion into the world's media, servicing 340 of the Fortune Global top 500 companies.

The WPP story began in 1985. Sorrell, like the Saatchi brothers, is a North London Jew, and until his £29 million divorce in 2005 he was strongly bonded to his religious heritage—even today you won't catch him tucking into a bacon butty on Yom Kippur. He read economics at Cambridge, and went on to Harvard Business School where he took an MBA, borrowing the cash to pay his way. These experiences made him a lifetime advocate of business school education, and gave him an unfeigned admiration for intellectual achievement. He himself is quick-thinking, clever, and surprisingly modest, but lays no claim to creativity: a desiccated calculating machine. He has an almost photographic memory, inexhaustible energy, and follows through on details meticulously. Woe betide those who do not remember every tiny decision taken at a Sorrell meeting. Martin will. Above all, Martin is a martinet. He is not gregarious, seems not to need close friends—which is as well as he is perpetually in flight—and has no difficulty being sharply acerbic. 'He expects people to dislike him,' says one of his former colleagues, 'so he doesn't worry about it. It's an invaluable armour.'

Leaving Harvard he first worked for the Glendinning consultancy in Connecticut, but left because, as he said, the trouble with consultancy is that 'you never end up running anything.' Sorrell likes running things. He returned to London to run the UK end of Mark McCormack's sport management company, then joined James Gulliver Associates as Gulliver's 'personal gopher and financial advisor'. There he became involved with the Saatchis, who were looking for their first ever financial director. Sorrell joined them in 1977. That was when he found his niche: advertising and marketing services. He stayed with Charles and Maurice for nine years, masterminding their finances and deals until March 1986.

Saatchi people say that before he left relations between Martin and Maurice grew acrimonious, as the media increasingly gave Sorrell the credit for Saatchi & Saatchi's strong financial performance—and Sorrell did not shun the applause. Sorrell's version of his departure is that when he reached 40 the male menopause kicked in, and he wanted to run his own show. Doubtless there are shards of truth in both versions. Anyway there is little love lost between Sorrell and the brothers today.

Sorrell began to plan his departure. Together with stockbroker Peston Rabl, he searched for a tiny public company which could be used as the shell for a marketing services holding company. It had to be tiny because they had little money. Having unearthed supermarket trolley-maker Wire & Plastic Products, in 1985 they bought just under 30 per cent of its equity for £400,000, which gave them control. Meanwhile, Sorrell continued working for the brothers while he got the trolley-maker up and running.

Sorrell and Rabl decided firmly against investing in advertising agencies. They believed marketing services companies—companies in sales promotion, graphic and pack design, market research, incentive marketing, public relations, and the like—were more profitable and were growing faster than advertising agencies. They saw an opportunity to put together the fragments of a variegated industry, and they made rapid progress. By 1987 WPP had bought 16 companies, its shares had climbed from 35p to £11, and its stock market valuation had leapt from £1.4 million to £135 million. Then Sorrell changed tack. He decided to acquire an advertising agency. There followed two expensive agency acquisitions which were to make and almost break him. Rabl bowed out.

But were they expensive, or were they cheap? The first buy, J. Walter Thompson, was unquestionably cheap. The agency, once called 'the university of advertising', was going through a torrid time, riven by internal strife. A public company, it was making a risible 4 per cent profit on turnover. Sorrell's Saatchi experience had taught him an averagely efficient advertising agency can make 12 per cent gross profit on turnover, and a more than averagely efficient agency can make 13–15 per cent without much difficulty. Many make more. Whatever else, Sorrell is a fine arithmetician. He knows—few others seem to—that an increase in margin from JWT's 4 per cent to 5 per cent equates to a 25 per cent increase in profits. If he could push the JWT margin from 4 per cent to a modest 12 per cent, overall profits would rocket up 200 per cent. He knew, everybody knew, JWT had run to fat, was over-staffed and under-managed. In a personal service industry, where tradition maintained that hostile takeovers were suicidal, Sorrell launched a hostile takeover. He had explained the financial logic to his backers, and they backed him all the way.

To get JWT, Sorrell paid £351 million, raising £213 million through a rights issue, and the debt had to be expensively serviced. He immediately set about increasing the JWT profit margin. A workaholic whose work is his life[6]—Sorrell has no significant outside interests, and describes himself as a fairly boring bloke—he swiftly restructured the JWT management, and installed his own rigid financial controls.

Simultaneously he met JWT's major clients and explained how the WPP takeover was in their best interests. At that time I happened to be at a dinner with Unilever chairman Sir Michael Angus, who had met Sorrell for the first time a few days earlier. Unilever was a worldwide JWT client. How on earth, I asked Michael Angus, would Sorrell's purchase of JWT, which would mean JWT slashing costs and firing staff, help the agency's clients? We always find, Angus answered benignly, that efficient suppliers help us more than inefficient suppliers—but the proof of the pudding will be in the eating: we will wait and watch . . . carefully.

Sorrell's pudding proved perfect. He simultaneously cut ingredient costs and improved the taste. JWT's margin zipped from 4 per cent to 6.3 per cent by the end of 1987. The agency was revitalized and Unilever, among

---

[6] When writing *Beating the 24/7*, my book on work–life balance, I asked Martin if he would agree to be interviewed. He provisionally acceded, then withdrew apologetically, saying his family would find it ludicrous for him to appear in a book on work–life balance, or even to express any views on the subject. He was right. His wife later cited his workaholism in their divorce.

many others, were delighted. Commentators emphasize Sorrell's tough cost controls. This is fair, but only half the story. Sorrell is also an exceptionally smart judge of what clients want, and ensures they get it. To quote Ross Johnson in *Barbarians at the Gate* (1988), saving money is easy—it is spending money that is difficult. Sorrell is accomplished at both.

But not so good at timing, perhaps. While putting JWT right, he continued his frenetic acquisition activity. He paid commissions to people who brought him good buys. He bought another 14 companies in the following 18 months, favouring investment in continental Europe and the Far East. He had a lucky windfall when the JWT building in Japan turned out to be worth an unexpected $200 million, cutting the cost of his original purchase by around one-fifth. Nonetheless his debt was heavy— and in 1989 he raised it several notches too high when he bought his second international advertising agency, David Ogilvy's agency Ogilvy & Mather International.

Once again the acquisition was contested—not least by David Ogilvy himself. With patrician disdain, Ogilvy sneered, 'God, the idea of being taken over by that odious little !!!! gives me the creeps. He's never written an advertisement in his life.' The !!!! stands for either 'shit', or 'jerk', or 'Jew'—take your pick. Ogilvy claimed it was the first; my money is on the last. Anyway Ogilvy later recanted. He had not met Sorrell when he made the remark, he said, and when he did meet him he was utterly won over. It transpired that Sorrell had read and greatly admired all Ogilvy's books. Sorrell then offered him the chairmanship of WPP. Ogilvy graciously accepted.

WPP's financiers were not so easily won over. Though Ogilvy & Mather had also run slightly to fat, its profits were hovering around the 6 per cent mark, and it was by no means as inefficiently managed as JWT had been. Improving a 6 per cent margin cannot be done as quickly and easily as improving a 4 per cent margin, nor is the arithmetic as dramatic. (An agency profitability of 12% is triple 4%, but only double 6%.) Too eager to do the O&M deal, Sorrell paid a hefty £560 million, which he again borrowed. And in the same year WPP bought two large market research companies, Research International and Millward Brown. His emphasis on research was shrewd and farsighted—for several years research enjoyed double-digit annual growth, while advertising was struggling to hit small single figures. But the buying spree saddled him with debts totalling about £1 billion. Then O&M lost some senior managers who had disliked the takeover, and lost a flurry of major clients, including Shell, Unilever,

Seagram, Nutrasweet, Campbell Soup, and American Express. (The traditional view of hostile takeovers is not wholly mythic.)

Then came the recession. For two years advertising was in the doldrums, worldwide. In 1990 Sorrell was forced to announce a profit warning. WPP shares plunged from 650p to 115p in two days, and continued sinking to 41p by 1992. It was touch and go whether the company would survive.

That it did so is another great feather in Sorrell's cap. He has both guts and resilience. He needed terrific guts to buy JWT and O&M—and he needed terrific resilience to keep going during the recession, while pondering whether to throw in the towel because he had made such a hash of things. Instead he restructured WPP's finances, switching his debt from bank loans to equity and longer term finance. He further screwed down his fiscal systems. He brought new management into O&M, which began to win new business. The non-advertising sectors of his portfolio, particularly the market research sector, raked in healthy profits. By 1994 WPP's business shares were back at 117p. The supermarket trolley business was on the move again.

Laughing All the Way

At the beginning of the twentieth century the leading writer on psychology in advertising was Professor Walter Dill Scott, of North-Western University, Chicago. In his book, *The Psychology of Advertising* (1909), he wrote:

> Advertising is a serious business and unless the advertisement is extremely clever it is unwise to attempt to present the humorous side of life.

In the United States, humour in advertising has always been professionally distrusted. Americans take salesmanship seriously. In the 1920s the great American copywriter, Claude Hopkins wrote: 'Nobody can cite a permanent success built on frivolity, people do not buy from clowns.' Well 'frivolity' is a pejorative word, at least in this context; and if people do not buy from clowns, they certainly buy from people who entertain them, as every salesman knows. (In 1981 a study by Karen O'Quin and Joel Aronoff showed that people who crack jokes during negotiations almost always get better deals than those who do not.)

Nonetheless, Hopkins's hostility to humorous advertising was still being echoed in the 1960s by no less an advertising potentate than David Ogilvy. Early in his career Ogilvy was profoundly sceptical about the use of humour.

He felt it was self-indulgent, and that it entertained the humorists but failed to sell products. Ogilvy later retracted this view when he saw an increasing number of amusing campaigns doing the business.

In Britain, following the Hardy and Hassall lead at the end of the nineteenth century, humorous advertising became fairly common. In 1909 Studdy's spirited Vim advertising for William Lever even brought some wit to household cleansers. During the 1930s the S H Benson agency was famous for the deftness of its humour. John Gilroy's celebrated campaigns for Guinness and Colman's Mustard were wonderfully witty.[7] Maybe the British predilection for amusing advertising is the obverse of our dislike of salesman and selling. If somebody is determined to sell things to us, blast them, they had best sweeten the pill by entertaining us while they are at it.

Many of the successful British campaigns identified in this book have been gently humorous. But some highly effective campaigns—a few, not many—go further, and are downright funny. They prompt not merely a wry smile, but a chuckle or even a belly laugh. Almost all of them are television campaigns. In fairness to Professor Dill Scott and Claude Hopkins, there was no television in their day and it is far more difficult to make humour work in print. The wit is almost always in the illustration, rather than in the words, which is why posters are more often amusing than press advertisements.

In the 1980s two of the twentieth century's funniest and longest-running television campaigns came to the fore, in wholly different ways: Benson & Hedges Hamlet Cigars and PG Tips.

The first was another CDP triumph. The 'Happiness is a cigar called Hamlet' campaign had been a popular favourite from its inception, and the 1986 'Photo Booth' commercial is, for many, the funniest commercial ever shot.

The 'Happiness' slogan was dreamed up by CDP copywriter Tim Warriner. Worrying about creating a campaign for Benson & Hedges' new small cigar, Warriner found himself atop a London bus and desperate for a smoke (smoking then being permitted upstairs, but not downstairs, on London busses). Finding a stale cigarette in his pack, he mumbled to himself, 'Happiness is a dry cigarette on the top of a 34 bus'—and promptly realized he could transpose the thought to Hamlet. In Warriner's debut Hamlet commercial a patient with a broken leg in plaster lights up his

---

[7] In 1936 the distinguished art and architectural historian Nicholas Pevsner noted that much Anglo-Saxon commercial art was far less serious minded than that of continental Europe.

small cigar and smiles seraphically, to the accompaniment of Jacques Loussier's orchestration of Bach's 'Air on a G String'. Hamlet inherited this music from B&H King Size, which had used it while cigarette advertising was still permitted on television—thus identifying Hamlet cigar's esteemed parentage (for those who remembered) without mentioning the forbidden cigarette brand. This was probably the first time classical music was used as an integral part of an advertising campaign, and the music—like the Hamlet campaign—survived for 27 years.

Once again CDP's creativity had made a hackneyed advertising idea—'our product will make you happy'—take flight. Hamlet became Britain's top-selling cigar, and over the decades CDP creative teams produced endless amusing and charming interpretations of the 'Happiness' theme. But for most people the funniest by far was 'Photo Booth', in which the Rab C. Nesbitt actor Gregor Fisher tries frantically to cover his bald pate with a few strands of straggly hair while simultaneously awaiting the photo booth flash. Fisher's performance is worthy of an Oscar, but he—and the commercial—had to make do with a galaxy of advertising creative awards.

Whether 'Photo Booth' is, or is not, more amusing than the PG Tips 'Piano Shifter' chimps commercial (1972) is hardly worth debating. Both are perfect examples of the commercial maker's art. 'Piano Shifter' was one of over 100 much loved chimps commercials—which sold a lot of tea. The chimps became PG Tips stars in 1956. Legend has it the agency copywriter had been so stumped for an idea he went for a relaxing stroll in Regent's Park Zoo, where he saw a chimps' tea party and—like Warriner on his 34 bus—immediately realized he could transform it into advertising. But using chimps to promote a human beverage—especially a premium brand tea—is a lot riskier than using happiness to promote a cigar. Norman Berry, creative director of the agency which ran the chimps campaign for many years (and was subject to a series of mergers, takeovers, and name changes) told me an American friend had been so appalled by the chimps that in their early days he repeatedly telephoned Berry from the USA, begging him to ditch the ugly creatures, for the good of the brand, and for the good of his own career—epitomizing Americans' suspicions of outlandish, funny advertising.

How wrong the American was was shown in 1989/90, when the IPA Effectiveness Awards introduced a new category, for long-running campaigns. As with so much else concerning the IPA Awards, this was catalysed by Dr Simon Broadbent, who wrote in *Marketing* magazine (22 September 1988) that to correct the short-term approach of many campaign planners:

Perhaps the IPA should introduce a class of entries which is about the long-term . . . effects of advertising.

The logic of Broadbent's case was accepted without demur. A new IPA Award category was introduced, and in 1990 the PG Tips chimp campaign was its first winner. The paper, titled 'PG Tips' 35 competitive years at the top of the tea market' is one of the most thoroughgoing IPA Award entries ever. The data is robust; the case unequivocal. The chimps lifted PG Tips from fourth place in the tea market in 1956 to number one in the market by 1958, and they helped PG Tips remain dominant brand leader for the following 35 years. Still, in the mid-1950s the American's anxieties about using chimps to sell a premium tea were wholly understandable. The IPA Awards paper admits that those involved were frankly astonished at how well sales responded to the anthropoids' salesmanship. Advertising, like every creative activity, involves risk. Creativity means doing things which have not been done before, and doing things which have not been done before inherently incurs dangers. It is possible, as John Hobson argued, to minimize the dangers, but not to eliminate them. Strand was a risk which bombed, the chimps were a risk which came off—triumphantly.

Even in Britain humour is not appropriate for every type of product.[8] It is doubtful whether it would be possible to produce, say, a successful funny campaign for a medicine. Sufferers would feel the advertiser was laughing at their illness. But many products are closely associated with fun and laughter—particularly beers, as Guinness proved in the 1930s and a barrel-full of other ales and lagers have proved since, including Boddington's, Carling Black Label, Castelmaine XXXX, Courage Best, Fosters, Heineken, John Smith's, and Stella Artois. British advertising excels at making people both laugh and buy. No other country does it nearly so much, or so well. But it can rarely, if ever, be internationalized.

The Hamlet and PG Tips stories, like several others related earlier, describe the conception of the campaigns as a Eureka (or 'light bulb') moment, when an incident unpredictably, and often inexplicably, triggers the kernel of the idea. No doubt this is the way the creators remember things happening—and it makes for a good yarn. But when ideas do materialize out of the blue, this almost always happens after a long period of ideation and worry. The advertising problem will have been fermenting in the creator's mind, and the creator will have had countless previous inspirations, but discarded them all as inadequate. It would be hard to

---

[8] See Giep Franzen, page 56.

exaggerate the obsessive desperation of the creative process when an original idea is needed by next Thursday but simply will not surface. It only takes, as detractors of the creative process frequently insist, a moment to have an idea. Indeed so. But such spur-of-the-moment ideas are seldom much good. Even more seldom, exceptional.

A Roller Coaster in Dreamland

While Sorrell raced onwards and upwards—apart from the glitch around 1990—his old mates Charles and Maurice Saatchi were riding a roller coaster. The first sickening downward lunge occurred soon after Sorrell left them.

With the acquisition of the British Airways account, and the major international clients which came via Compton, Saatchis were ready to go global—indeed they had no choice. In 1983 they obtained a share quotation on Wall Street, becoming only the third British company ever to do so. Maurice and Martin Sorrell then took a road show around the USA, explaining to financial analysts that Saatchi & Saatchi had long ago embraced Professor Theodore Levitt's philosophy of globalization, then all the rage. 'This global trend is something that Saatchi has been working on for years. We have a head start and are geared for it,' said Maurice. His agency, he explained, was already biggest in Britain, biggest in Europe, and tenth largest in the USA, with earnings growth averaging 34 per cent over the previous five years. How Saatchi had a head start when many American agencies had been operating globally for over half a century is unclear. But the analysts were apparently impressed.

In 1984 Saatchi bought two large American market research companies. Then came their biggest takeover yet, and it was outside marketing services. They bought the American-based management consultants Hay Group for £100 million, plus another $25 million on an earn-out, if Hay achieved agreed targets. Hay had 94 offices working with 5,000 clients in 27 countries. The rationale was clear. Management consultancy was growing rapidly. Hay clients would be brought into the Saatchi advertising agency (and vice versa) and the brothers would prove they could run personal service businesses of all kinds. This was a major symbolic step, possibly forward.

In 1985 the Saatchi buying spree accelerated. Twelve more advertising and marketing service companies were acquired at the rate of one a month (Sorrell was still at Saatchi's). The brothers then split their empire in two:

Saatchi & Saatchi Communications, comprising the advertising and marketing services companies, and Saatchi & Saatchi Consulting, headed by Milton Rock of Hay. To run the Communications side, headhunters suggested Anthony Simonds-Gooding. Simonds-Gooding was still at Whitbread, and happy there, but Maurice seduced him by 'climbing through the window with a rose between his teeth'—well anyway that is Simonds-Gooding's graphic description of the recruitment process.

On the day Simonds-Gooding announced he was leaving Whitbread, the brewer's shares fell sharply. On the day Simonds-Gooding joined Saatchi & Saatchi he found himself in a poky semi-basement office, behind the main Saatchi building, with no files, no secretary, and no instructions, engulfed in bouquets of roses on one of which was pinned a card saying 'Welcome Anthony. Over to you. Love, Maurice & Charles.' The brothers had skedaddled off on holiday. Simonds-Gooding had been thrown in at the deep end, with 4,000 Saatchi staff to manage. Within a year the number would be 14,000.

While Simonds-Gooding was trying to find out what he was supposed to be doing, the brothers renewed their shopping spree. At the beginning of 1986 they bought Dancer Fitzgerald Sample, the 13th largest American agency, founded in 1923, with substantial Procter & Gamble business to complement their own. It cost £75 million. This too was symbolically important. For the first time, a British agency had acquired a major American shop. New York, the world's advertising capital, was no longer impregnable. Dancer Fitzgerald was followed, a few months later, by Backer & Spielvogel, an attractive and fashionable young agency which had started only 8 years before but was already 23rd largest in America. However, it had begun to lose major accounts for want of an international network. Maurice was there to supply one. Saatchi's paid $56 million down, with more on an earn-out, depending on results over the following six years.

Then came Saatchi's nemesis: Ted Bates. The bloodcurdling saga of the Bates buy is splendidly related, at length, by Ivan Fallon in *The Brothers*. When it started I was chairman and chief executive of Bates in London, and on the board of Bates Europe. So I had a ringside seat, albeit with an obstructed view. The negotiations were on-and-off as fast as a Times Square neon sign. Not that I was party to the negotiations, far from it. Indeed I left Bates in 1985 because I believed the negotiations had broken down irretrievably. They had. For a few months.

The skeleton of the story can be swiftly told. After Theodore Bates & Rosser Reeves, the management of the Bates agency, and a fair slug of the ownership, fell to Robert E. Jacoby. Jacoby became its third chief executive in 1974. A cigar-chomping elfin of 5 feet 4½ inches—he makes Martin Sorrell look like Goliath—behind his happy, twinkling eyes lurked a far from benevolent despot. He toted a gun, and most of his colleagues were understandably petrified by him. Surprisingly, he had a streak of engaging self-denigration. After discussing a particularly intractable problem with me for a couple of hours, he said, 'OK, let's do nothing. That's what we're really good at.'[9]

Long before Jacoby became boss, Bates's USP philosophy had won them huge and highly profitable accounts, particularly from the Mars Group, Colgate, and Warner Lambert, and in the decade after he became boss Jacoby used the agency's well-filled piggy bank to swallow up other agencies—in America and abroad—with almost Saatchi-like gluttony. By the mid-1980s Bates was 3rd largest agency group in the world, and one of the most profitable. At this point Jacoby, and Bates, ran out of steam. Jacoby considered buying JWT and several other major shops, but client and/or management conflicts prevented him. He considered floating on Wall Street, but could already foresee Bates's future growth would be minimal. If there was no way to go up, Jacoby—who was approaching retirement age—knew he must get out. 'I'm going to sell this agency', Jacoby told his senior executives at a Hawaii beanfeast in March 1986, 'and I don't care what anybody says about it.'

Had they known this Charles and Maurice might have been more circumspect. But they were as desperate to buy as Jacoby was desperate to sell. They were frantic to become the world's largest agency group. They thought this would provide them with some kind of security, though the logic of this thinking is hard to grasp. They had explored all other possibilities, and kept returning to Bates as the only route to their nirvana. Maurice and Jacoby first met in London in spring 1985,[10] when Maurice spent some time explaining the philosophical and structural logic of a deal between them. When he eventually fell silent Jacoby removed his cigar and said:

That's very good Maurice. Now tell me about the dough.

Saatchi, like most others, valued Bates at around $300 million, which it offered. Jacoby wanted $500 million. Saatchi wanted an earn-out.

---

[9] At one riotous Ted Bates hoopla I told him he was as cunning as Stalin, but without the compassion. He thought this hilarious. Well he affected to.

[10] This was an absolutely top secret meeting, to which Jacoby was driven by my Bates driver, who immediately came back and told me he had taken Jacoby to Saatchi & Saatchi.

Jacoby would not countenance an earn-out. For six months there was a stand-off.[11]

Jacoby got his deal, personally trousering $110 million. He had nailed the brothers' aspirations, and their options, with deadly accuracy. Later he was to say:

> It would be fun to have something that would get me closer to knocking off the Saatchis. It'd be easy to do because these guys are amateurs.

Bates cost Saatchi more than twice as much as all their previous acquisitions added together, and they had paid almost double what it was worth. To raise the money Saatchi made a £406 million rights issue in London, the second largest the London stock market had seen to date.

And the brothers were most happy fellas. They had made it. In sixteen years Saatchi & Saatchi had become the largest advertising business in the world.

* * *

Within a year vicious infighting among Bates's top henchmen forced Simonds-Gooding to axe Jacoby, though not without apprehension, as he knew Jacoby was fond of a drink and had been warned about Jacoby's gun. Jacoby then trousered another $5 million for his broken contract—and Bates started to fall apart.

This did not show at first. In the year to September 1986, which included only a few months of Bates ownership, Saatchi profits leapt 73 per cent to £70 million. The following year profits rose another 77 per cent to £124 million, far beyond the dreams of any advertising company in history. Simonds-Gooding rationalized and restructured their frenzied acquisitions, merging the weakened Bates with Backer & Spielvogel to form Backer Spielvogel Bates. Today the remnants of the once mighty Bates comprise a modest chain of agencies in Asia owned, by a fine twist of fate, by Martin Sorrell's WPP.

Meanwhile there were advertising campaigns to be run. In the 1983 General Election the triumphant Falklands War—and the shambolic state of the Labour Party—had handed Mrs Thatcher victory on a plate. Saatchi, again the Tory agency, produced a couple of strong advertisements and

---

[11] This was when I quit. I had long decided that unless Bates was bought by Saatchi its future was untenable. The boozing and screwing in the New York agency were reminiscent of the last days of the Roman Empire, though less well organized. Not that my departure was due to any ethical distaste for the goings on. I simply thought the agency's future was parlous, and my future would be too, if I stayed.

garnered as much kudos as they could. But everyone knew the result was a foregone conclusion. The Saatchi strapline—'Britain's On The Right Track—Don't Turn Back'—was plumb in the tradition of positive–negative claims by parties in power. The Tories were so sure of winning they cancelled a newspaper campaign at the last minute, to save the money, and there was a row about who should pay the cancellation costs.

With two election victories under their belt Saatchi & Saatchi ought to have been a shoo-in to handle the Tories' 1987 election campaign. But during 1986 rumours spread that they were about to be sacked. Thatcher's favourite adman, Tim Bell, was no longer on their payroll. In December 1983 Bell had asked Charles for something he had long coveted: a seat on the Saatchi holdings board. Charles rejected the request out of hand. Bell, deeply hurt, began to disassociate himself from the agency. Frank Lowe offered him what the brothers had always denied him: a seat on his main board. He defected to Lowe. Charles's final coup was to ensure *Campaign* broke the news of Bell's departure on page 3—job moves by top agency people usually appear on the front page. For Bell this was the unkindest cut of all, and his break with the brothers was bitter. But despite his reputation as an account handler, he absconded with none of their clients. His career in advertising petered out, though he later set up a modestly successful public relations company—and burying the hatchet, for a while he ran the brothers' personal public relations. It seems he never quite shook off their spell.

For Saatchi's, the 1987 election was no bundle of fun. Mrs Thatcher threw out the agency's initial proposals, and querulously asked why Tim Bell was not working on her campaign. She knew he was no longer with Saatchi, but he was available as a consultant. Maurice would not countenance Bell being involved. Thatcher began to consult Bell privately. Unsurprisingly, Bell was delighted. But Thatcher was also holding private meetings with Young & Rubicam. News of Thatcher's meetings with Y&R soon spread, fuelling the rumours that Saatchi was about to be axed. In reality this was most unlikely, as within the Tory hierarchy Saatchi's reputation was still high, and anyway Y&R was an American agency. But it made the Saatchi people queasy.

The polls showed the Tories well ahead, but the early Saatchi posters were undistinguished, and came in for much Tory flak. Meanwhile Labour had got its act together, and its first party political broadcast, which glamorized their leader Neil Kinnock and was made by film director Hugh Hudson, was widely admired. Nonetheless most polls showed the Tory lead holding strong. A week before polling day, on Thursday 4 June, which became known as 'Wobbly Thursday', Thatcher—suffering from toothache—uncharacteristically lost her nerve. A rogue poll two days earlier had shown Labour pulling ahead. And Y&R had presented to the Tory panjandrums their own research, which showed the Tory lead falling fast. Thatcher ordered the Saatchi team to produce a new campaign for the last week before polling day.

Hearing this on the grapevine, Tim Bell set to work with Frank Lowe. Bell and Lowe came up with the line 'Britain is a success again—don't let Labour ruin it.' Thatcher loved it. She showed the Bell–Lowe advertisements to Maurice who, for some reason, was less enthusiastic. As instructed, Saatchi had produced their own advertisements. Thatcher insisted Saatchi blend the best of both lots—a recipe for disaster, which Saatchi somehow managed to skirt—and the final strapline was 'Britain is Great Again—Don't Let Labour Wreck It.' Despite the squabbling the Saatchi team put together some strong advertisements with extraordinary speed, and during the last weekend the Tories spent £2 million in the press—as much as had been spent on the entire 1983 election advertising. It was all pointless. Most of the polls had shown the Tories leading throughout, and Mrs Thatcher returned to Downing Street with only a slightly reduced majority.

By rights the next Saatchi escapade has no place in a history of advertising. But as it is one of the most famous—infamous—incidents in which a British agency has ever been involved, and contributed to Saatchi's disintegration, it can hardly be avoided. In the autumn of 1987 the brothers decided to buy the Midland Bank, the fourth largest bank in Britain (now part of HSBC). The rationale for this was never comprehensible to those less visionary. Having bought Hay Group, the brothers decided they were absolutely wizard at running service businesses, and having decided banking was a service business, they could not see why they should not snap up a bank. Saatchi's capitalization stood at £1 billion, the Midland Bank would call for capital of around £4 billion. But the brothers had often before bought trinkets they could not afford.

Having consulted friends in the City, Maurice went to see Midland's erudite chairman Sir Kit McMahon, to explain to him how Saatchi creativity would be synergistic with banking. McMahon's response to Maurice's proposal was an exemplary snub:

> You know, we depend for a great deal of our business on a lot of people who don't want us to be livened up or made more exciting. Our lifeblood is our deposit base, which comes from Swiss bankers and other very conservative people; we depend on the interbank market, and, as far as they are concerned, the duller we are the better. If that deposit base goes everything goes.

Then McMahon delivered his clincher. The Midland had been in financial difficulties in Latin America, and he quietly asked:

What happens when things go to pot in Latin America, and you have to put up another billion?

Maurice had done his homework fairly well, but was ignorant of technical banking processes. His nose was bloodied. McMahon and the Midland board rejected the Saatchi approach.

Yet again the brothers were down, but not out. They turned their hungry attention to merchant bank Hill Samuel. Hill Samuel, a much smaller apple, was in a spot of bother, and needed an injection of cash. Saatchi was willing to put in £200 million, which would double its existing capital. Hill Samuel was tempted, and its management agreed to recommend the Saatchi proposal to the board.

But City opinion had swung against the brothers. The election campaign squabbles had been well publicized, and the news of the Midland Bank shenanigans had leaked. The City hated it all. The *Financial Times* and *The Economist* were brutally sarcastic about the Saatchis' banking aspirations. The scuttlebutt said the brothers were being carried away by their own importance, not to say their megalomania. Maurice himself admits: 'People thought these upstarts have reached too far—they're too big for their boots.' Saatchi shares plunged, slashing the value of their offer for Hill Samuel. The deal fell through.

In the City, these moves profoundly shook investors' faith. But in adland everyone felt Charles, at least, had got what he wanted, and without the hassle of having to run a bank. For several days the brothers had been on the front page of every newspaper in Britain and around the world, and on every television and radio newscast. Bliss.

Through it all, almost unbelievably, Saatchi's creative output in London continued to bloom. Although the Saatchi creative reputation had been based, in some measure, on its brilliant anti-smoking advertisements, produced first at Cramer Saatchi and then at Saatchi & Saatchi, after parting company with the Health Education Council in 1983 the brothers promptly accepted the Benson & Hedges Silk Cut cigarette account from Gallaher. Gallaher's Peter Wilson appointed the agency without a pitch. He needed a worldwide agency to build the Silk Cut brand, and CDP had remained UK-based. 'We are confident Saatchi's will apply the success they have had themselves to our brand,' he said.

His confidence was vindicated. Charles Saatchi, Jeremy Sinclair, and art director Paul Arden created the 'slashed purple silk' campaign, which was almost as impenetrable and as radical as the CDP B&H King Size advertisements had been. The Saatchi Silk Cut campaign built sales and hauled in another horde of international creative trophies. Much of the Saatchi British Airways work was similarly garlanded, as were a handful of their 1983 and 1987 election advertisements. As the decade wore on they produced gong-winners for Abbey National, Alexon (gently beautiful—even though its sales effects were neither gentle nor beautiful), Anchor Butter, BP, British Rail Intercity, Castelmaine XXXX, Coal Traders ('the furry friends'), Jim Beam Bourbon, Nationwide Anglia, Pilkington Glass, the RAC, and *Time* magazine—plus work for a glut of charities including Amnesty International, Guide Dogs for the Blind, the Maritime Museum, NSPCC, Samaritans, and the V&A Museum. Charles Saatchi had cottoned on early to the dodge of using charities as loss-leading creative award winners. (Later, after the brothers had gone, their successors claimed the agency had lost a small fortune handling charity accounts, just to win awards. Probably. But perhaps it was money well spent. In addition to being award-winners, charity campaigns are much loved by agency people, who feel they balance the day-to-day commercial work.)

Campaign's 1993 Jubilee Issue Creativity League, based on awards won at top festivals, put Saatchi a nose ahead of CDP and BMP—though many of Saatchi's points were notched up by the aforementioned charity campaigns. Still, in 1987 at the Cannes Festival (where charity advertisements hardly count) Saatchi had won more awards than any other agency in the world. In 1988 *Campaign* noted 'Saatchis dominated most awards ceremonies during the last year.' Much of this was down to Jeremy Sinclair, one of the outstanding British creative directors of the period. But Charles Saatchi never ceased to exert his *éminence grise* influence on the agency's creative culture—whether or not he was anywhere to be seen.

While things were going sweetly on the creative front, they were fast turning sour financially. In October 1987 Simonds-Gooding left to become head of British Satellite Broadcasting, a short-lived private consortium which launched a satellite transmitter. His successor at Saatchi, Victor E. Millar, was head of the consulting group, now ailing, which he had joined in 1986. Millar claims he was not keen to take over the communications side of the business, but Charles played the old red roses trick on him. He was sent 'three or four dozen red roses', promised a rise in salary and said, 'I'll do it.' Millar knew nothing about the advertising business, but believed all the waffle about advertising and consulting being fundamentally the same. He changed the communications group's budgeting systems to match those of the consulting group, a seriously bad idea.

Ahead of the worldwide 1989 recession, advertising expenditures were already weakening in the United States. At Saatchi, Martin Sorrell's successor David Newlands concluded the agency was running out of cash. He was right, but nobody would listen. More money was borrowed. At the same time the brothers' spending habits began to resemble those of the late Marion Harper. Their joint cost to the company reached £6.5 million annually. Charles had 17 cars, many of which the company maintained. Maurice spent £60,000 on taxis, and threw a £50,000 party to launch the film of his wife's book *Damage*. They sought to pump up their personal 'golden parachutes', in case they were ever fired. By early 1989 Newlands was openly dismissive of both Maurice and Millar. In March he quit and was not replaced.

On 21 March 1989 Maurice was forced to deliver a profits warning. It was, he said later, 'the very worst moment of my career'. In 1989 profits plunged from £138 million the year before, to just £21.8 million. The glory days were over.

Wall Falls Down

As soon as the Berlin Wall crumbled, the ex-Communist countries hastened to set up their own advertising industries. The old regimes had fallen because their peoples had watched free enterprise bring Western consumers affluence, while they lagged far behind. The new regimes were not about to make the same mistakes. Their leaders knew that if their peoples were to get more and better consumer goods, advertising would be essential. Today there cannot be more than a handful of countries in the world which do not have a national advertising industry.

Keen to develop their advertising industry, and fast, in 1989 the Russians invited a party of 15 leading British advertising men to Moscow to run a two-day seminar. The Russians were eager—as they put it—'to get into advertising at the top of the learning curve'. They had heard, they said, British advertising was best, and so they hoped Britain's advertising leaders would help them. The seminar was held under the auspices of the IPA, and those who made the trip included John Hegarty, Rupert Howell (Managing Partner, Howell Henry Chaldecott Lury), Chris Jones (Managing Director, JWT London), Chris Powell (Chief Executive, BMP), as well as my partner Barry Delaney and myself. The Russians deemed the seminar a considerable success, and it was reported widely in their media. The British were more sceptical.

Naturally the British team strove to put across how advertising works, and what it achieves. But they were taken aback by just how little their hosts knew. As Chris Jones said afterwards: 'Advertising has to accept the premise that people have choices.' For 70 years Russian consumers had had precious few choices. Oleg Uralov, the head of VO Videofilm Productions, who had instigated the seminar, said: 'We are discussing commercials when there is almost nothing to sell in this country.' Chris Powell concurred: 'I wasn't aware of just how big a gulf there is.' Many commercial words and concepts simply did not exist in Communist Russia. There were no words for marketing, sponsorship, public relations, targeting, brand image, sales promotion, and so on. The Russians did not even have a specific word for advertising. They used the word *reklama*,[12] which then meant publicity of all kinds.

But the most revealing moment came when we showed a reel of British commercials. We had selected commercials of which we were especially proud—international award winners, which had bowled over juries around the globe. Most of the 300 Russian delegates, many of whom had flown to Moscow from afar, spoke pretty good English, and we ran the reel three times to ensure they got the gist. After which they all agreed the commercials would be useless in Russia. They were too indirect, too oblique. They did not say what the products were for. They did not say how to use them. Russian shoppers, the audience was sure, would simply want to know how the products worked, what they did. In Britain, I explained, the public already knows about the products—so we merely have to make everyone think good things about them. 'Ah,' the Russians replied, 'but if people already know about the products, why do they need to be advertised?'

With the British advertising industry fast sliding into its worst recession since the 1930s, it was a timely question.

---

[12] The *Oxford Russian Dictionary* (2000) now defines *reklama* as: 'publicity, advertisements, hype'.

7

The Nineteen-Nineties: Recession and Globalization

Cold Turkey

Towards the end of 1989 one of my younger, senior colleagues asked me how much his annual salary increase for 1990 would be. I said the future looked so dire there would be no salary increases until prospects were cheerier. He was furious.

'That's unacceptable!'
'Unacceptable?'
'I came into advertising in 1977 and I've had a salary increase every year since. I rely on it.'
'Sorry. There's a salary freeze. For everyone.'
'It's unacceptable.'

His attitude, if naive, was understandable. Advertising had been booming for fifteen years. Anyone who joined the industry during those years imagined the gravy train would keep going forever. In 1989 it ran into the buffers.

* * *

With the exception of 1984/5, when it held steady, advertising's share of the Gross National Product increased in every single year from 1975 to 1989, from 0.92 per cent to 1.53 per cent—an increase of 64 per cent, in a steadily expanding economy. Every year for the next four years it fell (Table 10). Expenditures then recovered again until the end of the century, when dot.com advertising first boomed, then burst.

Table 10. Total advertising expenditure as % of GNP

	Expenditure (at current prices) £million	% GNP (at market prices)
1989	7,883	1.53
1991	7,637	1.33
1993	8,232	1.30
1995	9,846	1.41
1997	11,695	1.44
1999	13,536	1.50
2001	14,320	1.44

Source: Advertising Association.

Naturally the advertising decline reflected the wider national economic picture. During the half century, as a percentage of the GNP, advertising expenditure has peaked at the top of economic booms (1973 and 1989) and bottomed at the bottom of recessions (1975 and 1993). This pattern mirrors international trends.

Parochially, the 1989 crash, which began in Japan and rapidly rippled round the globe, manifested itself in the number of people employed in IPA agencies. From 1989 to 1993 the numbers employed fell by very nearly one-third, and the number of IPA agencies also tumbled (Table 11).

From then on the number of employees slowly climbed back, reaching 14,000 by 2001—though the number of agencies did not recover until a few years later (when digital agencies, specializing in internet and text advertising, started to proliferate).

Rather than sit on its heels and whinge, early in 1990 the IPA ran an advertising campaign targeted at advertisers, warning them of the long-term

Table 11. IPA agencies: People employed and number of agencies

	Number of people employed	Number of agencies
1989	15,400	257
1991	13,000	245
1993	11,100	225

Source: Institute of Practitioners in Advertising.

dangers of slashing their advertising budgets in tough times. The campaign was written by my partner Barry Delaney, and this is how it opened:

IN A RECESSION, BUSINESSMEN NO LONGER HURL THEMSELVES FROM TALL BUILDINGS.

THEY JUST SHOOT THEMSELVES IN THE FOOT.

In every recession that has been analysed, those companies which cut their advertising performed badly compared to those which maintained or increased them.

They performed badly during the recession and for some years thereafter.

For example, a study by James Capel has shown that companies which maintained or increased their spending in the 1974/75 recession had 27% higher sales over two years and 30% higher sales over five years. But it doesn't stop with sales.

The authoritative Center for Research and Development has demonstrated how even a modest increase in advertising during a recession will buy brand share much more easily (and inexpensively) than in good times... In the USA there have been more studies, some taking in data from recessions as far back as the 1920s.

There, as here, the findings never vary. If a company cuts its adspend the money it expects to save may never appear on the bottom line. Chances are it will be outweighed by loss of sales attributable to lack of advertising.

The advertisement went on to offer a data-pack containing details of all the relevant research, and offering IPA guidance to any advertiser seeking additional information. As the media were suffering as much pain as the agencies, several newspapers provided free space for the campaign, which was launched in the *Financial Times*. The television companies soon followed suit, briefly running a commercial produced by Saatchi & Saatchi. The advertising generated a good deal of favourable editorial comment, and there was a heavy burst of requests for the IPA data-pack. But as with most short campaigns with no relevant data against which to benchmark them, whether or not the campaign had any real effect is, to be generous, unknown and unknowable; to be realistic, unlikely. (As it was my idea, I prefer to believe the former.)

For advertising—and for the nation—the recession seemed interminable. The national mood was grim and gloomy. House prices slumped, unemployment boomed. Despite constant, futile, optimistic pronouncements by government ministers, things did not get better until spring 1993, when three years' rising unemployment ground to a halt and output grew again after falling steadily for thirty months. Even then the emotional scars took a long time to heal, and few people truly believed the recession had ended until New Labour resoundingly kicked the Tories from power in May 1997.

'I'd Like To Teach The World To Sing In Perfect Harmony'

Once the recession was over, the two forces which dominated British advertising during the 1990s were globalization and, more slowly, new media. British creativity remained of an exceptionally high standard, and Bartle Bogle Hegarty's star shone brightly at Cannes. But for British creative agencies globalization is a tough nut to crack.

Like so much else in advertising that seems revolutionary, global advertising was not new. It was not new when John Metcalfe saw it coming in 1961, less still when Maurice Saatchi spoke so eloquently about it in 1983. Throughout the century global advertising grew—though the rate of growth was, and remains, impossible to quantify. The simplistic definition of a global campaign is one where the advertisements are the same in all, or anyway most, countries. But few so-called global campaigns are literally global: most are multinational, some running in many countries, some in a few. Some are simply regional—pan-European, pan-Asian, or whatever.

International cosmetics, perfumes, and fashion companies have been running 'global' campaigns since the 1930s, principally in top-class fashion magazines. But global campaigns for glamour products in printed media can be adapted for different countries relatively easily. It is much tougher to produce global campaigns for other products and in other media, particularly television.

In a shrinking world, the commercial benefits of global—or anyway multinational—advertising are indisputable. Central control of all advertising is easier. As international travel increases, and becomes ever more popular, travellers see the same campaign everywhere, instead of a mishmash of different campaigns in different countries. As national cultures become more homogenous, campaigns which succeed in one country usually succeed in others. The transference of such knowledge is one of most multinational companies' greatest strengths. And globalization means costs can be amortized—though the savings are usually far smaller than novitiate multinational advertisers expect. All these arguments impel global companies to globalize their advertising whenever they can.

But while the benefits are clear, the mechanics are complicated. In many ways still the boldest, and most seminal, attempt to produce a truly global television campaign was made in 1971, when Coca-Cola brought together a multi-racial choir of youngsters from thirty countries, all in their national dress, and filmed them singing 'I'd Like to Buy The World a Coke' on an Italian hillside. (Re-recorded by the New Seekers as 'I'd Like to Teach the World to Sing in Perfect Harmony', the track became a pop classic.)

The sales effects were shattering too. Within a decade vodka had overtaken gin in popularity.

In 1971 Coke aimed to teach the world to sing in perfect harmony—but this has proved far harder, and far slower, than global marketers predicted.

The Clunk! Click! campaign, using Jimmy Savile, almost doubled seat belt wearing among both drivers and front-seat passengers.

Campaign magazine chose the lovable Smash Martians as its 'Campaign of the Century', but I have nagging reservations about its long-term effects.

Here Heineken pay homage to a classic 1934 John Gilroy Guinness poster. Had I selected a 'Campaign of the Century' it would have been 'Refreshes The Parts Other Beers Cannot Reach'.

Tory Party grandee Lord Thorneycroft claimed this poster 'effectively won the election for the Conservatives' in 1979. Claptrap.

MIDDLE TAR As defined by H.M. Government H.M. Government Health Departments' WARNING: CIGARETTES CAN SERIOUSLY DAMAGE YOUR HEALTH

What did the surrealist Benson & Hedges advertisements mean? What were they getting at? What deep subconscious tricks were they playing? I wish I knew.

BA's Manhattan Island commercial might easily have been an embarrassing shambles, but it was breathtaking, and was rightly hailed an international creative triumph.

J. R. Hartley promoted Yellow Pages for eight years—extraordinary longevity for a single commercial.

Like several major retailers, Dixons would buy large spaces and in effect crowd them with its own semi-display classifieds.

Using pop songs in commercials goes a long way back, but none have done it better than Levi's 501s, when Nick Kamen stripped off in a launderette and Marvin Gaye heard about it through the grapevine.

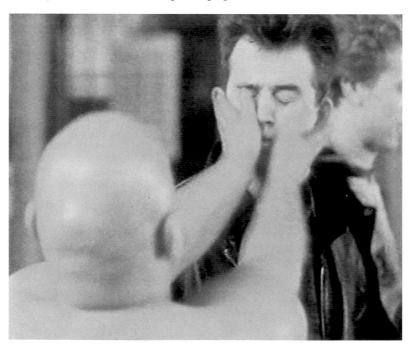

In playgrounds throughout the country kids started to Tango each other, and before long a Tango'd child ended up in hospital with perforated ear drums.

7mg TAR 0·7mg NICOTINE
SMOKING KILLS
Health Departments' Chief Medical Officers

During the 1990s Saatchi & Saatchi won numerous awards—for Silk Cut and other campaigns—an astounding performance for a creative organization in the throes of civil war.

The public voted Guinness Surfers 'The best British advertisement ever'—though 'ever' is a bizarre word here, as nobody under 35 would have remembered any advertisements from before the 1970s.

Created in London by an Anglo-American team (Bill Backer, Billy Davis, Roger Cook, and Roger Greenaway), it was a breathtaking statement of global leadership by one of the world's greatest brands, and was a defining commercial of the era.

But it implicitly spotlit the problems global commercials face. Which nationality or nationalities should be cast (not every commercial can have a cast of hundreds)? Which national costume should the cast wear (not every commercial can have people in varying national dress)? Which language should they speak (a simply worded pop song can easily go global, but dialogue is a whole lot trickier)? The Esso tiger, which prowled around the world in the 1960s, was born in an agency in Houston, Texas in 1964, but had to change his stripes in several of the countries he visited, to conform with local attitudes to tigers. The 'Top Breeders Recommend Chum'[1] campaign, which originated in Britain, ran successfully throughout the world—but with different dogs, and different breeders, in every country. Thinking global is fine, but everything must be right locally.

To this day there are but a tiny number of brands as uniform throughout the world as Coke, or as Esso. As they spin around the globe most brands have different national packs, many have different brand names, some come in different formulations, others are used differently in different countries. Nor are seemingly similar cultures always as similar as they seem. For a major brand in South East Asia, my agency filmed exactly the same commercial—well, almost—on three successive days: once for Malaysia, once for Singapore, once for Hong Kong. The indigenous peoples quickly spot each other's physical characteristics and dress, but more importantly, the benefits of the product were perceived differently in the three locations. Even in this small corner of the globe, the peoples did not sing in perfect harmony.

While the peoples of Hong Kong, Malaysia, and Singapore may be reluctant to share the same commercial, in many small countries throughout the world the local populations have no choice. Their commercials— and their television programmes and movies—are lip-synched, however badly. They have to put up with it. Small countries have never merited the cost of making separate commercials. Nonetheless most multinational advertisers now try hard to minimize ugly and awkward lip-synching, and nowadays try to write commercials which will minimize the problems from the start. But this in turn fetters the creators' freedom, making it impossible to use local idioms or traditions which will not travel.

---

[1] To further complicate matters, Chum is called Pal in some countries.

For all these reasons global advertising has taken off more slowly than John Metcalfe et al. predicted. Nobody today knows how much advertising has been 'globalized'. It is not even clear how global would be defined. In how many countries need a 'global' campaign run to be global? How much alteration would be acceptable from country to country, how many changes would be allowed before a commercial would be judged too local to be global? Were the commercials in Hong Kong, Malaysia, and Singapore global (the scripts were much the same), or were they local (they were individually filmed)? All this explains why nobody knows precisely how much 'global' advertising there is, nor how fast it is growing.

Despite these caveats, there is no doubt global advertising—however you define it—grew steadily throughout the second half of the last century. And the worldwide recession expedited the global trend, as multinational companies aimed to cut advertising costs by producing global campaigns (which they generally feel to be desirable, anyway). Before the recession global advertising had been steadily gaining ground. After it the advertising scene was transformed.

Campaign is a good barometer. From the mid-1990s onwards its international coverage swelled noticeably. London's adland had famously been a village. Now it was a global village. During the decade *Campaign* front-page headlines referred to international pitches and switches with increasing frequency, for both creative and media accounts—'Adidas in hunt for global network', 'Cisco calls for £80 million worldwide review', 'Lego to centralise £60 million worldwide account', 'Mediacom scoops $163 million global Shell business', 'Unilever calls for global Wall's pitch', and the like, quoting billings in dollars or in sterling, whichever was appropriate. A weekly international column was launched, new campaigns from around the world were routinely reviewed, and Worldwide Advertising Supplements began to appear regularly. A major series of features called 'Kings of Madison Avenue' ran for two years, featuring profiles and interviews with eighteen powerful chiefs of global holding companies and agency networks, including Allen Rosenshine (Omnicom founder), Phil Geier (Interpublic), John Wren (Rosenshine's successor at Omnicom), Ed Meyer (Grey), Charlotte Beers (Ogilvy & Mather—the only Queen of Madison Avenue on the list), as well as—though neither was strictly a Madison Avenue man—Maurice Levy (Publicis, France) and Martin Sorrell. All this would have been—literally—foreign to the magazine's founding editorial team in 1968, when half the top ten agencies were British, and even the American agencies mostly handled British clients. By the 1990s all top ten agencies in Britain were internationally owned.

To handle their booming international business, major agencies had to restructure themselves once again. They appointed Global Client Service Directors (whatever their exact title, which varies from agency to agency). These have immense power—for precisely the same reasons that Account Directors held immense power until the 1960s: they know far more about their client than anyone else. They will normally handle only a single large client, but the agency's overall income from that single advertiser may be much larger than a local branch agency's total revenue. Even in my days at Bates in the 1980s it was regularly rammed home to me that any one of our large international clients generated more revenue in the USA than Bates's London agency did in its entirety.

The Global Client Service Directors have to be on-call to their clients, 24/7, wherever they are. They travel with their clients, often for days at a time, learning everything about them, and more. Above all, they are responsible for ensuring the agency's work and its services are just what the client wants, all the time and everywhere. To handle their multinational clients, agencies have developed matrix management to a high level, with both local and international managers having interwoven and overlapping responsibilities for services and profitability. It is a complex game, calling for sympathetic personal relationships and close team work. Not every manager is good at it. Not every manager wants to be.

And not much of this helps British creativity, because most global companies look first to their national agencies for global campaigns, and only a small minority of global companies are British. Some international companies, occasionally, hold competitive pitches for new campaigns, between their agencies in different countries. Some decide their British agency is the best shop on their roster, and appoint it to handle all their work, everywhere. But these are the exceptions. It is hardly surprising global advertisers have a predisposition to appoint, as their main international agency, an agency from their own country. But it does not help British advertising. At present there are more than enough British advertisers to keep British agencies busy for the foreseeable future. But the middle-distance looks uncomfortably cloudy.

In the Playground

Despite the growing dominance of international business, after a lull during the recession young agency hopefuls started launching start-ups again, knowing there was sufficient local British business to get going—and well aware that, in the fullness of time, success would bring them offers from multinationals with deep pockets.

Outsiders find the fissiparous nature of the agency business, and the constant proliferation of new agencies, bewildering. They suspect the phenomenon simply reflects the egocentricity and vanity of advertising people, all of whom want to run their own show, preferably with their name on the door, and dislike working for others. There is some justice in this suspicion. But other important factors include the minimal capital needed to start up an agency; the opportunity for agency owners to sell out and make a capital killing quite quickly; and the natural desire of young people in a creative industry to want to do things differently from their elders. None of this should detract from the stress and risks involved in starting an advertising agency. Most new agencies fail. And mushrooming globalization increases the odds against them.

During the 1990s the three most significant new agencies were Howell Henry Chaldecott Lury, Rainey Kelley Campbell Roalfe, and M&C Saatchi. The first two never grew large in their own right, while M&C Saatchi was but another chapter in the long-running Charles & Maurice saga, to which we'll return later.

Howell Henry Chaldecott Lury had been launched in 1987, espousing some unusually iconoclastic beliefs. HHCL initially set out to make advertisements that were socially responsible, whenever possible using real people rather than actors, eschewing high quality production values—resulting in what is sometimes called 'grunge advertising'—and eschewing creative awards. Much of this thinking emanated from planning director Adam Lury, a radical, left-leaning thinker who had been one of BMP's brightest planners. But it was enthusiastically endorsed by his partners. Sceptics found it hard to believe Rupert Howell had truly embraced the Lury dogma, as grunge is not his style. He is an archetypical Ferrari-loving pinstripe-suited salesman—he had previously been a highly successful new business winner for Young & Rubicam. But the sceptics underestimated him. Howell is a flashy enthusiast, but is also thoughtful and shrewd, with something of a good politician's instinct for social change. Howell knew the Lury dogma would win HHCL the kind of publicity any new agency craves, but he also felt the time was ripe for it, as did the two talented creative partners, Steve Henry and Alex Chaldecott.

At the same time, with the traditional media commission system now in tatters, HHCL neatly reversed the Saatchi 1970 launch advertising by announcing the agency would not accept media commissions at all, and would only work for fees. The new shop immediately made waves and became—always a good sign—the agency everyone in the business loved to hate.

With Howell's new business know-how the agency set off at a cracking pace. HHCL soon won the Midland Bank's branch-less banking subsidiary First Direct, Fuji Films, Pepe jeans, Charles of the Ritz, and before long the Automobile Association, Mazda, Maxell, Tango, Molson, BHS, Pot Noodles, and Danepak. And yes, some of HHCL's early work was controversial, as promised. Their first Fuji campaign featured racism and mental handicap; their Pepe jeans advertising showed young people lying around and laughing 'Because one day you'll die'; their first campaign for Danepak revealed a nude family at a barbecue diffidently covering their private parts with cooking utensils; and their campaign for Maxell Tapes had a rough-looking guy hitching a lift on a busy road holding up placards—which got the lyrics of a Skids song hilariously wrong. But some of it was controversial for other reasons. The agency's high-profile launch of First Direct provoked responses ranging from 'mystifying' to 'appalling', with most in the latter category. Maybe HHCL believed the First Direct advertisements were heirs to the enigmatic B&H King Size campaign. If so, they were sadly mistaken.

But it was the 1991 Tango campaign which put HHCL on the map. Tango drinks come in a range of flavours, and HHCL decided to advertise each of them separately, dramatizing the taste and linking the flavours together with the line 'You Know When You've Been Tango'd'. The first commercial was for Tango Orange. A fat, bald, half-undressed plasticized orange genie jokily slapped a guy about the face, to illustrate 'the bite and buzz of real oranges'. It did this far too well. Emulating the slapping, in playgrounds throughout the country, kids started to Tango each other, and before long a Tango'd child ended up in hospital with perforated ear drums. Amid much media hubbub the commercial was pulled off air. The slap was changed to a kiss, but the Tango message had got through, and sales responded handsomely. Rupert Howell dextrously exploited the publicity, managing simultaneously to be overtly apologetic about the harm done and covertly proud of how effective the campaign had been. Despite the agency's distaste for awards, the Tango commercial was entered for and feted by D&DA, and was later described by former Campaign editor Stefano Hatfield as 'the seminal work of the decade'—which is overstating things a tad.

Though it was never a publicly declared agency policy, HHCL also made rather a specialty of losing clients shortly after they had won them, in the same way BBH had done but on a grander scale. HHCL's revolving-door clients included First Direct, the Prince's Trust, MTV, Fruit of the Loom, *Sunday Correspondent*, Red Mountain, Homepride, 3i, Avis, and National Savings. Despite this client churn, HHCL grew rapidly during the early 1990s, but ran into difficulties when it spawned a slew of subsidiaries. The agency set up its own media specialist, a promotional events company, and HHCL Brasserie—a project-based TV production boutique, while also acquiring an integrated marketing group called IMP. It was a miniature holding company. This took the partners' eye off their core agency business.

Ten years after its launch, HHCL went through a torrid patch and sold out to Tim Bell's PR Group, Chime Communications. The price was £24 million, the deal being bankrolled by Martin Sorrell, who bought 29.9 per cent of Chime to provide Bell with the necessary cash. Howell became joint chief executive of Chime, and was expected to succeed Bell as chairman. The other HHCL partners were intended to be locked into Chime for 2 years, but Adam Lury quit after about 18 months to become a writer. Nonetheless HHCL recovered from its torrid patch and started to win business again, climbing into the agency top twenty in 1999. But as Howell devoted more time to Chime, HHCL once more faltered and slipped back. In January 2003 Martin Sorrell bought HHCL—which during its short life had, risibly, been the *Campaign* Agency of the Year no less than three times—from Chime, for approximately £8 million, one-third of the price Chime had paid for it. Sorrell merged it into the London office of one of his international networks. HHCL staggered on for a while within the WPP empire, but is no more.

* * *

Rainey Kelly Campbell Roalfe started in 1993 and lasted just six years as an independent entity. Marie-Therese Rainey was the only woman to lead a successful agency start-up in Britain in the twentieth century. (Advertising is a far less female-friendly business than it should be, as successive IPA studies have shown.) Cool, unflappable, highly intelligent, and proudly Scottish, MT—as she liked to be called—came from what she describes as a 'totally non-commercial' background. After graduating at Glasgow University she gained an MSc at Aston. Her MSc dissertation on Signal Detection Theory was later published by NATO—a rare accolade for an agency boss. She trained with Bartle, Bogle, and Hegarty when they were at TBWA. Having become an account planner, she went to work with the radical American agency Chiat Day in California, when British account planning and account planners were becoming chic there. Returning to Britain she opened Chiat Day's London office, where her tenure was difficult, to put it kindly.

Launching a new agency in 1993, when the recession was still simmering, was bold, not to say reckless. Before starting the agency MT Rainey had a reputation for being too analytical, and unsympathetic to creative people. Moreover, although she claimed her partners Jim Kelly, Robert Campbell, and Mark Roalfe had all given up their jobs to launch the agency—which was true—they had all been stuck in less satisfactory positions than they doubtless aspired to. So the auguries for Rainey Kelly Campbell Roalfe were not auspicious.

Like HHCL, the new agency built itself on the demise of the commission system, with an innovative remuneration formula which, Rainey claimed, 'reinvented the advertising agency'. Advertisers wanted one fundamental thing from their agencies, declared RKCR: big ideas. Ideas which would work in different media, and in different countries. RKCR would therefore charge for its ideas, on a three-tier basis. There would be a basic payment for thinking and creative time; a second payment for the ideas themselves; a third payment related to the performance and success of the ideas. Though it appeared to relegate the role of advertisements to a back seat, the formula proved attractive to many advertisers.

RKCR took four anxious months to win its first assignment, a 'secret project' from BT. Then the clients crowded in. In 1994 the agency won business from Smith and Nephew, Emap, Virgin Atlantic, Scottish Courage, and Thornton's chocolates. It held onto its clients better than HHCL, though it too had a few brief encounters: Spillers Dogfood, M&G Investments, and Sun Microsystems came and swiftly went. But other clients—particularly Virgin—gave RKCR more and more business, always the litmus test of whether an agency is performing well. In 1994 the agency was 70th in the agency league table, and from there it rose in each successive year—to 58th (1995), 43rd (1996), 29th (1997), and 21st (1998) with billings that year of £64 million, much boosted by having won the pan-European launch of General Motors' Astra model. Their creative work, particularly for Virgin, won them some gongs, which gained the agency a modest but sufficient reputation for creativity.

Rapid growth brought a queue of suitors to their door. The partners had always made clear their intention to sell, in order to work on a bigger stage. ('To have a larger train set' as Robert Campbell put it.) In August 1999 RKCR sold themselves to Young & Rubicam—yet another great American agency which was sinking in London. In London its position had plunged from a highly respectable 4th in 1990 to a lowly 19th by 1998—falling almost as fast as RKCR had been rising. Following the Y&R purchase, the new agency was called Rainey Kelly Campbell Roalfe Y & R. Ever since Saatchi & Saatchi,

American international agencies have been forced, unwillingly, to accept that in Britain the British agency name should precede the name of the US owner. RKCR/Y&R jumped to 10th in the *Campaign* pecking order, where it consolidated under its new management and remained for several years.[2]

* * *

The short histories of HHCL and RKCR spotlight how hard it now is for new British agencies to grow and retain their independence, in an increasingly global advertising environment. But one agency launched in the 1990s successfully managed it. High above HHCL, RKCR, and other, lesser, new agencies, and making them all look like kids mucking around at advertising in the playground, has towered M&C Saatchi, launched in 1995. The brothers were no longer bright young things, and no longer made any pretence of being organizationally radical—but M&C Saatchi grew to be 9th largest agency in Britain within five years.

New Media for Old?

Though multi-channel television grew steadily, during the 1990s the most important media development from the advertising standpoint was the emergence of the internet. But the internet grew far more slowly than commercial television did in the 1950s. The internet first surfaced as an advertising medium in Britain in 1997, when it carried £8 million advertising, less than 0.1 per cent of the total. (1997 was also the first year in which D&AD accepted and judged internet advertisements as a separate category.) Five years later in 2001, the internet's advertising revenue had grown to £166 million, 1.0 per cent of the total—whereas after five years commercial television's slice of the cake was 20.9 per cent. The internet did not take hold as an advertising medium until 2006/7, a decade after it had started. Even then it lagged far behind television at the same stage of its life. Of course the internet's competition included television itself, by now deeply entrenched. Only time will tell if this is the entire explanation for its slower growth. The internet has proved its effectiveness in certain markets—especially travel and tourism, financial services, certain retail sectors, and automotive—as a cross between classified advertising and

---

[2] MT Rainey has since left advertising and launched an internet mentoring company, now bringing her full name Marie-Therese into play—presumably to sound friendlier and less austere than she chose to be in advertising.

direct marketing. But the jury is still out on whether it will become a major carrier of display advertising—an issue to which we will return.

The second important media development was the fragmentation of television viewing. Rupert Murdoch had launched Sky, initially transmitting four channels, in 1989. Sky was almost immediately challenged by British Satellite Broadcasting which offered a further five channels. With Anthony Simonds-Gooding at its head, BSB launched its distinctive 'squarials' in April 1990. A massive campaign announced that 'It's smart to be square'. The public disagreed. By November 1990, with debts approaching £1 billion and only 100,000 squarials sold, BSB merged with Sky—which already had a million viewers—to form BSkyB. In September 1993 Murdoch launched Sky's multi-channel package, followed in 1998 by Sky Digital's launch of 140 channels. Sky was now firmly in orbit, and was soon followed by a cluster of other satellite stations.

At the end of the twentieth century viewers could choose from 200 channels, causing much anxious discussion within advertising about how difficult this made reaching mass audiences, compared with the past when ITV had been the sole commercial station. This anxiety was ridiculous. Terrestrial stations then still reached over 80 per cent of households weekly. That figure has since been eroded, but even today any television time buyer who is not a complete blockhead has no difficulty reaching a mass audience. Nor is there any evidence that reaching television audiences in bite size chunks, rather than all at once, has a detrimental effect on advertising's efficacy. Not since the massive newspaper circulations of the 1940s has any other medium reached majority audiences in one fell swoop, but nobody has worried about newspapers, magazines, or posters being 'fragmented'.

For the worriers, more disconcerting fragmentation occurred in March 1997, with the launch of Channel 5. To give physical form to the new station's declared intention of offering 'exuberant family-oriented entertainment', it was launched by the Spice Girls, bouncing about innocuously on screen. But despite its family-oriented target, its programming was succinctly defined by its director of programmes Dawn Airey as 'films, fucking and football'. (In recognition of her pithy use of language Airey was shortly afterwards promoted to be Channel 5's chief executive, before leaving in 2002 to become managing director of Sky.) Because its reception necessitated set retuning, Channel 5 built its audience slowly, but steadily and successfully, though like all terrestrial channels it has recently struggled to hold onto its viewers in the face of satellite competition.

For most other media the 1990s were tough. The recession had bitten them hard at the start of the decade, but the 1999–2000 dot.com boom promised a new dawn. The dot.com hopefuls spent small fortunes in traditional media, to attract users and customers. Unfortunately the new dawn quickly changed to a stormy night. Most of the early dot.com companies imploded. The augury was e-tailer Boo.com, which was launched with much hullabaloo and went phut six months later. The dot.com companies, having been spending investors' money with abandon, were swiftly forced to curtail their campaigns. And by then the internet, as an advertising medium itself, was beginning to nibble at traditional media budgets. For traditional media and creative agencies the outlook grew gloomier.

A Good Thrashing

In 1994 I was thrashed by the late Keith Holloway. At a Marketing Society debate I tried to persuade an audience of about 400 that advertising creativity was not what it used to be. Holloway, a shrewd and experienced marketing man who was then Commercial Affairs Director at Grand Metropolitan, argued the opposite and beat me to pulp. The audience voted for the 1990s advertisements he had presented—for Haagen-Dazs, John Smith's (with Jack Dee), Levi's, Orange, Smirnoff, Sega, and Tango among others—rejecting the classic 1970s advertisements I presented, for B&H King Size, Dubonnet, Fiat Strada, Heineken, Hovis, John Smith's (Arkwright), and Smirnoff among others.

At first I suspected Holloway had deviously packed the audience with teeny-boppers, who were bound to vote for the latest and trendiest stuff rather than the eternally beautiful collection with which I had honoured them. Certainly the audience—though not teeny-boppers—were preponderantly in their 20s and 30s, and felt loyal to the current commercials they knew and loved, almost automatically preferring them to my blasts from the past.

But watching Holloway's 1990s selection I saw how advertising creativity had changed over years. Advertising messages had become much faster than in days of yore. Compared with Holloway's, many of my wonderful old commercials seemed to go on forever. Take the brilliant Fiat Strada 'Handmade by Robots' commercial, which was my *pièce de résistance*. When it appeared in 1979 many felt it to be perfection: the most fabulous commercial in the history of humankind. It scooped up gold and silver gongs everywhere. But boy does it take its time. When viewed now, that is. It didn't seem like that then.

Many of the campaigns Holloway presented were, indeed, targeted at the young. And the implicit presumption of the creativity was that young people can decode advertising faster than you can say cyberspace. This should not be surprising. They started watching television before they climbed out of their cots. By the age of 25 they had seen some 100,000 commercials (if they were average viewers), most of them six or more times. They had played computer games since infancy. They had watched heaven knows how many pop promos—which greatly influenced commercials during the 1990s. And today—if not then—they will have surfed the internet from as soon as they can read, if not before. Holloway's reel revealed how advertising creative people had absorbed all this intuitively, which explains why older folk increasingly find many new commercials baffling.[3]

Despite my thrashing, on the basis of Britain's performance at global awards festivals, we were at our peak in the 1970s and early 1980s. Still, during the 1990s British advertising continued to be internationally garlanded for such campaigns as (in alphabetical order, plus agency and launch date):[4]

- British Airways: Face (Saatchi: 1990)
- Boddingtons: 'The Cream of Manchester' (BBH: 1991)
- Carling Black Label: Dambusters (WCRS: 1992)
- Dunlop SP Tyres: Unexpected (AMV: 1992)
- Guinness: Surfers (AMV: 1999)
- Haagen Dazs: Ice Cream (BBH: 1992)
- John Smith's: Jack Dee (BMP: 1994)
- Levi's: Creek (BBH: 1994)
- Maxell: Mistakes (HHCL: 1990)
- Nike: Just Do It (Simons Palmer: 1992)
- Orange: The Future's Orange (WCRS: 1994)
- Reebok: The Edge (L H-S: 1990)
- RSPCA: Dog licences (AMV: 1990)
- Tango: You've Been Tango'd (HHCL: 1992)
- Wonderbra: Hello Boys (TBWA: 1995)

And in the 1990s a goodly number of fine long-running campaigns were being constantly replenished and revitalized with new executions, including B&H Silk Cut (Saatchi), Castlemaine XXXX (Saatchi), *The Economist*

---

[3] Much the same has happened to television crime thrillers—particularly American crime thrillers—which now move infinitely faster than they used to. Many early television thrillers seem veritably sluggish today.

[4] To minimize confusion the agency initials/names are those used throughout this book, and are usually the initials of the founding partners. Several of the agencies changed their names, some of them several times, over the years.

(AMV), Sainsbury's (AMV), Stella Artois (L H-S), Volkswagen (BMP), and Volvo (AMV).

Though it made for a fun debate, there can be no absolute judgements about which era's advertisements are 'best'. In any event, as Holloway's supporters rightly believed, British creativity approached the end of the century with a flourish.

Checking Out at the Checkout

By the 1990s the predominant advertisers in Britain were retailers. This was a sweeping reversal of the position in earlier decades. Each of the major multinational marketing companies—Procter & Gamble, Unilever, Nestlé, and L'Oreal in particular—spent more than any retailer in aggregate, on all their brands. But the retailers easily outspent most of their individual brands.

In 1970 there was only one retailer in the top 20—the Co-Op (15th). By 1990 retailers represented an astonishing 7 of the top 10 advertised brands (Table 12).

Moreover 5 of the next 10 brands in the top 20 were also retailers: Currys (11th), Comet (12th), WHSmith (13th), Sainsbury's (14th), and Dixons (18th). From then on retailers continued to be the dominant advertisers, year after year.

Retail advertising was, as has been seen, not at all new. The nineteenth-century antics of Glasgow grocer Thomas J. Lipton are sketched out in

Table 12. Television and press expenditure 1990

	Expenditure (£ '000s)
Tesco	26,313
McDonalds	16,930
Woolworths	16,322
ASDA	14,568
Benson & Hedges KS	14,317
B & Q	14,012
British Satellite Broadcasting	13,784
Whiskas	12,773
MFI Stores	12,745
Texas Home Care	12,528

Source: Advertising Association.

Chapter 2—and retailers have always recognized the need to advertise store openings, seasonal sales, and special promotions. But for the small independent shops which dominated the retail trade until well after the launch of commercial television, mass advertising made no sense. They could not afford it, nor did they have sufficient national coverage to justify it. The grand department stores had been big press advertisers since the 1890s, but their advertisements, mostly in local papers, featured the merchandise they carried: what today would be called 'line-and-price' advertising. They did not intentionally promote their stores as brands.

Though their coverage of the country was growing fast, the new multiple retailers—operating in a business sector which had traditionally seen no need for continuous campaigns—did not rush to start advertising. For some retailers the rejection of advertising became a matter of strategic principle. They felt it wrong to include a margin for advertising in their costs. Eschewing advertising, they believed, allowed them to keep their prices lower, which provided their customers with better value.

Marks & Spencer, then Britain's most admired and acclaimed retail chain by far, embraced this view religiously. M&S believed that for any retailer offering high quality goods at competitive prices, advertising was a millstone. John Lewis, Waitrose, and BHS similarly spurned advertising. NEXT was launched successfully with minimal advertising, exclusively in Vogue. Between 1983 and 1985 Tesco completely repositioned itself while simultaneously cutting back its advertising. And on the other side of the coin, the Co-Op spent heavily on advertising and watched its business plunge, while Woolworths' 'Wonder of Woollies' campaign—like the Strand campaign two decades earlier—achieved a high level of awareness but little commercial success.

To explain the apparent redundancy of retail advertising, several plausible hypotheses were advanced. Retailers owned sites and shop windows on high streets, which customers passed and visited constantly, so they had no need of advertising: they communicated with their customers directly, face to face. Anyway manufacturers' advertising, it was argued, created the consumer demand, retailers just had to make the goods available. And for retailers local word-of-mouth publicity was all-important: happy customers told each other where the bargains and best value were to be found. These points, it was widely believed, made retail advertising unnecessary.

The belief was buttressed by the powerful growth of retailers' own brands. Throughout the 1970s the battle between manufacturers' brands and retailers' brands was fierce. Almost universally, retailers' brands were cheaper, and their sole USP was their price: their quality was generally poor. But piling them high and selling them cheap kept retailers' margins as thin as a buyer's smile. Manufacturers had to advertise their brands heavily to force retailers to stock them, and to ensure consumers would pay for their added value. Retailers could not afford to advertise their own brands heavily, and did not believe they needed to. Smaller manufacturers, in particular, feared this would be a fight to the death: retailers would eventually dispense with their brands completely. (After all, M&S stocked no manufacturers' brands.)

But at the same time retailers were beginning to enjoy massive economies of scale. Self-service, computerization, juggernaut transportation, stock control, centralized purchasing, ruthless price negotiation, laser scanning, and large out-of-town stores started to take effect. Mass retailers could now afford to advertise (often forcing their suppliers to subsidize their campaigns) and still keep their prices low. And the siting of out-of-town stores made advertising all but essential: there was no longer any passing trade. In the 1970s several retail chains began to advertise, but with campaigns focused entirely on price: Tesco, ASDA, Dixons, and MFI advertised week after week, and built profitable businesses—simply and solely promoting their low prices. They still felt no need for 'image' advertising, advertising which carried general messages about their overall offering. They would have viewed such advertising as wastefully self-indulgent. The maxim of the time was 'Retail Is Detail'—and the only detail that mattered was price.

John Pearce had foreseen things would change as early as 1967, when CDP handled the relaunch of Selfridges. To quote David Puttnam, he briefed his team:

> Everyone will tell you store advertising is a nightmare. Don't believe it. You're going to change the old-fashioned image of Selfridges. You're going to do the best campaign that will appear next year. I've talked them into running whole pages in the Evening Standard every week.

Charles Saatchi and Ross Cramer responded by producing a witty campaign which included the memorable line 'The most valuable things shoplifters get off with in Selfridges are the girls on the cosmetic counter.' (Charles Saatchi is said to have personally researched the veracity of this claim himself.)

But Selfridges was a grand department store, and the flourish was a one-off. Most retailers continued to eschew image advertising, and most agencies continued to believe retail advertising was a nightmare: retail was detail. Much more importantly, few bright young marketing people wanted to work in retail. The best of the commercially inclined graduates with advertising and marketing aspirations went to the large marketing companies, or to advertising agencies. Retail marketing was unappealing, unglamorous, unexciting.[5]

The dearth of bright marketing people working in retail exacerbated agencies' lack of interest in handling retail accounts. Agencies felt line-and-price campaigns to be wearisome: verbally unimaginative, visually crude, and boringly detailed. The advertisements incessantly required amendment, and they mostly ran in dozens of local newspapers. Few agencies had either the organizational systems or the staff to handle constantly changing detailed advertisements in a gamut of local papers. No matter how much they spent, retailers were the poor relations. (In the mid-1970s the Managing Director of MFI said to me, 'If I fired half a dozen agencies in as many weeks, the trade press wouldn't even mention it. If Guinness tests a new ad in Wigan it is front page news.' He was only slightly exaggerating.) Even today few creative agencies feel a burning yearning to handle retailers' line-and-price advertising. But it is only fair to add that many agency people do not choose a career in advertising in order to handle crude, laborious, unimaginative advertising—no matter how effective, or how lucrative it may be.

Sainsbury's broke the mould. Sainsbury's had always understood people choose where they shop on the basis of both price and brand image. While Tesco and other multiple retailers' stores had looked liked bargain basements, Sainsbury stores exuded sensible, affordable quality—at low prices. Led by Sainsbury's shrewd marketing chief Peter Davis, from the beginning of the 1980s the supermarketer employed separate agencies to run the different parts of its advertising. First Saatchi & Saatchi and then Abbott Mead Vickers created elegant brand campaigns, built around the slogan 'Good Food Costs Less at Sainsbury's'. These were as innovative and stylish as any manufacturer's brand advertisements, and in due course added further to David Abbott's sizeable cache of creative gongs. Simultaneously Sainsbury's employed an agency called Broadbent[6] to produce its run-of-the-mill line-and-price advertising, mostly in local newspapers, using the same slogan. Davis spent four times as much on his line-and-price advertising as on the brand advertising, relying on the two campaigns to reinforce

---

[5] While at university I regularly topped up my inadequate grant by working at Selfridges during vacations, and they regularly offered me a permanent job—not because I was any good, but because they were desperate to recruit graduate trainees. But I wouldn't countenance doing anything so prosaic!

[6] Nothing at all to do with Dr Simon Broadbent.

each other symbiotically. In 1983 Sainsbury's was *Campaign*'s 'Advertiser of the Year'. For a retailer to win this accolade would have been unthinkable in earlier years.

Far more tellingly, Sainsbury's advertising was helping make its checkouts ping. Between 1980 and 1986 Sainsbury's pre-tax profits increased more than 20 per cent annually for six years running. Watching and learning, other retailers, particularly Tesco, found their own ways to combine brand imagery and price competitiveness in their campaigns. Bright young marketing people found themselves attracted to retailing. Retail advertising boomed, and has done so ever since.

Many retailers continue to rely on line-and-price advertisements—particularly the electrical, furniture, and D-I-Y chains—and for good reason. Long before visiting a store (or today, a website) customers decide they want a new television set, or a carpet, or household paint. These are rarely impulse purchases. Having made the decision to buy, the customer will search for where the product can be bought most cheaply. Both the prices and the style of the line-and-price advertisements say 'Come to us, we're cheapest.' Sceptics who question the effectiveness of these retail campaigns should read Gary Davies's fine paper 'Retailer Advertising Strategies' (1991), which establishes a clear and statistically significant correlation between advertising and the number of shoppers visiting electrical and D-I-Y stores, and furniture stores (excluding Habitat, where the picture is more complicated).

Retail brand advertising is not so very different from manufacturer brand advertising. Both, in William Lever's words, 'build a halo' around what they are selling. The art is to ensure that the halo reflects what the brand offers, and that its glow communicates what the consumer wants (which may, or may not, be the lowest prices).

Nobody has now grasped this better than Marks & Spencer. M&S belatedly became a convert to brand advertising. And as their commercials might say, today their increasing profits are not just any profits, they are M&S profits. In 2006 the Marks & Spencer campaign deservedly won an IPA Advertising Effectiveness Award.

'TV Pollutes the Penis'

The retailer whose advertising created most controversy in Britain at the end of the century was not British, nor was his advertising. The Italian knitwear company Benetton's advertising set out to be contentious, not to say notorious. In this it succeeded brilliantly. Whether it helped boost Benetton's sales remains a woolly question.

In 1983 Luciano Benetton, president of the eponymous retail chain, appointed the Italian photographer Oliviero Toscani to create all the company's advertising. Toscani was a fashion photographer who had worked for Vogue, and for Fiorucci and Esprit, before being given carte blanche by Benetton to do pretty well as he liked. Owning 7,000 shops in more than 100 countries Benetton needed a truly global campaign, dependent on visual rather than verbal impact.

Toscani's response was to create a series of posters designed to shock all nationalities. They did. Benetton posters showed a blood-smeared new-born baby, coloured condoms, a dying AIDS victim, a black horse mounting a white mare, a baby with Down's syndrome, a blood-stained T-shirt riddled with bullet holes, and a black woman suckling a white baby, among many others. Different countries banned different posters—invariably generating much local sound and fury in the process. This ruse is often employed by advertisers with small budgets, to make their money go further. In Britain, as the ASA has grown stronger, the ruse has been used increasingly, usually by political and pressure groups—but it was also used for some time by the fashion retailer French Connection ('fcuk'). It infuriates the more staid and respectable sectors of the advertising industry—but there is nothing they can do about it.

In Britain, complaints about Benetton flowed into the ASA thick and fast. The bloodied baby, still attached to its placenta, prompted over 800 complaints in 1991, the largest number ever provoked by a single advertisement at that time. It resulted in the ASA creating a new, fast-track system for banning advertisements that cause excessive public outrage. Toscani assumed disingenuous surprise. 'Why is traditional advertising acceptable, with its fake images, yet reality is not?' he asked. 'These sorts of images are seen every day on television and in newspapers, but as soon as we use them for advertising everybody gets upset.' (How he knew this is unclear, as he claimed 'I don't watch TV. TV pollutes the mind, the brain, the heart and the penis.') The answer to his *faux naïf* question is that the public chooses which newspapers and television programmes it wants to read and watch, but advertisements are thrust upon them. Despite Toscani's grab for the moral—even ethical—high ground, this was blunt-instrument advertising: he pummelled the public's sensibilities and hoped it would make them buy. It seems certain Benetton never bothered to research public reactions to their posters.

But like the B&H King Size surrealist advertisements a generation earlier, the Benetton posters soon became instantly recognizable, generating voluble word-of-mouth publicity and public awareness, for much less money than B&H had spent. Did they increase sales? It seems doubtful. Perhaps Benetton came to the same conclusion, as Toscani and his client parted company in 2000. The analogy with Benson & Hedges is misleading. The public accepts that advertisements exist to sell products and make profits. But many deplore commercial businesses exploiting shocking—not to say horrifying—social issues for financial gain. Toscani's answer to such criticism was characteristically robust: 'I am not a salesman. Selling is the company's problem, not mine.'

Predictably, advertising (and especially predictable advertising) inspired Toscani's wrath: 'Advertising is a dead body which keeps on smiling,' he opined. But he generously threw a tiny crumb of comfort to the Anglo-Saxons: 'In England, you are the most creative, you have the most feeling for ads. It must be part of your Anglo-Saxon heritage,' he said when he came here in 1995. We were duly flattered.

On the Track

Though they began in the 1950s, tracking studies did not become the dominant form of advertising evaluation until the 1990s. As their name implies, tracking studies track the impact of a campaign as it progresses, with regular surveys. The survey questions can cover many areas: respondents' recall of the advertising campaign, or of different parts of the campaign; respondents' attitudes to the campaign—what they thought good/bad, what they found interesting/uninteresting, what they liked/disliked, what they found persuasive/unpersuasive and so on.

Successive tracking surveys must use precisely the same questions, to be comparable, and they must interview exactly matched samples of respondents. Tiny changes in question wording or sample structure can produce wild and seemingly inexplicable changes in response levels. Consistency also makes possible the aggregation of normative data. Over the years research companies and advertisers have learned what levels of response are averagely achievable, for any given level of advertising expenditure, in any given market.

Generally speaking, the tracking data which carries most weight is advertising awareness: what percentage of the public remembers the brand's advertising at all? The presupposition is that consumers will not respond to advertisements they cannot remember. As Giep Franzen writes in *Advertising Effectiveness*:

> Over the years research has shown a strong correlation exists between brand aware-
> ness and buying behaviour... also a strong correlation between brand awareness and
> market share.

But the borders between brand awareness and advertising awareness are
often blurred. People may know about a brand but not recall its advertising, or recall advertising but not remember which brand it is for. It has also
been argued, by Dr Robert Heath, Paul Feldwick, and others, that people
may well be influenced by advertising they do not remember, or may
never have even been conscious of. Feldwick has written (*Admap*, 1990):

> We [BMP] know of a number of campaigns with high scores for advertising aware-
> ness which have not achieved their objectives, and campaigns with low awareness
> scores which have proved very effective in the marketplace... a high aware-
> ness score is neither essential nor sufficient for effective campaigns.

Past chapters have told of several campaigns which achieved high awareness but nugatory sales. Campaigns which achieve low awareness but
which are nonetheless highly effective need more explanation. Like all
other media, advertising certainly works at the subconscious level—currently jargonized as 'low-attention awareness'. You will seldom consciously remember the advertising when you choose to buy a brand. But
the principal reason for campaigns with low awareness levels achieving
sales success is that for the great majority of brands a minuscule number of
additional consumers will generate a notable increase in sales. Persuading
an additional 1 per cent of the adult population to buy your brand will add
some 400,000 new customers. (For a car manufacturer that would be
nirvana.) Low overall awareness can thus produce massive sales—as long
as the awareness is among exactly the right people. And awareness tracking is insufficiently sensitive to measure such small percentages.

Nor is 'awareness' as straightforward as it sounds. There are immense
differences between spontaneous (or top-of-mind) awareness and prompted
awareness. ('Do you remember any advertising for petfoods...?' versus 'Do
you remember this advertising for Whiskas...?') Verbal advertising messages are easier to remember, or anyway easier to relate during research
interviews, than visual or emotive messages. Awareness is generated more
successfully by 'public' media—television, print, posters, for example—
than by 'private' and tightly targeted media (direct mail, e-mails, and text
messages, for example). Though tightly targeted media generate low total
awareness, they may be highly sales effective among those to whom they
have been addressed.

Awareness is also strongly influenced by 'feedback'. Feedback is the propensity for regular users of a brand, or even of a generic product, to notice and remember the advertising for their brand (or product). So major brands, used by large swathes of the population, tend automatically to achieve higher awareness levels than minor brands. (Incidentally, feedback also muddies all those studies which claim that because, say, beer drinkers are aware of beer advertisements, this proves beer advertisements cause them to drink beer. Not so. It is the other way round. They are aware of beer advertisements because they drink beer.)

Despite these caveats, most major advertisers now use tracking studies as a useful, relatively inexpensive, rough check on whether their advertising is or is not getting through. Many advertisers set Key Performance Indicators based on tracking results: the KPI for the campaign is a prompted awareness level of xx per cent, which must be achieved, or else! Tracking studies are generally carried out monthly or quarterly, and agencies live in mortal fear of the next tracking result being a lousy one. This is not unwarranted: agencies have been fired for consistently achieving poor tracking ratings.

The first major research company to specialize in tracking studies was formed in 1975 by Maurice Millward and Gordon Brown. Millward Brown, now owned by WPP, is still the largest in the field, but today there are at least a dozen significant research companies specializing in tracking studies, employing more than 600 market research executives between them (excluding interviewers). Each week *Marketing* magazine publishes awareness tracking data for the top television campaigns. (Q: 'Which of the following TV commercials do you remember seeing recently?') The results bounce about, as new campaigns come on stream and old campaigns go off air. With consumers bombarded by approximately 1,000 new commercials (or adaptations) every week, it is hardly surprising their memories are fleeting. Few experienced marketing people believe tracking studies are the be-all and end-all of campaign evaluation—but they have become much the most widely used advertising measurement system.

'Man with Glasses Quits Job'

'When the going gets tough,' runs the corny adage, 'the tough get going.' As things got tougher for Saatchi & Saatchi Charles and Maurice certainly got going—but perhaps not quite in the way the maxim means. In March 1989 when Maurice delivered his profits warning, with the sky about to fall on them, they took a 25-year lease on a ludicrously expensive top-floor office suite in Berkeley Square, to be occupied solely by the group holding company. Bestriding the top of the building they hoisted the name Saatchi & Saatchi, in big black block letters. Kevin Goldman says this cost them £70 million. Berkeley Square had long and famously been J Walter Thompson's London home, and the preposterous big black letters threw a yah-boo V-sign at JWT, across the tops of the trees. Though the letters nominally spelt Saatchi & Saatchi, in translation they spelt *folie de grandeur*.

Maurice rationalized all this in predictable ways: the advertising business is a fashion business, a confidence business, where an agency's image counts for everything. But the gesture of confidence did nothing to shore up their profits. By the following year things had gone so far awry even the brothers accepted the need to bring in an outside group chief executive, to take over the job from Maurice. Maurice would remain chairman.

In October 1989 Robert Louis-Dreyfus was named the group chief executive. This was a puzzling appointment. Unknown in Britain, Louis-Dreyfus came from a wealthy French family and had a reputation as a flamboyant playboy, though he had built a successful market research company (and has since proved himself an effective businessman in other fields). Louis-Dreyfus brought with him to Saatchi his finance director Charles Scott, who was neither flamboyant nor a playboy, and had a reputation as an unimaginative bean-counter. Neither had ever worked in advertising, nor shown any predilection for it.

Still, Louis-Dreyfus and Scott initially did the right things. They sold off the management consultancy business, and they slashed the worldwide headcount, which had reached 18,000, down to 12,800. They did less well reorganizing the subsidiary advertising agencies, which began to leech clients. These were merged and remerged in different configurations, as though they were jigsaw pieces nobody could find ways to fit together. And the newcomers failed to tackle Charles and Maurice, who continued to treat the company as an intriguing hobby. In Maurice's case this meant dabbling in politics—he was ennobled in 1996—and dealing with a small but important group of advertisers with whom he had built close personal relationships, particularly British Airways, Procter & Gamble, and Mars. In Charles's case it meant occasionally looking at new creative work, playing chess, going go-karting, and tending to his increasingly substantial art collection.

For both it meant generous pay and rations. Accustomed to lavish expenses the brothers were unwilling to cut back. In 1989 they cost the company £2 million in direct compensation, and a further £3.5 million in other expenses—big dough for a company in financial trouble. In the following year they agreed to cut their remuneration, but their total costs still exceeded £2 million. From 1990 the company was haemorrhaging money and heavily in debt. It did not post a pre-tax profit between June 1989 and August 1992. Yet some £20 million a year continued to be spent on the group holding company, including £1 million on the rent and overheads in Berkeley Square.

Enter David Herro. Herro was a successful young fund manager at the State of Wisconsin Investment Board when he made his first purchase of Saatchi stock—4 per cent of the company—in autumn 1990. Herro specialized in buying rubbish stock, and he felt Saatchi & Saatchi PLC fitted the definition admirably. Between 1987 and 1990 Saatchi shares had fallen 97 per cent, and a new management team had been brought in. Now, Herro felt, was the time to buy. Louis-Dreyfus told Herro that Maurice and Charles were 'out of the picture', so the company was poised to recover. 'If the brothers were still in the picture', Herro said later, 'we wouldn't have touched it. They destroyed the company once, so why give them the chance to do it again?' This statement is a mite disingenuous, as Herro built up the Wisconsin holding to 8.11 per cent. And after he left Wisconsin in 1992 to set up his own investment fund, Oakmark International, he acquired a further 9.64 per cent of Saatchi's stock in 1993. By then Herro most certainly knew of the brothers' continued involvement, but he invested Oakmark funds to the hilt. Together with Wisconsin, with which he still had strong ties, Herro now influenced 17.75 per cent of Saatchi stock, and was the largest shareholder by many transatlantic miles.

In some ways Herro is an amalgam of both Charles and Maurice. Intense and obstinate, when he was young his friends said he was a wild man whenever things did not go his way—like Charles. Like Maurice he graduated in economics, and showed a similarly remarkable talent for strategic analysis when in his twenties. Like both he came from humble beginnings and enjoys an expensive lifestyle. But unlike the brothers, Herro had a puritanical attitude to money. So when he discovered how much the brothers were taking out of the company, and how little they were putting in, he was incensed. The first time they met, Maurice compounded the problem by lunching Herro privately in the luxurious Berkeley Square offices, smoking large Havana cigars, grumbling about the company's costs as though they had nothing to do with him, and refusing to agree to invest in Saatchi & Saatchi PLC himself—from which Herro deduced he had little confidence in the future of his own company.

Herro deplored the brothers' costs, but what distressed him far more was that Maurice had begun waging open war on Charles Scott. After a relatively short stay Louis-Dreyfus resigned, fed up, and the brothers appointed Scott as his successor as group chief executive. This too was a puzzling appointment: Scott had even fewer qualifications than Louis-Dreyfus for running an international advertising business. Indeed the brothers had to persuade him to take the post, as he himself was not keen. Having persuaded him, they swiftly concluded he was not up to the job, of which Maurice made no secret. To Herro, for the chairman of a public company openly to attack his chief executive was inexcusable. But Scott fought back, and proved a tougher fighter than might have been expected. Before long each side was, incredibly, employing its own PR consultants to rubbish the other side. Maurice used an old friend called David Burnside, who the company paid £25,000 for his work. Scott used Grandfield Rork Collins Financial.

The media had a ball. *The Guardian* headlined an article: 'Maurice Sets Out to Fill the Sails of the becalmed Saatchi Yacht.' *The Times* responded with: 'The board of Saatchi & Saatchi is expected shortly to tackle the vexed issue of the generous remuneration package enjoyed by Maurice Saatchi.' Supporting Maurice, the *Evening Standard* said: 'Saatchi (the company) should be moving steadily forward. It is not.' Scott gave an interview to *The Guardian* in which he criticized the top management he had inherited from Maurice, implying it was not up to scratch. Ivan Fallon—whose book *The Brothers* is a Maurice eulogy—attempted to deliver the *coup de grâce* in the *Sunday Times*, calling Scott a 'good-natured and guileless accountant who should never have been put in to run an advertising group'. (But who put him in?) This article was picked up by the US press, and the *New York Post* headlined its report 'Civil War at Saatchi & Saatchi'. David Herro was not amused. Several of the agency's largest clients wrote to the non-executive directors on the group board, stressing their strong support for Maurice. This further fuelled Herro's fury, as he was sure Maurice had orchestrated the letters. (He may well have done.)

Though still abysmally low, the Saatchi profit margin improved from 4.7 per cent to 5.7 per cent during 1994, and the share price rose 17 per cent. This strengthened Scott's standing with investors. Rapprochements, usually brokered by creative director Jeremy Sinclair, led to temporary truces between the warring factions. Maurice began putting in the hours again, new business came in again, and Scott claimed they were all buddy-buddy again. Then hostilities broke out again. Maurice wanted a package of 'super-options' to reflect his greater input, his salary having been slashed to a measly £200,000 a year. Once again Herro was not amused. This leaked into the *Financial Times*, which on 13 December 1994 wrote: 'Maurice Saatchi's future as chairman . . . hangs in the balance following an explosive row between the company and leading shareholders over a £5 million option package.' Maurice was sure Charles Scott had leaked the story. (He may well have done.)

Like an old fashioned Western, by late 1994 the melodrama was fast stumbling towards its final showdown. Herro—the tall, dark, and fairly handsome gunslinger from Wisconsin—was determined to settle the varmint's hash once and for all: Maurice must be gunned down. In an interview with the *Wall Street Journal* on 16 December 1994 Herro was adamant: 'He must stand down as chairman...He may continue to work for the company, but not as chairman.' After an 8½-hour meeting on the same day, the Saatchi board finally ousted Maurice as chairman of the holding company. Instead he was offered the chairmanship of the subsidiary agency he and his brother had founded in 1970. Maurice demanded time to think it over. It was an offer he could, and did, refuse.

* * *

There, almost, ended one of the more bizarre episodes in British advertising history. In retrospect it is easy to argue Charles and Maurice Saatchi were inspired builders but lousy managers. They kept close to their pals and their favourites, but ignored the rest of their staff and clients completely. At his first agency Xmas party Louis-Dreyfus ironically quipped that Charles had sent a message saying how profoundly sorry he was that he was unable to attend the party that year. He had never attended. Organization and discipline had been lax to the point of chaotic. Saatchi staffers used to boast that agency meetings were revolving doors: the same people were never present when a meeting ended as had been there at its start. It was not only Charles and Maurice whose personal expenses were cavalier: other senior people's financial excesses were legendary. The brothers threw titles about like twinkling confetti. During the late 1980s, when things were beginning to get rough, a wag in the creative department sent out an all-staff memo saying there would be no Xmas bonus that year but everyone in the agency would be made a board director.

Nonetheless, as Maurice would grumpily point out when things first started to go wrong, for two decades their turnover and profits grew every year without exception: not bad going. And through all the shenanigans, under the indefatigable leadership of Jeremy Sinclair, the agency continued to produce outstanding—and award-winning—creative work for many of its clients. During the first half of the 1990s Saatchi & Saatchi collected numerous awards for its work for B&H Silk Cut, British Airways, BT, Castelmaine XXXX, Club 18–30, Fuji Films, NSPCC, Selfridges, and the

COI—for both the Army and Nurses recruitment. An astounding performance from a creative organization in the throes of civil war.

The Charles and Maurice story only 'almost' ended with their departure
from Saatchi & Saatch. Three of their closest associates—Jeremy Sinclair,
Bill Muirhead, and David Kershaw, christened by the press 'the three
amigos', quit the agency too. All three made statements saying they did
not want to work for a company that was, as Sinclair put it, 'in the grip of
people who do not understand the advertising business'. The departing
trio were soon joined by another half a dozen top Saatchi executives. It was
manifest such senior people were not about to sit on their hands forever—
and doubly manifest when it became known that Maurice's contract had
included no restrictive covenants to stop him poaching clients from his
old agency. Almost immediately other agency bosses made contact with
him in the hope of forging an alliance. In quick succession Maurice talked
to D'Arcy Masius Benton & Bowles, Grey, Lintas, Chiat Day, and Publicis—
but all the discussions came to nought.

The three amigos decided to set up a new agency themselves. They then
signed a secret agreement with Maurice and put it into escrow while their
contractual situations with their ex-agency were resolved. Unlike its predecessor, the new agency was to be a partnership of five equals. The amigos
were in a far stronger position to set up a new agency than the brothers
were, and they all knew it. As Muirhead said, 'I wasn't interested in being a
serf again.' On 11 January 1995 Maurice announced the establishment of The
New Saatchi Agency—a typically cheeky name, which nimbly positioned
their previous shop as the old Saatchi agency. Charles Scott immediately
took restraining legal action. But as legal fees headed towards £1 million on
each side, they agreed to settle. There was a 'lopsided truce', as the *New York
Post* described it, which was rightly seen as a victory for the brothers.

On 22 May the name of The New Saatchi Agency, which had been one of
the trickiest issues for the sides to agree upon, was announced: M&C
Saatchi. The amigos did not like it much. Charles and Maurice did not
like it much. Scott was less than delighted with it. But it was the only name
on which all parties could agree. At more or less the same time Saatchi &
Saatchi PLC was renamed Cordiant, which nobody much liked either.

During the first few months of its existence M&C Saatchi snatched
British Airways, B&H Silk Cut, the Mirror Group, and Dixons from Saatchi
& Saatchi, which Maurice now called OldCo. Additionally, Maurice's
departure cost the Cordiant Group the $400 million worldwide Mars
account, which had been with Bates. Maurice had been close to Mars,
though at first no Mars business followed him to M&C Saatchi. (Some

did later.) The Mars loss forced Cordiant to cut 470 jobs, with severance costs of about £10 million. Nor did Maurice win any Procter & Gamble business. The great Cincinnati behemoth, it seems, had been less than impressed by Maurice's all-too-public dogfights. Instead it gave additional business to his old agency, which had done excellent work for it—excellent, that is, within the P&G canon.

Even without P&G or Mars business, M&C Saatchi's take-off was meteoric. In 1995, during which year the agency only traded for about 7 months, its billings reached £65 million, taking it straight into the agency league top twenty. During the next year it started to win new business of its own, rather than from its predecessor. In 1996 M&C billings hit £174 million, and it vaulted to 8th in the agency league, where it hovered until the end of the century, when it climbed to 5th. M&C's creative work has never quite matched that of its forebear, perhaps because Charles has never paid it that much attention, while Jeremy Sinclair had passed his creative peak. But they have won their share of creative awards—as indeed has Saatchi & Saatchi itself in the years since the bloodletting.

In April 1997 it was announced that Cordiant would be dissolved, and its two major advertising agencies—the Saatchi & Saatchi Group and the Bates Group—would be demerged. Since then Bates has all but disappeared, but Saatchi & Saatchi—now owned by the French holding company Publicis—is still doing fairly well, despite the defections of so many key people and a slide in billings at the beginning of the twenty-first century. Perhaps Herro was right: by the mid-1990s the company Charles and Maurice had created no longer needed them, nor could afford them.

More than a decade after the brothers' departure, the original agency they created is still in business, and they have created another that is almost equally successful, employing 800 people in 13 international offices. M&C Saatchi went public in London on AIM in 2004, and is now the only independent British agency publicly listed. The brothers have two agencies named after them in Britain's top ten. No other advertising men have ever achieved anything remotely comparable.

Private Eye, referring to Maurice's trademark spectacles, headlined the tipping point in the saga: 'Man With Glasses Quits Job'. Enough said.

£30 Million Down the Drain

If general election advertising ever makes any difference, it must have done so in April 1992—though as always the evidence is hazy. In the run-up to that election the two major parties spent £6.5 million each, about the same in real terms as had been spent in 1979. The Labour advertising was highly praised, by both political commentators and media pundits, and polls showed that it enhanced the public's opinion of Labour leader Neil Kinnock. The Tory advertising, which stressed the likelihood of increased taxation under Labour, was generally thought uninspired. Most polls consistently showed Labour in the lead, albeit by the narrowest of margins. But the Tories won, albeit by the narrowest of margins. The advertising may have tipped the balance, and post-election research suggests the Tories' taxation threats—uninspired or not—struck home. The Tory campaign may have influenced sufficient voters to have won them the election by a few ballot papers.

The May 1997 general election could not have been more different. Labour had been far ahead in the polls since Black Wednesday, 16 September 1992, when the Tory government abandoned the European Exchange Rate Mechanism, and effectively devalued sterling. The voters never forgave them. From then until the 1997 election was called, Labour's lead in the polls was never less than 20 per cent. The outcome of the election was a foregone conclusion. Curiously, this made the parties spend more than ever on advertising. Labour were desperate to avoid a replay of the last-minute slip-up in 1992, and the Tories were desperate to reverse the voters' antipathy.

The Conservatives spent £13.1 million on advertising, Labour spent £7.4 million, Sir James Goldsmith's single-issue Referendum Party—dedicated to holding a referendum on Britain's relationship with the European Community—spent £7.2 million. Others spent about £3 million, bringing the total to over £30 million. This was a quantum leap above any previous spend. What did it achieve? The turnout of voters, at 71.3 per cent, was the lowest at any election since 1935. The Labour lead over the Conservatives fell steadily from 22 per cent in the polls in the first week of the campaign to 13 per cent on voting day. This might be taken to prove the Tory campaign had worked, but in 'Why Labour Won the General Election of 1997' Steve Hilton, who ran the Tory advertising, through M&C Saatchi, concluded: 'There is one simple, salutary lesson . . . directed particularly at those who argue modern elections can be bought by heavy advertising expenditure. The general election of 1997 shows that advertising . . . cannot make all the difference.' Hilton's conclusion, one feels, would have been heartily endorsed by Sir James Goldsmith. His Referendum Party garnered 800,000 votes at a cost of about £10 per vote. It would have been simpler to hand out £10 notes at the polling booths.

Perhaps the parties' advertisements were particularly feeble? With one exception, they were indubitably unmemorable. Indeed it is hard to find anyone—even among those who worked on the campaigns—who can now remember much about them. Determined to avoid a repetition of the Tories' 1992 taxation attack, and guided by a battery of focus groups each week, Labour pressed home the message that the Tories had themselves increased taxes 22 times since 1992, and were likely to introduce VAT on food. The Tories began by claiming 'Yes It Hurt. Yes It worked.' When that message failed to dent Labour's poll lead they switched to 'New Labour. New Danger'. This did no better. Hence Steve Hilton's gloomy conclusion above.

The single well-remembered Tory advertisement was the 'Demon Eyes' poster, a personal attack on Tony Blair dreamed up by Maurice Saatchi. The advertisement made Blair look demonic, with red eyes and a scary glare. Once again Maurice hit the headlines, as Demon Eyes was banned by the ASA, and there was a clamorous brouhaha. The ASA had minimal jurisdiction over general election advertising, partly because its judgements would not normally take effect until the election was done and dusted, and partly because it might be seen to be interfering with the freedom of political debate. However, this freedom did not extend to the unfair depiction of individuals in advertisements, political or otherwise. The ASA judged Demon Eyes was an unfair depiction of Blair.[7] Nonetheless *Campaign* voted it Advertisement of the Year—one of its wonkier judgements—on the grounds that it had achieved its purpose by raising questions about Blair's character.

Despite *Campaign*'s plaudits, and despite the clamorous brouhaha, Demon Eyes did not register as even a blip in the polls.

---

[7] As a result of this brouhaha the ASA withdrew from all regulation of election advertising shortly afterwards.

8

Crystal Balling: Peering into a Cloudy Future

What Are Holding Companies For?

While the Saatchi brothers were playing phoenixes, Martin Sorrell pushed WPP forward with a steady, if impatient, hand. In 2000 WPP bought Young & Rubicam, and its shares zoomed to 1323p, more than ten times higher than they had been five years earlier. Its growth has hardly faltered since. In 2005 Sorrell bought Grey Global, thereby achieving a trick many had believed impossible: servicing arch enemies Unilever (at JWT) and Procter & Gamble (at Grey) within the same holding company. In addition to its considerable market research and public relations holdings, WPP is now the largest advertising media-buyer in the world, owning two of the three biggest global buying companies. It has significant agency invest-ments in the fast emerging BRIC countries—Brazil, Russia, India, and China. It jockeys for the position of the world's largest marketing services holding company with Omnicom, usually running it a close second. Third comes Interpublic, with the two French holding companies, Publicis and Havas, in 4th and 6th positions, separated by Dentsu (Japan) in 5th spot. Currently WPP's revenue equals the revenue of Publicis, Dentsu, and Havas combined. WPP is another mammoth British advertising success story. Sorrell was deservedly knighted for his services to communications in 2000.

But the gist of the question I asked Sir Michael Angus in 1987, when WPP acquired JWT, remains unanswered. How do advertisers benefit when their agency is owned by a holding company? The holding companies have provided handsome returns to investors—holding companies usually do, for a while—but what do they offer their clients? Sir Michael's 1987 answer was valid, but insufficient. He posited that WPP would improve JWT's efficiency, and an efficient agency serves its clients better than an inefficient one. Yes, but an advertising agency need not be owned by a holding company to be run efficiently. JWT had grown fat and wasteful, but many large independent agencies have been managed excellently. Nor are holding companies inherently competent. The management of Interpublic has been almost as woeful of recent years as it was under Marvel Marion.

Sorrell claims holding companies wrest nitty-gritty administration and financial management from their subsidiaries' shoulders, allowing them to deploy their creative talents full-time, for their clients' benefit. This won't wash. With or without holding companies, agency managers handle the administrative and financial aspects of agency operations, without involving the creative guys. The best holding companies make their subsidiaries run efficiently by introducing another layer of managerial reporting into the mix. Nobody working for a holding company subsidiary believes the holding company saves either time or money. Most believe precisely the opposite: the holding company wastes time on additional meetings and reporting.

After acquiring JWT in 1987, Sorrell smartly appointed Jeremy Bullmore—the wise and perceptive ex-chairman of JWT London—to the WPP main board. How, he asked Bullmore, could WPP make the best use of the many talented people it employed, and the many more it planned to employ over the coming years? In response Bullmore produced a ten-page report titled 'Networking, synergy, cross-referral: And what's in it for the customer'. This addressed the holy grail of holding companies: how to bundle the services of their various subsidiaries together, in ways that will be attractive, and advantageous to advertisers.

In the report Bullmore noted, 'All WPP companies put their own performance and their own client relationships before any consideration of a Greater Good for the group... Traditionally, it's been extremely difficult for a service company with a primary skill to charge a client realistically for the provision of secondary skills.' (This harked back to the 1960s full-service agency bugaboo.)

To overcome these 'difficulties and inhibitions' Bullmore recommended the building of personal and professional relationships across the WPP group, and he himself worked hard at bringing such relationships into being. But, his report concluded, unless collaboration was seen to be in the interests of advertisers 'it won't last long'. Two decades after Bullmore's report, advertisers are indeed demanding integrated services, and noisily. But they are still not convinced internal collaborations between holding company subsidiaries are the best way to get them—so the integration of services within holding companies remains a pipe dream.

Sorrell is undaunted. As recently as April 2005, 20 years after WPP started, he said: 'Integration is fundamental. There is no point in [holding] companies existing unless they get the benefit of their constituent parts. The thing that bedevils us and our clients is the unwillingness of people to work together.' Well the first point is spot-on—but the second is simplistic. Many have tried to hoe this field. For seven years Young & Rubicam put immense effort into a sophisticated multi-service integration system. At first stockbrokers Merrill Lynch were highly enthusiastic about the Y&R approach. But Merrill Lynch confessed in 2005: 'The market didn't buy it . . . the theory sounded great, until it didn't.' The market hasn't bought it from WPP either. In recent years Sorrell has managed to sell some small collaborative multi-service packages, but precious few.

Like Young & Rubicam, Bullmore, and countless others, I too have tried to build collaborative business within a holding company—and failed. I now believe the concept inherently doomed because advertisers are unwilling to meet the costs involved. Advertisers believe that because the holding company is getting more business from them, the overall package should cost them less. The truth is the opposite. The coordination and integration of different facets of a marketing campaign are time-consuming and costly. Somebody has to foot the bill. The notion that separate companies, within a group, will simply get together and a viable idea will materialize out of thin air, and instantly be executed in all its different aspects, is cloud-cuckoo land. The appropriate individuals within the separate companies will need to work closely together for weeks, or months. Their time costs money. But clients don't want to meet the cost. And they are right, because they can, and should, manage such integration themselves: it is their job.

So what do holding companies offer advertisers? As long as they are well run, they offer financial stability to the subsidiaries they own, from which clients indirectly benefit—but no more stability than any well run agency can offer. Their massive media-buying subsidiaries provide advertisers with excellent media research and the lowest possible media costs, but no more so than Aegis—the 5th largest global media-buyer, which has so far remained independent despite being constantly courted by the holding companies. Maybe the holding companies can sweat their property and cash assets better than independent agencies, and pass on such savings to their clients, but these are minimal.

Well, if marketing holding companies like Procter & Gamble, Nestlé, L'Oreal, and Unilever make sense, why don't marketing service holding companies? The comparison highlights the weaknesses of the latter. The marketing companies have huge raw material buying power, which (except for media) the service companies do not, as there are precious few economies of scale in personal service businesses. The marketing companies can and do attract high quality young people, which Omnicom and the rest do not (though their subsidiary agencies do). The marketing companies provide career paths across their trading subsidiaries, which the service holding companies cannot emulate.

My crystal ball suspects the days—or anyway the years—of the marketing service holding companies are numbered. Today the might of the marketing service holding companies is substantial: the revenues of Omnicom alone exceed the revenues of the eight largest global advertising agencies (three of which it owns). But far mightier industrial conglomerates have bitten the dust and been broken up in recent times. The marketing service holding companies' organic growth has been modest of late, around 5 per cent at best. They have squeezed every penny they can from their margins. And there are no more huge independent agency or marketing service company acquisitions to be had.

Perhaps they should buy a bank or two?

Fatties and Guzzlers

When Lord Borrie became chairman of the Advertising Standards Authority in 2000 he initiated a legal review of Britain's self-regulatory system, and sought leading counsel's opinion on whether it was watertight under European law. After an exhaustive investigation the high-powered legal eagles recommended some minor process adjustments, but otherwise declared the self-regulatory system safe.

At about the same time the ASA took on responsibility for internet advertising (but not for websites), and for telephone advertising (but not for telephone selling). In 2004 the UK government showed its faith in advertising self-regulation when it allowed the newly launched Office of Communications (OFCOM) to delegate the regulation of broadcast advertising to an expanded and restructured ASA. This was a significant step: ever since the launch of ITV in 1955, television advertising had been statutorily controlled. Initially OFCOM's delegation was for a two-year probationary period, but in 2006 the contract was extended for a further eight years. As a result the ASA, with over 100 staff, today handles some 25,000–30,000 complaints each year, across all media.

With an annual ASA budget of around £9 million, Britain now has much the best financed and most thoroughgoing advertising self-regulatory system in the world—perhaps the best financed and most thoroughgoing self-regulatory system of any industry in the world.

The ASA's writ, however, extends only to the content of individual advertisements. It has no jurisdiction over the broad influence of advertising on society. The ban on tobacco advertising, which finally took effect across all media in 2003, was outside its bailiwick. So, largely, have been the subsequent debates concerning the influence of advertising on heavy drinking and—following the government's 2004 white paper 'Choosing Health'—on childhood obesity.

Alcohol advertising has been under pressure for some 40 years. In 1970 the Codes of Practice relating to alcohol were first toughened to ensure—as far as this is possible—that advertisements only sell brands, and do not encourage drinking per se. The Codes have been further tightened since. However, the growth of binge drinking—excessive guzzling, once or twice a week—combined with increasing (but not wholly reliable[1]) medical evidence that alcohol is causing more illness than had previously been thought, brought increasing criticism from both doctors and pressure groups intent on restraining alcohol advertising still further. If there was little evidence to prove cigarette advertising made people smoke, there is even less evidence alcohol advertising makes people drink. In Britain by far the fastest growing sector of alcohol consumption has been wine drinking. There is very little advertising of wines, and wine advertising at constant prices per litre fell by 50 per cent between 1996 and 2005. Beer and spirit advertising fell similarly, though not quite so steeply, with only cider showing any increase. Nonetheless, under direction from OFCOM, the broadcast advertising Codes were again toughened in 2005, in order to minimize any possibility that advertising might encourage heavy drinking.

Whether certain types of food advertising do, or do not, encourage children to eat too much, or too unhealthily, is still more confused, and more hotly contested. Many children are growing dangerously obese, but how far this is genetic rather than environmental is unresolved. Much the strongest influence on children's food consumption, as would be expected, is parental, with schools the next most influential. Children's average calorie consumption has been falling rather than rising—but so has the amount of exercise they take. It is probable that less than half their

---

[1] Increased diagnostic speed and accuracy bedevil many of these apparent statistical 'increases', though doctors seem loath to admit this.

food intake is accounted for by advertised brands (the exact figure is currently unknown). All this means that restraining the advertising of certain foods to children is unlikely to make a jot of difference. Nonetheless in 2007 OFCOM ruled that on television the timing of food advertising to children must be restricted, and that Codes governing food advertisements in broadcast media must be toughened. The new rules are almost precisely the same as those imposed on cigarette advertising in the mid-1960s. Once again advertising has been cast as villain and paid the price— albeit not a very large one. As with the 1960s cigarette restrictions, the effects of the advertising restrictions on drinking and on child obesity will be nugatory.

The experimental approach taken by the early road safety advertising— in which different campaigns were tested and re-tested until effective advertising solutions were found—has largely been discarded. Instead governments and government agencies bulldoze into place cosmetic regulations and restrictions, with no evidence they will achieve anything at all. A symptom of all this is that at the very end of 2007 the government announced a ministerial inquiry into the 'commercialization of childhood' (whatever that may be), with particular emphasis on the influence of television advertising, *in toto*, on children. So my crystal ball feels safe in predicting that more and more of the woes of the world will be blamed on advertising, and restraints will burgeon.

Long-Term Forecast: Foggy but Sunny

During the first decade of the twenty-first century, the British advertising industry split into two lopsided halves. One half, which accounted for 90 per cent or so of all advertising, comprised the traditional media and traditional campaigns: 'the old advertising'. The other half, accounting for around 10 per cent, was based on the new media, particularly the internet: 'the advertising of the future'. Those involved in 'old advertising' were generally uneasy about their prospects; those involved in new media were gung-ho and full of themselves. Steve Henry (Creative Director, TBWA London, and formally of Howell Henry Chaldecott Lury) expressed the situation graphically, if ironically, in *Campaign* in March 2007: 'Does worrying about television advertising really matter any more?' he asked, 'Aren't we moving into the new digital world?'

To put this question in perspective, the previous year some £460 million was spent on display advertising on the internet—and £3,929 million was spent on television advertising. But as the head of a major agency said to me, talking about his digital staffers, whom he was trying to integrate within his traditional agency structure: 'To them I'm an old fogey, clinging to the wreckage—and they're where it's at.' He is in his early forties.

The traditional media sectors have some justifiable grounds for concern, but these are small. As people migrated to the net, television viewership dropped a tad—though not much. In early 2007 the average number of television hours people watched climbed back to 2004 levels. Taking a long view, the average number of viewing hours has hardly changed since records began. Meanwhile viewers are buying bigger and bigger sets—the size of the average TV screen increases by an inch a year, which hardly suggests people are falling out of love with television.

Another much discussed threat to television advertising is the Personal Video Recorder (PVR), which allows viewers to fast-forward through commercials or skip them entirely. How much this will happen is questionable. At present the use of PVRs is small, but is steadily increasing, and there have already been numerous research studies into PVRs' effects on television viewing—and particularly into their effects on the viewing of commercials. The situation is still fluid, but almost all the studies show, paradoxically, that those who zap some commercials still see more commercials in total, because using PVRs increases the total hours of viewing. This was confirmed by three separate studies, carried out by the London Business School, Sky, and BARB towards the end of 2006. Nor, as Erik du Plessis has shown, is it certain switching off commercials negates their impact—the viewer has to notice them before switching them off (Admap, 2007). A Nielsen study in the United States, where PVR usage is more advanced than it is in the UK, has come to much the same conclusions. Nonetheless, in the USA the PVR threat has caused some leading advertisers to desert spot advertising and increase their use of sponsorship and product placement in programmes.

On the plus side for television, the increasing number of channels has resulted in more effective targeting, and has greatly reduced the real cost of advertising. An IPA study in June 2007 showed that TV advertising in Britain was 42 per cent more cost-effective than it had been in the 1980s.

Against print media the internet not only provides 24-hour news in depth, but is grabbing a major share of classified advertising. This is severely hurting the quality press, and many magazines. Pessimistic media soothsayers foretell the decimation, or even the imminent demise, of print media. Bill Gates, perhaps not the most objective of voices, has claimed newspapers will be dead as dodos by 2012.

Despite these glum presentiments, most forecasts predict continuing overall growth in advertising in Britain. In January 2007 the Advertising Association predicted expenditure growth in real terms (at constant prices) of 36 per cent over the 12 years to 2018. The AA's clairvoyant record has been pretty good. But according to the AA, most of the 36 per cent growth will come from the internet. Remove internet expenditure, and the 12-year increase in traditional media drops to 12 per cent: hardly a bonanza, but not a decline. The AA forecast claims the advertising revenues of newspapers and magazines will begin to fall, in real terms, from 2012. Also in 2012, the AA sees the internet overtaking television, and becoming the largest advertising medium by 2018. No wonder my chum's digital staffers feel they are the future.

But in the USA the internet still takes less than 6 per cent of the advertising cake. In the UK there is not, at present, one single packaged goods brand among the top 20 internet advertisers. The internet is excellent for targeting minority groups. It works well in markets where customers require a lot of information before they make expensive purchase decisions—finance, travel and tourism, automobiles, certain retail sectors. And it works well with customers who are already interested in what is being sold. Emails to existing customers who have bought before are exceptionally cost-effective in several markets—wines, books, holidays, entertainments; but the volumes of business are minuscule.

The internet is essentially a search medium. Over 50 per cent of internet revenue comes from sponsored search, from 'clicks'. Internet operators boast that sponsored search expenditure is accountable. The advertiser pays per search, and knows exactly what he is getting for his money. But this is a two-edged sword, and there is strong evidence many advertisers are finding that the cost of search is beginning to exceed the value of the response. So my crystal ball stubbornly insists internet advertising will neither grow as fast, nor as huge, as other gypsies' balls foretell.

In any event, you only search for information you know you want. For a company or a brand to grow over the long haul, it must constantly win new customers—customers who were previously uninterested in it. Winning totally new customers calls, at least in part, for intrusive communication. Television, display space in newspapers and magazines, posters, radio, and cinema are all proven intrusive media. They introduce people to products they did not know about, or did not know they might be interested in. In my crystal ball, their future is safe.

Meanwhile internet display advertising, which accounts for just 25 per cent of internet revenue, faces creative agencies with challenges similar to those television faced them with half a century ago. Hardly any creative people brought up with 'the old media' feel even comfortable, let alone confident, working in digital media. Consequently specialist digital agencies have sprung up—some wholly independent, some spawned by existing creative agencies. But this separation of 'old' creativity and 'new' digital creativity has not been welcomed by advertisers. Advertisers want their 'old' and 'new' campaigns to be integrated. Creative agencies have responded by attempting to embrace digital creative people within their operations—as my chum was doing. ('Will Digital Agencies Exist In Five Years?' *Campaign* asked in June 2007, but failed to answer.)

Meanwhile there is a widespread feeling that British advertising creativity is not what it was, even as recently as the mid-1990s—when I was trounced by Keith Holloway for suggesting the same thing. During 1999 the Cannes Festival President Donald Gunn, a former Leo Burnett creative boss (page 73), launched a system for aggregating the awards won by creative campaigns at all the world's leading festivals. Gunn publishes the winners, and tots up each country's winnings. Between 1999 and 2005 Britain did not once come out on top.

A spate of news features shuddered at this downturn. 'Has the ad biz lost its lustre?' asked *Management Today* anxiously in August 2007. Several *Campaign* articles bemoaned British advertising's predicament: 'Has adland run out of original ideas?' and 'Have [British] creative standards diminished?' the magazine has asked—headlines unthinkable in earlier decades. While most of those interviewed for the features admitted they tend to look back nostalgically, they accepted the truth of the implicit thesis. They blamed the drop in creativity on there being too much stifling market research nowadays, a long-standing creative grouse. In contrast, I blame the conflict between 'old' and 'new' media.

It is great when a campaign idea, like 'Heineken Refreshes The Parts Other Beers Cannot Reach', is translatable into a multiplicity of media. But lots of successful advertising ideas resist being adapted to different media. They only work in the media for which they were intended. To insist a creative idea must work in all media frequently ensures it excels in none. Though advertisers seem pig-headedly unaware of it, this is not in their best interest. The fragmented message in my crystal ball is that British advertising creativity will not be pre-eminent again until its creators stop wearing prismatic spectacles.

In the 2006 Gunn Report, Britain won back its leadership at global creative festivals, shoving the US off the top spot for the first time since

1999. Regrettably, my crystal ball is too murky to reveal whether or not we are going to stay there.

* * *

When I started out in advertising I asked my elders and betters whether there was macroeconomic proof that advertising increased the gross national product. Could it be shown that the more a country spent on advertising, the wealthier its population became? Sadly not, they replied, though wealthier countries broadly spend more on advertising than poorer countries, as you might expect. The number and complexity of factors that drive a modern economy make such correlations unverifiable. Anyway, I later realized, if display advertising accounts for about 1.0 per cent of the GNP, even if it consistently generates a 10 per cent return on investment, which would be vast, this would account for but 0.1 per cent of the GNP, which would not be identifiable.

Anyway it was a daft question. Nobody would ask: does expenditure on architecture or accounting increase the GNP? How could you know? Over recent years various attempts have been made to prove advertising helps strengthen Britain's balance of payments. The most recent, produced by Will Hutton's Work Foundation in July 2007, suggests advertising accounted for exports of £1.1 billion in 2004. I happen to believe the figures are specious, but anyway they are irrelevant to my original question. Most advertising expenditure has nothing to do with the balance of payments, and the balance of payments is only indirectly related to the GNP.

The vital question is whether advertising—like architecture and accounting—delivers a worthwhile service to the public, notionally (but unquantifiably) on a cost-efficient basis.

Society, economists, critics, and the industry itself put far too much emphasis on the benefits of advertising to companies, to advertisers. But advertising would not exist—as Montaigne pointed out in 1595—if it were not, above all, of benefit to consumers. Indeed it has no right to exist, as Lord Beveridge stressed in 1951, if does not fulfil this prime role:

> the service of advertising to the community is to enable citizens to get the most and best out of . . . the consumer's freedom in spending his income . . . those who conduct advertising shall take service to the consumer as their over-riding purpose.

The principal way in which advertising serves consumers is by helping them deal with the abundance of available choices. There is now copious evidence—as Barry Schwartz shows in *The Paradox of Choice: Why More is*

COLEG LLANDRILLO COLLEGE
LIBRARY RESOURCE CENTRE
CANOLFAN ADNODDAU LLYFRGELL

Less—that many if not most consumers find the panoply of choices facing them today bewildering. Moreover the internet often exacerbates people's difficulties, as Damian Thompson's recent multinational study has shown. Consumers move from website to website, gathering new waves of information along the way which Thompson shows 'can be overwhelming and make purchasing decisions harder'.

Yes, companies need advertising to keep them running. As the plenitude of brands and products in every market grows—and this is not going to stop—businesses will increasingly need advertising to differentiate their brands from the myriads of others, and to draw their brands to consumers' attention. And yes, the media will continue to need advertising to subsidize their production costs and thus keep their consumer prices low, or nil.

But above all, consumers need advertising. Consumers need advertising to let them know what products and services are on offer, and to help them sort out quickly and easily which of those on offer might be of interest to them. Not everybody approves of this process, but the public wants it, likes it, and unequivocally needs it. Ecological and environmental pressures will not change any of this; they may even make advertising more, rather than less, necessary, as consumers use it to help them sort what they want from an even greater number of options.

Without brand advertising, profusion brings confusion. Brands are a shorthand way of encapsulating what a product is, and what it offers. Very, very few people want to explore the chemical formulations of their detergents, or dog foods, or deodorants. Few want to, fewer still would be able to. Very, very few people want to investigate the workings of their mobile, or automobile, or washing machine. Few want to, fewer still would be able to. Advertisements identify, encapsulate, and provide the key information most people want, in ways that will interest and engage them—information which could be about the formulation, or the halo, or both. In doing so, advertising helps people simplify, organize, and structure their daily lives. Advertisements continuously remind people about established products and introduce them to new ones, speedily and often entertainingly. In an advanced economy, people could not cope without this service. And as the proliferation of choices and options grows ever greater, people will need it more and more—and more. My crystal ball is radiant. The future of advertising is assured.

Select Bibliography

As a 'history' *Powers of Persuasion* is a mite unusual, as I lived through, and was occasionally personally involved in, many of the events described. Some of the story is therefore dependent on memories: my own and other people's, recounted in interviews and casual conversations. Wherever possible these memories have been checked and verified. But all the essential reference data is identified in the text and comes from the following key sources, listed alphabetically.

Abbreviations

HBR: *Harvard Business Review*
IJA: *International Journal of Advertising*
IJMR: *International Journal of Market Research*
IPA: Institute of Practitioners in Advertising
ISBA: Incorporated Society of British Advertisers
JAR: *Journal of Advertising Research*
WARC: World Advertising Research Center

Published Documents

'Ad-tracking Buyers' Guide 2007', *Admap*, September 2007.
Advertising and Advertising Agencies: A Survey of Advertisers' Opinions, IPA & British Market Research Bureau, 1972.
Advertising Agencies: Their service and their relationship with advertisers and the media, ICC report, 1976.
Advertising Expenditure: 1956 & 1960, Advertising Association.
Advertising: Opposition Green Paper, The Labour Party, 1972.
Advertising Standards Authority Annual Reports, 1974–2007.
Advertising: Today, Yesterday and Tomorrow, Printers' Ink, 1963.
Advertisers' Weekly (from November 1972, *AdWeek*), 1951–75.
Advertising Statistics Yearbooks, Advertising Association and NTC Publications.
Advertising Works, Vols 1–15, IPA Advertising Effectiveness Awards, 1980–2006, IPA and various publishers.
Alps, Tess, and Brennan, David, 'Five myths about television advertising', *Market Leader*, Autumn 2007.
Ambler, Tim, 'Do Brands Benefit Consumers?', *IJA*, Volume 16, Number 3, 1997.
—— 'Myths About The Mind: Time To End Some Popular Beliefs About How Advertising Works', *IJA*, Volume 17, Number 4, 1998.

—— 'Does the UK Promotion of Food and Drink Effect Child Obesity', *JAR*, Volume 46, 2006.

Ash, Brian, *Tiger In Your Tank*, Cassell, 1969.

Baddeley, Alan, *Human Memory: Theory and Practice*, Lawrence Erlbaum Associates, 1990.

Barnes, Micky, *Ad: An Inside View of Advertising*, Bachman & Turner, 1973.

Barnicoat, John, *Posters: A Concise History*, Thames & Hudson, 1997.

Barton, Roger, *Advertising Agency Operations and Management*, McGraw-Hill, 1955.

Barwise, Patrick, 'Brands in a Digital World', *Journal of Brand Management*, Volume 4, Number 4, 1997.

Batra, Rajeev, Lehman, Donald R., Burke, Joanne, and Pae, Jae, 'When Does Advertising Have an Impact? A Study of Tracking Data', *JAR*, Volume 35, 1995.

BDO Stoy Hayward, *The Advertising Sector: An Analysis for the Department of Trade and Industry*, 1994.

Benady, Alex, 'Has The Ad Biz Lost Its Lustre?', *Management Today*, August 2007.

Berger, Warren, *Advertising Today*, Phaidon, 2001.

Bernstein, David, *Creative Advertising*, Longman, 1974.

—— *Advertising Outdoors: Watch This Space*, Phaidon, 1997.

Biel, Alex L., 'Love the Ad. Buy the Product?', *Admap*, September 1990.

—— and Bridgewater, C. A., 'Attributes of Likeable Television Commercials', *JAR*, Volume 30, 1990.

Bishop, Matthew, Kay, John, and Mayer, Colin, *Privatization and Economic Performance*, Oxford University Press, 1994.

Borrie, Gordon, Director General of Fair Trading, *Review of the UK self-regulatory system of advertising control*, OFT 1978.

Bower, Joseph L., 'WPP: Integrating Icons to Leverage Knowledge', *HBR*, November 2001.

Braithwaite, Brian, and Barrell, Joan, *The Business of Women's Magazines*, Associated Business Press, 1979.

Broadbent, Simon, *The Advertising Budget*, IPA with NTC Publications, 1989.

—— *Accountable Advertising*, Admap Publications with IPA and ISBA, 1997.

—— (ed.), *Does Advertising Affect Market Size?*, Advertising Association, 1997.

Brown, Gordon, 'Facts from Tracking Studies: And Old Advertising Chestnuts', *Admap*, June 1988.

Bullmore, J., and Waterson, M. (eds), *The Advertising Association Handbook*, Holt, Rinehart and Winston with the Advertising Association, 1983.

Bullmore, Jeremy, *Behind the Scenes in Advertising* (3rd edn), WARC, 2003.

Burden, Sue, 'Ad Creatives' Relationship with Ad Research', *Admap*, April 2003.

Burrough, Bryan, and Helyar, John, *Barbarians At The Gate*, Arrow Books, 1990.

Butler, David, and Kavanagh, Dennis, *The British General Election of 1987*, MacMillan, 1988.

Butterfield, Leslie, and Haigh, David, *Understanding the Financial Value of Brands*, IPA, 1998.

Burke, Jeffrey, and Stanton, John L., 'Comparing the effectiveness of executional elements in TV advertising: 15- versus 30-second commercials', *Journal of Advertising Research*, November/December 1988.

Campaign, Silver Jubilee Issue, 1993.

Campaign's Annual Agency League Tables, 1970–2007.

Cappo, Joe, *The Future of Advertising*, McGraw-Hill, 2002.

Carter, Stephen, 'Retail Advertising: The Third Way', *Admap*, July 1999.

Caves, Richard E., *Creative Industries: Contacts Between Art and Commerce*, Harvard University Press, 2000.

Channon, Charles, 'Agency Thinking and Agencies as Brands', *Admap*, March 1981.

—— (ed.), *20 Advertising Case Histories*, Cassell, 1989.

—— 'Russia: "Another Country" for Marketing', *Admap*, June 1990.

Chong, Mark, 'How Do Advertising Creative Directors Perceive Research?', *IJA*, Volume 25, Number 3, 2006.

Clark, Eric, *The Want Makers*, Hodder & Stoughton, 1988.

Colley, Russell H., *Defining Advertising Goals for Measured Advertising Results*, Association of National Advertisers, first published 1961.

Commentary on the Labour Party 'Green Paper' on Advertising March 1962, Advertising Association, 1972.

Commercial Radio Pocket Book, CRCA, 2005.

'Commercials', *JAR*, Volume 28, 1988.

Cook, Louise, 'Using Econometric Analysis to Evaluate Retail Advertising', *Admap*, July 1998.

Cowen, Tyler, *In Praise of Commercial Culture*, Harvard University Press, 1998.

Crewe, Ivor, Gosschalk, Brian, and Bartle, John, *Why Labour Won the General Election of 1997*, Frank Cass, 1998.

Cross, Jennifer, *The Supermarket Trap*, Indiana University Press, 1970.

Damasio, A. R., *Descartes' Error: Emotion, Reason and the Human Brain*, Macmillan, 1994.

D&AD, 'Creativity Works', selected from the D&AD Awards 2003.

D'Arcy-MacManus & Masius, *The ITV Strike: Its Effect on Sales*, D-M&M, 1989.

Davidson, J. H., *Offensive Marketing*, Cassell, 1972.

Davies, Gary, 'Retailer Advertising Strategies', *IJA*, Volume 10, Number 3, 1991.

Davis, E., Kay, J., and Star, J., 'Is Advertising Rational?', *Business Strategy Review*, Autumn 1991.

Day, Barry (ed.), *100 Great Advertisements*, Times Newspapers, Mirror Group Newspapers, and *Campaign*, 1978.

Delaney, Sam, *Get Smashed*, Sceptre, 2007.

Della Femina, Jerry, *From Those Wonderful Folks Who Gave You Pearl Harbour*, Simon & Schuster, 1970.

Design and Art Directors Awards Annuals, 1964–2007.

de Vries, Leonard, and Laver, James, *Victorian Advertisements*, John Murray, 1968.

—— and Van Amstel, Ilonka, *American Advertisements 1865–1900*, John Murray, 1973.

Dewey, John, *Art as Experience*, G. Puttnam's Sons, 1934.

'Digital Report', *Marketing*, May 2007.

Donaghey, Brian, and Williamson, Mick, 'Thinking "Through The Line"', *Admap*, April 2003.

Dru, Jean-Marie, *Disruption*, John Wiley & Sons, 1996.

Dunbar, David S., 'The Agency Commission System in Britain: Its History to 1941', *Journal of Advertising History*, Number 2, 1979.

Du Plessis, Erik C., 'Memory and Likeability: Keys to Understanding Ad Effects', *Admap*, July–August 1998.

—— 'Advertising Likeability', *Admap*, October 1998.

—— 'DVRs, Fast-forwarding and Advertising Attention', *Admap*, September 2007.

Economics of Advertising, The Economists Advisory Group and Advertising Association, 1967.

Edwards, H. R., *Competition and Monopoly in the British Soap Industry*, Clarendon Press, 1962.

Ehrenberg, A. S. C., *Repeat Buying*, Charles Griffin & Company, London, 1988.

—— 'Towards an integrated theory of consumer behaviour', *Journal of the Market Research Society*, Volume 38, October 1996.

Elliott, Richard, and Wattanasuwan, Kritsadarat, 'Brands as Symbolic Resources for the Construction of Identity', *IJA*, Volume 17, Number 2, 1998.

Englis, Basil G., *Global and Multinational Advertising*, Lawrence Erlbaum Associates, 1994.

Fallon, Ivan, *The Brothers*, Hutchinson, 1988.

Feagin, Susan, and Maynard, Patrick (eds), *Aesthetics*, Oxford University Press, 1997.

Feldwick, Paul, 'What should we measure?', *Admap*, April 1990.

—— and Heath, Dr Robert, '50 years of using the wrong model of advertising', MRS Annual Conference, 2007.

Fendley, Alison, *Saatchi & Saatchi: The Inside Story*, Arcade, 1995.

Fine, Laura Rich, and others, *Advertising & Marketing Services: Global Ad Primer*, Merrill Lynch, 2005.

Fletcher, Winston, *A Glittering Haze*, NTC Publications, 1992.

—— *Advertising Advertising*, Profile, 1999.

—— *Introduction to Gilroy Centenary Catalogue*, History of Advertising Trust, 1998.

—— 'John Webster Obituary', *The Guardian*, 17 January 2006.

Fox, Stephen, *The Mirror Makers: A History of American Advertising and its Creators*, University of Illinois Press, 1997.

Franzen, Giep, *Advertising Effectiveness: Findings from Empirical Research*, NTC Publications, 1994.

Gable, Jo, *The Tuppenny Punch and Judy Show: 25 Years of TV Commercials*, Michael Joseph, 1980.

Galbraith, John Kenneth, *The Affluent Society*, Hamish Hamilton, 1958.

—— *The Anatomy of Power*, Hamish Hamilton, 1984.

Gardner, Burleigh, and Levy, S. J., 'The Product and the Brand', *HBR*, March/April 1955.

Goldman, Kevin, *Conflicting Accounts: The Creation and Crash of the Saatchi & Saatchi Advertising Empire*, Simon & Schuster, 1997.

Goldstein, Jeffrey, *Children and Advertising: Policy Implications of Scholarly Research*, Advertising Association, 1994.

—— 'Children and Advertising: The Research', *Commercial Communications*, 1998.

Goldstein, W. M., and Hogarth, R. M., (eds), *Research on Judgement and Decision Making*, Cambridge University Press, 1997.

Gordon, Wendy, and Valentine, Virginia, 'Buying the Brand at Point of Choice', *Journal of Brand Management*, Volume 4, Number 1, 1997.

Green, Laurence (ed.), *Advertising Works and How*, WARC & IPA, 2005.

Griffiths, Dennis, *A History of the NPA 1906–2006*, Newspaper Publishers Association, 2006.

Guirdham, Maureen, and Tan, Siew Choo, 'Tracking the British Telecom Share Campaign', *Admap*, September 1986.

Gunn, Donald, 'Do Creative Commercials Sell?', *Campaign*, 22 September 1955.

Gutteridge, Bernard, *The Agency Game*, Weidenfeld & Nicolson, 1954.

Haliberg, Garth, *All Consumers Are Not Created Equal*, John Wiley, 1996.

Harris, Ralph, and Seldon, Arthur, *Advertising in a Free Society*, Institute of Economic Affairs, 1959.

—— —— *Advertising in Action*, Hutchinson, 1962.

—— —— *Advertising and the Public*, Andre Deutsch, 1962.

Healey, Tim, *Unforgettable Ads*, Reader's Digest Association, 1992.

Heath, Dr Robert, 'Can Tracking Studies Tell Lies?', *IJA*, Volume 18, Number 2, 1999.

Henry, Brian (ed.), *British Television Advertising: The First 30 Years*, Century Benham, 1986.

Henry, Harry, *The Dynamics of the British Press 1961–1984*, Advertising Association, 1986.

—— 'Advertising: A Necessary Expense or just a Residual?', *Admap*, January 1978.

Hilton, Steve, 'The Conservative Party's Advertising Strategy', in *Why Labour Won the General Election of 1997*, Frank Cass, 1998.

Himmelweit, Hilde T., and others, *How Voters Decide*, Open University Press, 1985.

Hindley, Diana, and Hindley, Geoffrey, *Advertising in Victorian England 1837–1901*, Wayland Publishers, 1972.

Hobson, John W., *The Selection of Advertising Media*, IPA, 1955.

Hollis, Nigel, 'Like it or not, Liking is not Enough', *JAR*, September/October 1995.

—— 'The Future of Tracking Studies', *Admap*, October 2004.

Hopkins, Claude, *Scientific Advertising*, MacGibbon and Kee, 1968, first published 1923.

Inglis, Fred, *The Imagery of Power: A Critique of Advertising*, Heinemann, 1972.

Iosifides, Petros, *Public Television in the Digital Era*, Palgrave Macmillan, 2007.

IPA, *Advertisers' Opinions of Advertising and Advertising Agencies: A Survey*, 1972.

IPA Seminar report, *Consumerism—a threat or a challenge?*, IPA, 1973.

IPA Effectiveness Awards Papers (selected):

Smirnoff Vodka: They Said Anything Could Happen (1980).

Privatisation of British Telecom (1986).

British Gas Flotation (1988).

Drinking and Driving Wrecks Lives (1988).

Rolls-Royce: The Most Cost-Effective Privatisation (1988).

Smirnoff: The Effect is Shattering (1990).

Consistency & Chimpanzees (1991).

BA: 10 Years of the World's Favourite Advertising (1994).

Isaacs, Jeremy, *Look Me In The Eye*, Little, Brown, 2006.

James, Ros, 'Integrated Marketing: The Big Picture', *Media & Marketing Europe*, November 1998.

Johnson-Cartee, Karen S., and Copeland, Gary A., *Negative Political Advertising*, Lawrence Erlbaum Associates, 1991.

Jones, John Philip, *When Ads Work*, Lexington Books, 1995.

—— 'Is advertising salesmanship?', *Commercial Communications*, July 1998.

Joyce, T., 'Models of the Advertising Process', ESOMAR seminar, April 1991.

Kaid, Lynda Lee, 'Measures of Political Advertising', *JAR*, Volume 16, 1976.

Kavanagh, Dennis, *Election Campaigning: The New Marketing of Politics*, Blackwell, 1995.

Keegan, Sheila, 'The Commercial–Academic Divide: Never the Twain Shall Meet?', *IJMR*, Volume 49, Number 1, 2007.

Kehoe, Louise, 'Agents who sift the information overload', *Financial Times*, 29 October 1998.

Kelvin, R. P., *Advertising and Human Memory*, Business Publications, 1962.

Key, Professor Wilson Bryan, *Subliminal Seduction*, Signet, 1974.

King, Stephen, 'The Anatomy of Account Planning', *Admap*, November 1989.

—— *A Master Class in Brand Planning*, edited by Judie Lannon and Merry Baskin, John Wiley & Sons, October 2007.

Klein, Naomi, *No Logo*, HarperCollins, 2000.

Kleinman, Philip, *Advertising Inside Out*, W.H. Allen, 1977.

—— *The Saatchi & Saatchi Story*, Weidenfeld & Nicolson, 1987.

Kover, Arthur J., Goldberg, Stephen M., and James, William L., 'Creativity Vs. Effectiveness', *JAR*, Volume 35, 1995.

Lace, Jonathan M., *Payment By Results*, ISBA and the Advertising Research Consortium, 1999.

Lamb, Larry, *Sunrise*, Macmillan, 1989.

Law, Andy, *Open Minds*, Thomson Texere, 2001.

Layton Awards Annuals 1955–1962, C&E Layton.

Le Bas, Hedley (ed.), *The Lord Kitchener Memorial Book*, Hodder and Stoughton, date unknown.

Leigh, Adam, 'How to make retail advertising work harder', *Admap*, July 1998.

Lester, Tom, 'How WPP Wants To Win', *Finance Magazine*, November/December 1989.

Levitt, Theodore, *The Marketing Imagination*, MacMillan, 1983.

Lind, Harold, *Making Sense of Advertising*, Advertising Association, 1998.

Luik, J. C., and Waterson, M. J. (eds), *Advertising & Markets*, NTC Publications, 1996.

Lynn, Matthew, 'The World According to Martin Sorrell', *Management Today*, June 2003.

McDonald, Colin, *How Advertising Works*, Advertising Association, with NTC Publications, 1992.

McLuhan, Marshall, *Understanding Media*, Routledge, 1964.

Marcantonio, Alfredo, *Well-written and red: The Economist Poster Campaign*, Dakinibooks, 2001.

Marketing Pocket Books, Advertising Association with NTC Publications.

Marketing Week, '20 Years', 1988.

Marketing Week, 'Horizons: Silver Jubilee Issue', 1993.

Marshall, Caroline, 'WPP at Twenty', *Campaign*, 29 April 2005.

Martineau, Pierre, *Motivation in Advertising*, McGraw-Hill, 1957.

Mayer, Martin, *Madison Avenue U.S.A.*, Penguin, 1960.

—— *Whatever Happened to Madison Avenue?*, Little Brown & Company, 1991.

Media Pocket Books, Advertising Association with NTC Publications.

Mediaedge:cia adstats, 'Is Advertising Making us Drink More?', *Admap*, April 2007.

Mintel, *The Marketing Services Business*, Special Report, 1987.

Mitchell, Alan, 'Brand Strategies in the Information Age', *Financial Times*, Management Reports, 1997.

Montaigne, Michel de (translated by J. M. Cohen), *Essays*, Penguin Books, 1958, first published 1595.

Morris, J. P., *Road Safety Publicity*, Advertising Association, 1972.

Moses, Brian, *The War Years: The Home Front*, Hodder Wayland, 1995.

Myerson, Jeremy, and Vickers, Graham, *Rewind: Forty Years of Design & Advertising*, Phaidon, 2002.

National Consumer Council, 'Advertising: Legislate or Persuade?' Consumer Statement, 1978.

Nevett, Terry R., *Advertising in Britain: A History*, William Heinemann, 1982.

—— 'Thomas Barrett and the Development of British Advertising', *IJA*, Volume 7, Number 3, 1988.

Nyilasy, Gergely, and Reid, Leonard, 'The academician–practitioner gap in advertising', *IJA*, Volume 26, Number 4, 2007.

Ogden, John, *Advertising: Introduction to Catalogue*, Bernard Quaritch, 1998.

Ogilvy, David, *Confessions of an Advertising Man*, Atheneum, 1963.

—— *Ogilvy on Advertising*, Pan Books, 1983.

—— *The Unpublished David Ogilvy: A Selection of his Writings from the Files of his Partners*, The Ogilvy Group, 1986.

Olins, Wally, *Corporate Identity*, Thames & Hudson, 1989.

—— *Wally Olins On Brand*, Thames & Hudson, 2003.

O'Quin, Karen, and Aronoff, Joel, 'Humor as a Technique of Social Influence', *Social Psychology Quarterly*, Volume 44, Number 4, 1981.

Packard,Vance, *The Hidden Persuaders*, Penguin, 1960.

Pearson, John, and Turner, Graham, *The Persuasion Industry*, Eyre & Spottiswoode, 1965.

Penniman, Howard R. (ed.), *Britain at the Polls, 1979*, American Enterprise Institute for Public Policy Research, 1979.

Perry, Michael, *The Brand: Vehicle for Value in a Changing Marketplace*, Advertising Association, 1994.

Pincas, Stephane, & Loiseau, Marc, *Born in 1842. A History of Advertising*, Mundocom, 2006.

Porritt, Jonathon, *Where on Earth are we Going?*, BBC Books, 1990.

Pringle, Hamish, *Celebrity Sells*, John Wiley, 2004.

Reeks, Toby, 'European Advertising Agencies: Accessing Growth', Merrill Lynch Industry Overview, 2006.

Reeves, Rosser, *Reality in Advertising*, Alfred Knopf, 1961.

Reichheld, Frederick F, *The Loyalty Effect: The Hidden Force Behind Growth, Profits and Lasting Value*, Thomas Teal, 1996.

Ritchie, John, and Salmon, John, *Inside Collett Dickenson Pearce*, Batsford, 2000.

Robinson, Jeffrey, *The Manipulators: A Conspiracy To Make Us Buy*, Simon & Schuster, 1998.

Rose, Richard, *Influencing Voters*, Faber & Faber, 1967.

Rothenberg, Randell, 'Brits Buy Up The Ad Business', *New York Times Magazine*, 2 July 1989.

Sampson, Henry, *History of Advertising*, Chatto and Windus, 1874.

Saunders, Dave, *20th Century Advertising*, Carlton, 1999.

Saxon Mills, G. H., *There Is A Tide . . .*, William Heinemann, 1954.

Sayers, Dorothy L., *Murder Must Advertise*, Victor Gollancz, 1933.

Schudson, Michael, *Advertising, The Uneasy Persuasion*, HarperCollins, 1984.

Schwartz, Barry, *The Paradox of Choice: Why More Is Less*, HarperCollins, 2004.

Scott, Walter Dill, *The Psychology of Advertising*, North-Western University Press, Chicago, 1909.

Sellers, Patricia, 'Martin Sorrell: Adman On Fire', *Fortune*, 10 July 2000.

Sendell, Bernard, *Independent Television in Britain*, Palgrave MacMillan, 1983.

Sibley, Brian, *The Book of Guinness Advertising*, Guinness Books, 1985.

Simmons, Douglas A., *Schweppes: The First 200 Years*, Springwood Books, 1983.

Simms, Jane, 'Martin Sorrell: The Last Emperor', *The Director*, October 2000.

Sinaiko, Eve, *Posters: Turn-of-the-Century*, Shorewood Fine Art Books, 1980.

Sleight, Peter, *Targeting Customers*, NTC Publications, 1997.

Smit, Erica G., Meurs, Lex Van, and Neijens, Peter C., 'Effects of Advertising Likeability: A 10 Year Perspective', *JAR*, Volume 46, 2006.

Smith, Adam, *The Wealth of Nations*, Oxford World Classics, 1776.

Stout, David, *Of Brands and Growth*, National Economic Research Associates, 1998.

Superbrands, Vols 1–9, 1998–2007.

Sweet, Matthew, *Inventing the Victorians*, Faber & Faber, 2001.

Teasdale, Mike, 'How Users Respond to Internet Advertising', *Admap*, May 2007.

Tellis, Gerard J., and Ambler, Tim (eds), *The SAGE Handbook of Advertising*, Sage, 2007.

Thompson, Damian, 'Aping Natural Selection Online', *Admap*, June 2007.

Thorson, E., 'Likeability: 10 Years of Academic Research', Advertising Research Foundation seminar paper, 1991.

Timmers, Margaret (ed.), *The Power of the Poster*, V&A Publications, 1998.

Treasure, John, *Advertising Expenditure in 1962: A re-appraisal*, IPA, 1963.

Trollope, Anthony, *The Struggles of Smith, Brown and Robinson*, Penguin Books, 1993.

Tumber, Howard (ed.), *Media Power, Professionals and Policies*, Routledge, 2000.

Tungate, Mark, *Adland: A Global History of Advertising*, Kogan Page, 2007.

Tunstall, Jeremy, *The Advertising Man*, Chapman & Hall, 1964.

Turner, E. S., *The Shocking History of Advertising*, Michael Joseph, 1951.

Tusa, John, *On Creativity: Interviews Exploring the Process*, Methuen, 2003.

Unilever Marketing Division, *Unilever Plan for Great Advertising*, UMD, 1988.

Vakratsas, Demetrios, and Ambler, Tim, *Advertising Effects: A Taxonomy and Review of the Literature*, London Business School Centre for Marketing, July 1995.

WARC, 1999–2007.

Watkins, Julian Lewis, *The 100 Greatest Advertisements*, Dover, 1959.

White, Roderick (ed.), 'The Future of Communications', *Admap* 40th Anniversary issue, October 2004.

—— 'Understanding Ad Avoidance and Ad Rejection', *Admap*, January 2007.

—— 'Paying the Ad Agency', *Admap*, February 2007.

Whitworth, Damien, 'The Persuader: Martin Sorrell', *The Times*, 20 October 2007.

Who's Who in Advertising & Public Relations, New Homes Press, 1963.

Wight, Robin, *The Day the Pigs Refused to be Driven to Market: Advertising and the Consumer Revolution*, Hart-Davis, MacGibbon, 1972.

Williams, Raymond, *Problems in Materialism and Culture*, Verso, 1980.

Windlesham, David, *Communication and Political Power*, Jonathon Cape, 1966.

World's Press News, 1951–1968.

Young, James Webb, *How to Become an Advertising Man*, Advertising Publications, 1963.

Private and Unpublished Documents (in chronological order)

'The Story of the Advertising Association', author unknown, 1950.

'Speech by Lord Beveridge', AA Conference 1951.

'Background to Launch of John Hobson & Partners', confidential paper by John Hobson, 1960.

'About Collett, Dickenson, Pearce & Partners', probably drafted by John Pearce, 1961.

'The History of Advertising: A Proper Subject of Study?', paper by Brian Smith, 1965.

'Fifty Years of Advertising: What Next?', James O'Connor for the IPA, 1967.

'Irritation in Advertising: Next Battleground for Advertisers?', speech given by Stephen A. Greyser, Toronto, 1972.

'Speech by Shirley Williams', AA Conference 1974.

'Speech by John Methven', AA Conference 1974.

'OBM: 125 Years', by Stanley Piggott, published by Ogilvy Benson & Mather, 1975.

'How Much, How Many? IPA Vital Statistics 1960–1975', 1977.

'Top 30 Ad Agencies: Reputation Study', by Gerry Levens & Company, circa 1982/3.

'Cigarette Marketing and Sales', confidential paper by Mark Ramage, 1985.

'The unpublished David Ogilvy: Writings from the files of his partners', The Ogilvy Group, 1986.

'Networking, synergy, cross-referral: And what's in it for the customer', WPP paper by Jeremy Bullmore, 1987, selectively quoted in *HBR*, November 2001.

'The Thirty Club of London', by Jeremy Bullmore and Michael Cudlipp, 1999.

'Anatomy of Successful Retail Advertising', presentation by Delaney Lund Knox Warren, March 2004.

'David Ogilvy: The Most Famous Advertising Man In The World', speech by Kenneth Roman, New York, November 2004.

'John Webster's Memorial Service', speech by Martin Boase, April 2006.

Index